Rock Life in the Sixties

Augmented Edition

ELLEN SANDER

DOVER PUBLICATIONS, INC.
Mineola, New York

Bibliographical Note

This Dover edition, first published in 2019, is an augmented and revised republication of the work originally published by Charles Scribner's Sons, New York, in 1973. Four stories appeared originally in slightly different format in *Hit Parader, Vogue, Saturday Review,* and *The Realist.* Copyright © 1968, 1969, 1970 Ellen Sander.

Library of Congress Cataloging-in-Publication Data

Names: Sander, Ellen, author.
Title: Trips : rock life in the sixties / Ellen Sander.
Description: Augmented edition. | Mineola, New York : Dover Publications, 2019.
Identifiers: LCCN 2018040284| ISBN 9780486828473 | ISBN 0486828476
Subjects: LCSH: Rock music—United States—1961–1970—History and criticism.
| Sander, Ellen. | Rock music fans—United States.
Classification: LCC ML3534.3 .S22 2019 | DDC 781.6609/046—dc23
LC record available at https://lccn.loc.gov/2018040284

Manufactured in the United States by LSC Communications
82847601   2019
www.doverpublications.com

Contents

For each age is a dream that is dying,
Or one that is coming to birth.

—Arthur O'Shaughnessy,
"Ode," 1874

STONE

Step on this rock
that moves underfoot

Spite the street
(that is dancing)

Lashing bodies on
the oracle

Black Vinyl Mandala
the howl of the circle

It comes,
it rocks

—Ellen Sander

Preface

It took more than two years and the support of scores of people when I originally wrote *Trips: Rock Life in the Sixties*. I was the collector of anecdotes, the detective of detail, a nibbler concocting a feast of my favorite adventures and everyone's pet road stories, tracking down tales, cross-interviewing, drawing on my own travels as a rock journalist, critic, and fan. Except for minor editing, intermittent commentary, and excising things I now know to be erroneous, ill-considered, or gratuitous, this enhanced reissue is fundamentally as originally written, with other *in situ* journalism merged in here and there as additional chapters or portions of chapters.

Trips is a memoir, a sourcebook, and a love letter; a recollection of a time, parenthesized by ambivalence and apathy, a search for the ultimate high, a generation with an irrepressible vision, its art, artists, its audience, and the substance of its statement. Most importantly, it was written during the period it describes, and not subject to analytic hindsight, even in this second edition. It was important to retain the essence, the enthusiasm, and the naïveté of the era. It was especially important to retain the exuberant feminine *esprit*.

When rock was young, in the 1950s, it was swarms of infatuated girls in the audience that first registered the impact of those songs, artists, and records, and made for cheerfully unruly live shows. Most of the hits were lovelorn songs about or addressed to girls. Girls were the reason for rock 'n' roll. The girls adored the pop stars, so the boys all wanted to be pop stars. From that primal combination of fuel and spark came a lineage of passion and rebellion that resounded exponentially for decades. Rock absorbed rock 'n' roll, integrating a social conscience and a generational call for moral evolution, moving from AM radio to the massive penetration of FM radio, and from there into the consciousness and the imagination of the enormous population of young adults in the 1960s.

I have compiled a smattering of personalities and impressions as events of the rock 'n' roll Sixties were happening into a sampler of rock journalism in its first generation. What came to be known as "new journalism" ignited reviews, features, and cultural commentary focused on rock music. The pain of racism, civil rights abuses, and the Vietnam War inflamed artistic expression in the 1960s. Those years generated the women's movement, black power, gay rights, legal birth control, and the right to vote for eighteen-year-old Americans. Those issues, especially the war and the draft, tore families apart as ferociously as did the U.S. Civil War.

This original work and the additional journalism that has been merged into this edition are part of the maiden run of rock journalism, a pioneering effort on behalf of a dozen or so writers in the Sixties that believed in rock as an art form, as a social force, and as a creative ethic. Our work was not only to represent the music authentically, but also to convince the editors of major periodicals to publish it alongside critical and reportorial coverage of other fine and popular arts.

The alternative press, counterculture peer group reportage, came to prominence with rock coverage during the years this book traverses. Rock criticism, features, news, and rankings are now a part of many more publications in print and online. What has since come to be known as "classic rock"—and writings about it—is taught in universities in American Studies, History, Music, Women's Studies, and Journalism departments. Courses in writing about pop culture are offered by many colleges. If you are a student in one of those classes and your question to me would be "What advice would you give to an aspiring cultural journalist/critic?" this is for you: Write with intimacy, informed context, and abandon. Pop culture is fiercely and intimately beloved by its aficionados. It deserves to be written about with imagination and devotion, ardency, and yearning.

Trips offers a sunlit glimpse of a face of the Sixties—often hilarious, sometimes tragic, rarely in repose, but always erupting. It was a unique time. Its music stands apart in the landscape of American and English popular music and has never—much to my surprise—been equaled, much less eclipsed.

A frontier of changes opened up in the Sixties. No American decade was more rife with cultural and political change than the Sixties and no time more enlightening for its changes. The people intimately involved with its vanguard were talented, visionary, and courageous. There is little left of it but the backlash.

—E. S., 2018

Acknowledgments

The late Paul Williams, founder and publisher of *Crawdaddy!* and the innovator of serious, in-depth, inventive writing about rock music and culture, was an active, encouraging, and loving muse. I miss him every day.

For many hours of recorded interviews for the original edition, my thanks still and always will go to David Crosby, Jim Dickson, Billy James, and Roger (aka Jim) McGuinn, who provided a great deal of inside information on the Byrds and their times and never tried to gloss over their difficulties with one another. Cass Elliot was warm and helpful with memories and her own ineffable wisdom. Paul Krassner and Abbie Hoffman inadvertently gave me a good look before an abortive, short-lived, and quickly retracted leap, as is accounted herein. Moreover, Krassner, with his gnome-wit and encouragement by implication, has been an influence on my writing as well as an editor who published one of my proudest moments.

Eric Burdon allowed himself to be scrupulously interviewed while suffering one beast of a hangover. Grace

Slick, Paul Kantner, and Bill Thompson were always available for a quip, a hit, and a good time. The late DJ Peter Fornatale played soothing music on the radio after I'd been up all night. Wherever I went I found rock 'n' roll, and whomever I asked helped. The original editor was Norbert Slepyan at Scribner's.

Jac Holzman, for the original edition, proofread some of the sections, recounted several of his own experiences for use in the book, and provided intelligent and ruthless criticism, which I used and appreciated.

The original of this manuscript was stolen and held for ransom. During an argument with Jac Holzman, with whom I'd been traveling, we forgot my briefcase in an airport parking lot, where it was snatched. Jac hired a detective, who tracked it down. The thief threatened to turn me in for the few joints that were in the briefcase. Jac graciously and willingly paid a pricey ransom, and we got the manuscript back; otherwise this book would never have been finished.

Allison J. Boron, a few years ago, traveled six hundred miles to sort through, arrange, and file my archives. Without that work, putting this edition of *Trips* together would have been so much more difficult. It does me proud to see what she has added to current coverage of mid-century music and pop culture.

Thanks to Rick Stockton, a complete stranger, a fan of the original *Trips*, for helping me out with clippings from his collection of *Hit Parader*.

Thanks to David Geffen for help, for friendship, for everything, and especially for being such a patient, forgiving soul.

Thanks to all, too many to name, who've quoted, cited, praised, and used *Trips* in their classes. To my detractors, even more thanks.

To all the makers of myths and music, living and lost, the dazzling highs and the crushing comedowns and the things learned in between, what follows is a love letter to you and the times we lived together. There was a significant shift in awareness during these times and our world has never been the same.

Finally, significantly and sincerely, many thanks to Jeff Golick and everyone at Dover who've helped make this edition of *Trips* what it is after forty-some-odd years.

—E. S.

Teenism in the Fifties

Coming of age in the Fifties was pure pain. Adolescence is hard enough; boys get grabby, gawky self-consciousness invades every waking hour like a lecherous Peeping Tom. So many secrets too intimate to reveal, too terrifying to keep, real agonies everyone around thought were cute or, worse yet, hilarious. Families got divorced; the immediate structure of life was shaken, shattered beyond comprehension as emotional turbulence crackled in crosscurrents through half-homes like mine.

Later in the decade there were Little Rock and *Sputnik*, body blows to the myth of American supremacy internationally and American complacency internally. The smug self-righteousness of the entire social system began to crumble before our eyes. We were jolted, shocked from our troubled, changing insides, TV the perimeters of perception, and our world was set spinning to the edge of sexual awareness and global annihilation at the same time. I don't know how we could have made it through the acceleration of shocks without our trusty companions: transistor radios tuned to the rock 'n' roll in the air and a stack of 45s, as intimate as a diary, the common denominator of a Fifties teen social life.

Everything else happening was beyond us, forced upon us by circumstances beyond our control. But our music was ours; it was us, it represented us and it created us. It gave us something wholly our own, young, youth-oriented, and inviolate.

There was that sweet soul music, the sexy, sassy rubber-bumping rhythm and blues to dance to, those beautiful boys undulating their bodies in a dance of delight. There was the syrupy sentimentalism of country singers spreading young men's fancies and God's good word across the land like hayseed in the wind. Sex and romantic languors, the first pain of love, rebelliousness, the symbolism of youth chauvinism, the fire water and soul of the temper of our times. Chuck Berry was the prophet and Elvis the shaman-God; rockabilly rhythm and blues to set your life a-movin'. Berry with his cars and girls, his guitarboy "Johnny B. Goode," and insinuating beat; Elvis, upper lip and humping hips forever.

History provides for retaliation. Nuclear weapons dropped on Hiroshima on August 6, 1945. Ten years later to the day, "Rock Around the Clock" was the nationwide number one hit song, *Blackboard Jungle* was showing all over, and we sensed a feeling of identity, an identity tinged with rebellion, resentment, and fired by sound.

It was fun to put the local town movie theater managers uptight by mobbing *Blackboard Jungle* and *Love Me Tender*. Bill Haley and the Comets were originally Bill Haley and the Saddlemen, a country and western band covering race records until Haley sang the title song from *Blackboard Jungle*. The film caused riots in theaters, which became total teen experiences: suddenly there was a movie as noisy and as rebellious as we were feeling, and its music urged us on. That first flash of being in an unruly crowd, that first rush of power. Out of that mob would come a young, contained culture of which rock 'n' roll radio was the first indigenous tonic and weapon. "Rock 'n' Roll Music," "Hound Dog," "Sweet Little

Sixteen," "Bo Diddley," and "Rock Around the Clock" were like passwords between us, the movement of our minds and bodies together. We were, after all, just beginning to realize that we were young, misunderstood, tipsy with incipient power, and in it all together.

Somewhere around the time I was approaching puberty I was taught about nuclear power. As if a hormonal crisis erupting into manic moodiness and engrossing daydreams of seduction were not enough, I had obliteration to deal with. Under a tiny nipple, which had all these tomboy years lain so taut and quiet on my chest, a painful little gland about the size of a grape protruded— only one—and I could not be consoled into believing I would ever have another. I was destined, oh woe, to be a unibreasted freak.

I was dismayed as much as relieved when, five months later, the other breast fully emerged and, Lord, to find them so sensitive to pain. Sometimes I'd bump into a chair, clumsy, aware of the eyes of the boys in the classroom upon me and—ow!—chest first then chin, I'd crumple to avoid the humiliation as pain shot through my chest like a comic-strip zinger.

Some of the girls who wore bras already, they laughed. They knew. They were the girls in the locker room who told us less mature ones what it was like to get your period. Those bull sessions were pure hell. How would I ever make it, I wondered.

The world was going through its time of the month. Or was it menopause? At the very least it was in full, flaring heat and we were all virgins. Going to school with The Bomb was as real as dirty jokes, ducktail haircuts, crinolines, marks, first nylons, and jive talk. The social studies teacher tried to be kind. He saw us freaking out. When gunpowder was first invented, he reassured us, they thought it was the end of the world, too.

One day, in "hygiene" class, the girls were shown a film on menstruation. The same day, in "shop," the boys saw a film on V.D.

The next day we all saw a film of Hiroshima together. I learned to menstruate and live in terror of The Bomb the same week. The mushroom cloud blazed; it rose and crested in magnificent bursts of fire and power. It was one of the most movingly beautiful sights any one of us had ever seen. Our minds broke in terror and awe. We walked out of the auditorium changed children. Our pants were hot and we were full of paranoia. The cycle of anger, fear, and rebellion had started. We'd had our illusions busted and it was only the beginning.

The original "Sh-Boom" was a rhythm and blues record by the Chords released in 1954. It was one of the first R&B hits to be covered by a white group (the Crew Cuts, in this case). The ad for the single in music trade magazines had a photo of a mushroom cloud, and a huge BOOM ended the song. It sold a million copies on the white pop market.

We all danced to it and roared with the boom. We danced so hard we couldn't think anymore; we danced in sexual frenzy and grateful relief. We didn't know whether to be thankful for the interruption of classwork by air raid drills or not. Single file out of the room, down to the basement halls, huddled against walls, waiting for the flash, the boom, the final apocalyptic dance. Was it really happening or were they trying to frighten us into submission for study hall? The lunchtime smell of peanut butter and jelly hung stickily in the air, floating though the cafeteria door. Whom would I crouch with, to whom would I run? Myra, who promised not to tell how I stuffed one cup of my tiny brassiere to make my breasts look even? Or Betsy, who had "done it," and confided that it hurt like hell? Linda, the Elvis nut, at least had her hayloft fantasies to die with. Sylvia was going steady and would die beloved. Donald, the class president, would be blasted to hell, most likely to succeed. I would die alone, relieved at last of the complication of committing suicide.

The door broke loose in the spring wind, sprang open, and cracked sharply against the inside wall. We yipped and started. Our minds leaped to the ultimate conclusion. Could it really be? We huddled next to the walls, arms over heads. It was fearing not just being killed, but the end of the meaning of life, and we never outgrew it.

We experienced a planetary anxiety that was awakening a global consciousness in every adolescent of the time. We not only knew of the 1956 Hungarian revolution, we saw it on TV. We experienced it; we felt the lapse of time and space over distance and instantly identified with those students, rocks in hands, being mowed down by tanks and machine guns. It was instant, that change: our awareness was increased geometrically and everything that touched that awareness was evil, destructive, and frightening but the one thing we had for ourselves, that rock 'n' roll. It sustained us. And more.

We were television children, the first generation of them. We would be the last generation to remember way back in our childhood the tiny lapse of time before TV. We'd been placed in custody of the living screen almost from our earliest memories. *Howdy Doody, Dragnet, Sky King, Disneyland, The Lone Ranger*— they would all figure prominently in our fantasies as we broke free to wander in a rock 'n' roll world. *American Bandstand*, hosted by good clean Dick Clark and guested with contemporary Philadelphia teens all dippy and dancing, was our show, a media mirror with which we checked ourselves out each day. No generation before us had that.

And we rocked and rolled, and we petted in cars, and we talked of Elvis and Connie and Dion and Annette, and we grew into one another in self-defense against The Bomb, against the fear of Soviet supremacy in space, sexual discovery, and having to let the junior high guidance counselors know of our choice of college. If we wanted admittance to The World we had to decide and begin planning for it at fifteen.

It struck some of us that it was their world and we didn't care much about admittance to it. There had to be a better way and we had to find it. We looked in other directions. The only thing specifically and exclusively for us was that rock 'n' roll.

We trembled on the brink of self-awareness while TV, movies, rock 'n' roll, and other media were introducing us to the shuddering of the world. The music grew louder, raunchier; dancing grew crazier, and our bodies and minds convulsed in a rapturous motion that was both an escape from, and a direct response to, the precarious spasms of events. We were a generation cut off from the past by total absorption with the present. And our parents thought surely that it was a phase, that we would outgrow it.

Fat chance.

Teenism had been born. Teenism means running silly and scared, the result of an information assault, the world pouring in on us from every orifice of the media and all of it bad news. It is idealism coming smack up against reality, impatience, frustration; being more than children without the power of adults; being a part of something—*special*!

Entire industries bend for your favor; singers wail tunes you alone would understand and appreciate. There was a whole language, a colorful vernacular jive of black musicians, an ethnic parlance hip kids understood. It was the birth of hip, the birth of cool, a newly discovered road away from the path leading into the quiet desperation to which our parents and teachers resigned themselves, a direction away from chaos. Teenism was being a part of a special subspecies, an age span of irate, affluent white kids, a culture born to the renegade ballsy beat of rock 'n' roll music, half-put-together outcasts learning to make the best of it together.

"I don't care what people say, rock and roll is here to stay!"

It was a metaphor for our commitment to one another and to finding another way to live. And the bond that held us together distinct from the rest of humanity was the smug, deep-down certain knowledge that that was the truth, baby, you betta believe it!

Music would break off an absurd edge: the stupid "See You Later, Alligator" (after 'while, crocodile), the goony "Flying Saucer" record. Sweet harmonies of the Everly Brothers, like sliding between satin sheets. Paul Anka and his problems with "Diana." The Coasters' "Searchin,"—we knew what that was all about. Woo-woo. "Peggy Sue-oo-oo." Goony falsetto of "Little Star," David Seville and the "Witch Doctor" (*oo-ee-oo-ah-ah, ting-tang-walla-walla-bing-bang*). You want lyrics with Significance? Those are lyrics with Significance. Oh, yes, there was the "Purple People Eater," who wanted to be a rock 'n' roll star, and "Yakety Yak" (don't talk back!).

Is it any wonder we got a little strange behind it all?

"Way Down Yonder in New Orleans" reinforced the sensation of being part of something teenistic and nationwide. The music gave spunk to our belligerence; adult distaste kept it going. The most unique and repercussive generation gap was busy being born between the throbs of a big black dirty beat.

Teens wrote millions of fan letters, voted for records, and influenced play lists of major radio stations. They mobbed rock 'n' roll road shows, inside to writhe and scream, fall on their knees, worshiping the makers of music with shrieks of sexual release. Major magazines struggled to bring the crazed antics of teenism into focus. When Elvis was on *The Ed Sullivan Show* in September

1956 and the camera was forbidden to reveal him below the waist where the action was, it was an insult, an outrage. You could tell by the tempo of the screams of the live audience when he would give it a little shake, but they wouldn't let us see it on the screen. In a backhanded way it asserted our power. They were afraid to see, afraid to show, afraid to acknowledge that years of sexual repressiveness in the care and feeding of adolescents were exploding in hysteria and joy, breaking the bounds of acceptable morality, touching every teenager within earshot to his very forbidden genitals. For rock 'n' roll changed our sex lives. It spoke a language that included girls in its frantic, rebellious sexual need, and the response to it was largely sexual. We discovered the delights of each other's bodies and minds through music in the crucible of the Fifties, creating an open arena from which a wholly personal morality could emerge.

Clergy begged that this flood of degradation be stemmed; parents threw up their arms in helpless anger. They couldn't stand the thought that we were getting it, liking it, and doing it, feverishly, happily, and openly. They envied us our lean young bodies and our pleasures, and we dug it all. Along with all that loving and coming it was delicious and fitting spite, the critical slap back at authority losing control of its children. We were spoiled, unrestrainable, and sexually in control. We didn't have to take any of what they were laying out, not even school, seriously. Eccentric attire identified a peer, bosstalk was the language, music was the connecting wave of an age style that would take us from self-consciousness to generational consciousness to global consciousness over the following decade.

Music has always had the power to break down barriers and now it erected one. To be young was cool, to be old was a drag, and we were discovering it all at fifteen, sixteen—with enough time to live in the myth of eternal youth until we saw beyond it.

The presence of blackness in the rock 'n' roll of the times, the black rhythm roots and the black performers, integrated our minds. Black kids were white teen sex idols, and, in the alarm adults expressed, we sensed the racist implications. It was action and reaction with no real conscious consideration until much later. TV news would interview a southern cracker during the integration upheaval and he'd bluster about how "next they'll be wanting to marry our daughters." What they really were scared of, and what in fact was happening, was that their darling daughters wanted to get it on with black boys. Miscegenation is not the result of integration; it is one of the bases.

With the music of the Fifties, teens had the first taste of full boogie. Despite everything else happening (because of it, probably), we were learning to feel good among one another. We had to, it was about the only outlet available that consumed as much energy as we had.

Adults agonized over the future of youth. They never knew what the agonies were. They couldn't relate to the increase in awareness we were responding to; it was totally beyond their experience. We got a long hard look at how it was out there, competitiveness motivating a dreary lifestyle, money being an end and not a means, nations hustling ultimate doom, and it stunk. We had the first good full global view of it any young generation was ever given. We could hardly be expected to respond with gratitude. We didn't know what the answer was, but we knew better. With that frame of reference they weren't going to teach us a thing. That's what hip was born as: knowing better. We felt adrift in a sea of utter bullshit and we could really perceive it. Soon we would learn to articulate it.

In a society lacking in values attractive to its horny, idealistic young, rock 'n' roll energized a need to find some.

Those needs found some relief in the behavioral accoutrements of being a teenager, those car songs, those Blue Suede Shoes. All those material aspects of teenism filled our vocabulary, our wardrobes, our ears, our dreams, and our lives, only to show us there was something more to be had. There was still so much missing. And we were growing older, high school was drawing to an end. The music, toward the end, began to lag, the industry was manufacturing endless hours of facsimile rock, all those Italian kids and their featureless rock late in the Fifties just didn't cut it beyond a superficial level. Although the culture had seemed superficial to that point, it was beginning to experience a lack of substance, and out of that we began to feel that the rebelliousness of teenism was not rebelliousness without a cause but without a center. It was invigorating but ephemeral, transient, and beginning to sound lousy.

From that partial vacuum college kids were digging on "Tom Dooley" by the Kingston Trio in 1958 and getting into fretted instruments. Pop took a quantum leap, and when it fell to the street, rebelliousness had at last found a cause.

In 1977 NASA launched space probes Voyager 1 *and 2 to explore the outer solar system. Aboard are golden records filled with information about Earth, including images, sounds, and music intended to represent our planet. There's only one rock 'n' roll song in that collection, which Carl Sagan curated. It is Chuck Berry's 1958 hit, "Johnny B. Goode." Chuck Berry lived long enough to learn that the* Voyagers *made it to interstellar space in 2012. He passed away on March 18, 2017, at the age of ninety.*

MacDougal's Farm

Decades somehow have the personality of an age contained in them. The Fifties were bitterly alienating. We'd been spewed into the Sixties powerless in outrage. Our education had been pointless. . . . What can you do with logarithms and gerunds when you're out of high school, mad at the world, surrounded by contemporaries that feel the same way, and sure you're right?

The Fifties ended a few weeks late. In February 1960, in Albany, Georgia, the first freedom ride civil rights sit-in took place. It was a milestone for change in the music that became popular and the lifestyle of its audience. At once, there was a movement, and its music would be an integral, often a motivating, force.

It began with discovering ourselves; it led to discovering one another. It was overwhelming, discouraging, frightening, and demanding. We were on the street.

There was a migration from homes and campuses to the street. Whatever it was that was making us so unhappy pulled us toward the street. It was the only way out and it was completely open.

The street was the place to meet kindred souls of every physical description, the place to score dope, the place to hang out and find out what was happening. It was dotted with shops and coffeehouses where you could find anything from a chess game to every conceivable assortment of sexual partner or partners. It was where we lived, learned, worked, played, taught, and survived; it was where you oriented yourself among it all. Naturally, it was the best place that anyone who wanted to could find and play and make and go to hear music.

It was an intimate scene. Homemade music in homestyle settings, a surrogate home for thousands of children of the Fifties who felt like orphans elsewhere. On the West Coast it was Venice or Berkeley. The street was in Denver, Philadelphia, Chicago, and, importantly, Cambridge; music people came from and through and by way of all of them, ending up in Greenwich Village.

The music was acoustic and fresh, simple rhythms and gentle voices, a relief from the vinyl love masquerading as radio rock 'n' roll. Audiences would clap and stomp along and participate in the music they were experiencing. When it was over, audience and performers would applaud each other with an ovation that was as lusty as it was genuine.

Traditional material came largely from ethnic sources and most young folksingers started out interpreting the traditional folk figures, singing "Wildwood Flower," "Banks of the Ohio," "Pretty Peggy-O"—railroad songs, union songs, and the like. Words, verses, and structures were changed—the folk process. Soon hybrids would develop, like Paul Clayton's "Gotta Travel On," so tasty it was often mistaken for a traditional song.

Entirely new songs, adapted from older ones (like Bob Dylan's "Masters of War," adapted from "Nottamun Town"), then free and on their own (like Phil Ochs's "Changes" or Dylan's "Blowin' in the Wind"), would develop out of young gifted troubadours who populated the street. Their following was cultish, composed mostly of street people who were a part of the creation of this rebirth of song stylings. The flow of ideas, people, and music was very real and regenerating.

There were a half-dozen or so girls with apartments around all the centers of music without whom many young folksingers never would have gotten along. Beatific lovelies, young matriarchs of the scene, they'd care for and house the music boys who didn't have rent or supper for themselves. It was a wise little coterie; within hours of the first report of the clap the word was on the street: "Don't ball no boys with guitars."

"People say, 'Boy, those must have been tough days,'" reminisced Cass Elliot. "I lived in a $36 a month apartment that had a john in the hall and was constantly being burglarized. But I had a great time. I worked for $40 a week under the table as a hat-check girl in a night club. At the Night Owl singing with Tim Rose I was making $2 every other night, when the year before I had made $50,000 as an actress. That was when the Spoonful were just starting out, Tim Hardin and Richie Havens were also working there. It was fresh and wonderful, we were all young kids feeling the wind in our hair. We were making music and listening and doing a *lot* of walking. We were free! We did what we had to do to keep ourselves alive. My apartment was on Fourth Street and Avenue C, the electricity had been turned off 'cause I couldn't pay the bill. But it was fine; I used candles. There was an innocence you just don't find that way again. Later on when it got successful, when it got down to money, that innocence was all gone. We all learned a lot from each other back then. But rock 'n' roll is a tremendously competitive business. There's no reciprocity in it; when it came down to dollars everyone got uptight. Probably the biggest bringdown in my life—it's so hypocritical—was being in a big pop group and finding out just how much it was like everything it was supposed to be against."

In the Fifties, coffeehouses had hired folksingers to turn the house over for the beat poets. In the Sixties the situation was reversed. The beats had been brained into existentialism, but the folkniks were full of piss and vinegar and ready to make a lot of noise about change. Greenwich Village was alive and radiating young talent and enthusiasm, fucked-over kids of the Fifties, in from wherever, disgusted with what they'd left behind, open to whatever was waiting for them, with a burning desire to express themselves with music of their own making, with a lifestyle of their own contrivance. It meant being broke most of the time, maybe working in a shoe store by day, or running lights at the Bitter End at night, maybe both just to get hamburgers together. But it meant being into something that did not entail constant digestion of the *New York Times* and the world outside the street it symbolized. Even on those nights when we'd huddle together over a corner table in a coffeehouse and talk about where it all came from and where it all could go, nobody in his wildest fantasies came close. We had found a very gratifying way of living among ourselves and we were looking for ways to make it grow.

Nine steps down from MacDougal Street was a cellar lodge, bricked, wooded, benched, with a small stage at the far end of the room, and a single chair. Two microphones stood in front of the chair in the glare of a single spotlight. Upstairs there was an apartment where Hugh Romney, then a beat poet, lived. In this attic room, which had as its furnishings a battered red couch and a chandelier, musicians who played the Gaslight would turn on, tune up, and prepare for their set downstairs.

At one time, Bobby Dylan, a grandiloquent kid with a lot of hair, would wait until a set was over and play unannounced and unpaid as a trailer. He would turn over the house but fast (which was one of the reasons the management had him there in the first place). Audiences would sit bewildered through the unfamiliar first part of the first song (his songs, then primitive, had monotonous melodies and went on forever) and walk out. They seemed completely uninterested in this intense but nondescript young man who sang as if each syllable were a struggle for breath. If the boy minded, he didn't show it. In fact, he didn't even seem to notice most of the time. He was just working out, after bumming his way halfway across the country to get there. He'd sing on hootenanny nights at Gerde's Folk City in between hundreds of young folksingers who waited just to try their talents out on a live audience.

He had just begun to write his own material, and his songs quickly departed from what his colleagues were singing. His meter was ever changing, his timing was impeccable. His lyric sense was off the wall. But you could see something going on: he was working very hard at the science of affecting minds by eloquently unreeling his own. You could see his face screw up as he concentrated his energy. You could feel the intensity even when he hid his face. He was exercising a bizarre twist in language and inflection that later would earmark his style and he was deliberately, calculatingly, and brilliantly creating an entirely new idiom for artistic comment. But most of all—he said so himself— he was trying to see if he could remember all the words.

The music at the Gaslight was good. Pickers and strummers and songs of what we were all feeling in the tradition of people's music. That's what the folk boomlet did; it left commercial pop behind and brought music back to the people. It was music that anyone could and did make. Folk music had always been indigenous, incestuous, and local, passed on hand to hand. With records, radio, microphones, and huge concert halls it was pop; from its source it boomed to millions with immediacy, power, and scope, losing none of its intimacy in the process, and the kids who were singing it could perceive their impact.

It was becoming clear that mass music through mass media could be a powerful tool for enlightenment. It was basically the mass media that had messed up our lives in the first place; the world had always had its troubles, but young people didn't have to live with them on a continuous, daily, immediate basis. Came the Sixties and the streets, thousands of young makers of music were learning how to use the very same mass media to amplify what they all had to say about it.

Up the street from the Gaslight was the Folklore Center, where a young but paunchy, balding, and very good-natured proprietor, Izzy Young, provided a place—a tiny storefront and back room—for musical exchange. Everyone hung out there at some time or another, picking over the bins of folk records, fondling a row of Martin guitars that played like heaven, cost like hell, but hung there if you wanted to play them. And if Izzy liked your music or your laugh and you needed an ax for a set at one of the local cafés, your credit was good.

Next door was the Kettle of Fish, a bar where there were always drink and gossip and camaraderie. Sometimes even music. Late at night, when the folk houses closed down, some singer who hadn't wound down after his last set would come in and do another, maybe joined by whoever was around, and of course the house chorus and clapping section.

Around the corner on Bleecker were the Bitter End, a folk house, and the Dugout, another hamburger and beer meeting place. There were always people around and it was good times.

Almost every music place had hoots at least one night a week, and they were evenings of great to-do. Handmade music crafted by musicians aged and traditional, singing of the simplicities of day-to-day life and the basics of being human ran side by side with troubadours young and growing, growing so fast they couldn't keep up with themselves. They would sing of torment, of being raw and exposed, of having to cope with everything at once, of the complexity and insanity of life in the outside world.

It was either cope or go crazy and we all did some of each, vision and insanity overlapping, creating some of the most bizarrely expressed perceptions that have graced Caucasian mass art since William Shakespeare was a pop artist.

The songs had their teeth into racism and war, America's social and political hypocrisies, and they bit hard. Between the traditionalists and the new troubadours things would get grim now and then; accusations were hurled by people blind to the possibility that there was more in common than different between the two forms of music. But there was always a saving edge of tomfoolery, a harbinger of the time very shortly at hand when American complacency was going to get a good swift kick in the ass.

Phil Ochs, a rangy journalist turned troubadour, moved hundreds of thousands of young people in his audience to think about the society into which they would graduate. Dave Van Ronk was a bearded boho whose brewsy ballads could make you feel like you were born in a bar and would die in a bar, having lived your whole life in a bar. He'd sing and stomp all night long, like some gigantic circus bear, gruff and tender and somehow always there. Billy Faier and Patrick Sky with outrageous guffaws would keep a room in stitches all night long with the lowest, but the lowest, humor. Albert Grossman put two folksingers and a stand-up comic together and came up with Peter, Paul and Mary, who would sing at the Bitter End and break Bob Dylan songs into the mainstream. The Smothers Brothers were a folk act with more yucks than music; there were those around who'd refer to them as the Village idiots. Simon and Garfunkel sang in subways. Ramblin' Jack Elliott was once called a poor man's Woody Guthrie and Bobby Dylan was called a poor man's Jack Elliott. Midnight at the Kettle of Fish, they'd all hang out, backslap, drink, bullshit, and gossip, a soft edge of warmth surrounding the crowd. Off in the corner the cacophony of Van Ronk and his kazoo buzzed through the muted sounds of the protected night. There wasn't much luxury to be had, but it was a good life.

Nights would turn into parties, instantly, magically, the sounds of guitars and voices, the gleam of candles, incense, and the slip of grenadine and wine down a hashish-parched throat. The wisp of marijuana smoke, in a room pillowed all around the floor, floated through the soft laughter and the sounds of people making love in dark corners.

Grass was a hushed scene then, but it was definitely around. You got high within hours of hitting the street. Someone turned you on or you scored, took the stuff home inside your clothes, lovingly separated the flowers from the stems and seeds, put it in a pipe or rolled it in some papers, and inhaled deep. All the way down, hold your breath. High.

Soft and elated, the night was happy and welcome. Perceptions sharp as a razor. The feel of soft old jeans being rubbed against the insides of your legs by a fierce and beautiful lover, the beauty of a hand-tooled belt as its contours caught the candlelight. The way things instantly were what they seemed; the mirth when it all fell apart; hours and hours of intense rapping. The sound of voices next to you, inside you close. The snuggle of a Navy surplus peacoat against the bitter winter chill; and the smile—contented and happy, optimistic, bursting open with ideas, friendship, and hope; free, easy, and full of laughter.

The combination of the music, the outright honesty it elicited, being away from home and among souls in the same situation on the street, broke down sexual inhibitions. You could live with a roommate or with a lover—the latter was often more practical and always more fun. Music was the ingredient that brought out the flavor and we were beginning to understand that we cared more about one another and our life together than anything else. It became our world, our morality, our standards of integrity and it was quite an improvement. Our most terrifying secret fears and hopes were as common a denominator between us as grass, and while the music and the grass were helping us to feel, to respond and react, we realized that what we were feeling was the way it simply was and we alone could keep it going.

Electronics had increased our awareness of each other and what made us tick, and this awareness forged our relationships with our peers. We didn't have to face our fears, either about ourselves or about the universe, single-handedly anymore. People were creating out of the heart of their inner changes unafraid. A whole new breed of young citizens of the Sixties— enthusiastic, determined, and high—were discovering what it was like to live among one another as human beings, successfully and by their own rules. It was a flash to realize that it could happen. Without interference it was so simple. The level and amount of creativity spiraled. The energy that was organized on that level would take that scene much further than anyone ever dreamed.

On Third Street a new café opened called the Third Side. One day the owner, Charley Washburn, was approached by Albert Grossman, manager of Odetta and Peter, Paul and Mary. He had a new client, Bobby Dylan, and the boy had no place to go, nothing to eat during the day, and could he use the café to compose, rehearse, and be alone? Grossman secured a tab so Dylan could eat—the bill came to about $20 a week—and he had a place to be and work. It was arranged.

In 1961 Ramblin' Jack Elliott's album of Woody Guthrie songs was released; it was like a primer in American folk for learning musicians. On the tail end of a bitter 1962 New York winter, Bobby Dylan's first album was released containing, among traditional material, his poignant "Song to Woody."

Fred Neil was about. Thin to the point of emaciation. A freckled towhead with one of God's most perfect baritones and a huge Adam's apple that bobbled in the middle of it, he sang so movingly that, years later, Stephen Stills spoke for many a boy when he said that Freddy had taught him how to feel. The younger music boys would flock around wherever Freddy was performing just to hear him sing. He was a walking event.

He had written a tune called "Candy Man" that Roy Orbison recorded and made into a big hit in 1958. Neil came to New York from Coconut Grove, Florida, to make it as a singer-songwriter in the wake of that one hit. He spent two weeks in an uptown hotel compliments of a record company, got fed up with the music business, and spent the next few nights in a park. He rambled around like a lost noonday cowboy until he checked out the Village. He was a legendary figure the moment he hit the street.

One winter Freddy took the whole Village back with him to Coconut Grove, then a tiny hamlet on the periphery of Miami where the weather was warm. There were lots of music places and boats and musicians around and it became a mini-scene of its own, the magic and laziness of which is captured in John Sebastian's song "Coconut Grove," recorded a couple of years later by the Lovin' Spoonful.

Trouble was, Freddy had a chronic case of functional confusion and cranial nada. It would come over him at odd times and he got a reputation for being professionally unreliable. Regardless, he was well loved and welcome whenever and wherever he showed. He was a musician's musician, one of the most magnetic inspirations of the time. Even those young boys fast becoming stars would make it a point not to miss him. Bob Dylan felt privileged on several occasions to back Freddy up on harmonica when he did sets at the Playhouse for a few bucks out of pocket. Fred Neil would acknowledge applause with a well-meant, mumbled, "Fuck you very much."

They were lean days; it was scufflin' times. We were threadbare, hungry in so many ways, but basically happy, among peers, kindred minds, and a growing sense of something, somewhere, somehow getting better and that we had something to do with it all. We just lived the shit out of the times, soaking up days and nights of experience.

We were getting turned on in so many ways, lit up to new experiences, discoveries, adventures, music, all of which had something very tangibly related to the drugs available. The drugs were enjoyed, used, abused, taken, given, bought, sold, and stolen. We never questioned them; we did drugs because they were there. They felt good, they were fun, and they were a part of our existence. They helped us over some mighty humps and they stood in the way of some others. Most of all they were a stone groove, for making and hearing music, for making love, for getting silly or serious and down to it among ourselves.

High and grooving for the first time, we were above the narrow-minded puritanism that held them illegal. Legal for us was what we chose in good conscience. Smoke sweet and high, it couldn't hurt. And out of this the mutual contempt between us and the heat was born, developed, and grew. It seemed such a humorless, pleasure-denying society, one that took its kicks behind excuses. We had no excuses; we were just getting as high as we could in every conceivable way and out of it a whole scheme of local dealing developed.

Grass, hashish, acid, and pills were cool; we knew their limits. Cocaine, it was so fine, a breathtakingly exhilarating high, too expensive to keep enough around to do any harm. Not in the shape we were in, for Chrissake! Bumming coin from one another, chipping in for Chinese takeout or pizza, cooking brown rice and seaweed, short on everything but dope.

For anything really important there was money, or other means, around. Any trip that got you off was cool, the higher the better, the happier the better, the funnier, the freer, the more and the more and the more. It was for now, for nothing else but now, for us, for our thing; no other dimension of time, space, or responsibility existed. The past was a bummer, the future completely uncertain, and nobody would then really admit to feeling secure as to whether or not the future would even be. If there was to be a future, we would create it out of the flat-out-balls-against-the-wall good time we were having in the great now. The pageant that was our lives had no past and no future; it was always in the process of becoming. It was not goals that stimulated us; it was the experience of being and becoming, the journey there rather than the end haul. We had no precedents that we knew of, we made it up as we went along; anything that proved uncool fell by the wayside of our circus.

We were certainly aware of the hassles. Paranoia fired our thinking and imagination into outrageous hooliganism. It got so that we could just smell trouble coming. A signal would go round the street like electricity whenever the heat was on. They had their informers and we had ours. The only difference was that they were running scared and we weren't.

Nicky was a great connection, still is. He knew a rookie cop who did a little dealing on the side to support his Catholic family and kids in season. Sometimes Nicky would buy from him, sometimes sell. Depended. Information was always extracted about where and when to expect heat, a friendly little exchange of goods and services. When the heat was on you never saw such a clean street in your life.

We'd hear about a bust somewhere, usually a setup, and it would be cool for a while after that. It got to be a joke, a cynical cops-and-uppers game played for tempting stakes.

No matter how hard to come by, dope was always shared. Before 1965 it was relatively scarce on the East Coast, which created a situation where the really cool dealers emerged as community heroes. If you could handle it, you bought some; if you couldn't, there was always a free taste around. It was part of taking care of one another. It was just a better way to live, and nobody was looking back.

"Hang together or hang separately" was an expression passed around and examined in the light of what we were doing. Pete Seeger's agreeable "Take it easy but take it" was a greeting, a farewell, a verbal contact point. New language developed—a colorful, living language, growing, changing, borrowing from the songs and style and contributing to them. Everything we had to do with one another was reciprocal, cyclic, change feeding on itself and causing more in an upward spiral of change whose end was not known or cared about as long as it got higher. The vernacular of the day was a sign between us. The two-fingered V became the parting "peace."

Clothing was warmth and body decoration expressing a love of beauty, individuality, and humor. A leathercrafter in from Colorado went around the Village in a black-and-brown suede jacket he'd made, beautifully tailored with a huge question mark welted into the back. His old lady would walk beside him, the back of her identical jacket adorned with an exclamation point. *Zap-pow*. Walking comic book.

Clothes were inspired by traditions we assimilated—field-hand funk, nomadism, tribalism, and whatever hybrid that mixture produced. Before department store hippie garb was around, some discomfort with the gear he was wearing would give an undercover cop away.

Dealers emerged out of the demand for a constant dependable source of good dope. Andy and Marietta, he a bass player—portly, bearded, wiry, dark hair with a mind of its own and he of no mind to tame it—she a waitress at the Bitter End, had a deal going with Matt, a former accountant in his thirties who was always clad in jeans and a work shirt except when he took planes. Periodically he'd go down to Mexico and bring back twenty to fifty kilos of Acapulco Gold for $60 to $75 a kilo. They'd meet in a motel room in Juarez, complete the transaction. Matt would come back through Nogales. Once, when the grass wasn't up to usual standards, we accused him of passing off as Acapulco Gold what was merely Tijuana Brass.

From Texas, Matt would jet to New York and deliver to Andy and Marietta for $100 to $125 a key. The pair (she was into peasant dress and they were fast becoming known as Raggedy Ann and Andy) would break off the extra two-tenths of a pound in each kilo and accrue their own stash and send the remainder of the "extra" around as a taste, a sample for prospective customers. Usually it was the best around, far superior to the Harlem or Mafia shit, which was likely to be cut with sugar to bring up the weight. Great golden flakes and flowers of smooth-smoking billowy grass. It would get the ultimate rating: dynamite.

Most of the keys would be sold off for anywhere from $175 to $250, depending on how much was ordered (quantity meriting discount is called "weight"), how scarce grass was, and what the traffic would bear. They'd get to keep a considerable stash for themselves, usually giving half of it to friends. You dealt for a living, for status, for the pleasure of being needed and to keep yourself and friends supplied.

Eventually they had enough saved to buy a camper and gear and a pregnant Raggedy Ann and Andy were married by a friend who owned the incense store and they took off for a trip across the country. They arrived back over a year later with something new: acid.

An enormously entertaining Israeli, a one-legged loudmouth—who for the longest time had everyone on the street convinced he was Dennis Weaver, to whom he bore a great resemblance and with whom he shared a common first name—brought hashish back from Lebanon in his prosthetic leg. Seventy-five dollars an ounce if you had the bread, a taste for friendship's sake if you didn't.

Dennis Sheldon was one of the original full-blast groupies. He was always bragging about his heavy clientele of stars. He'd tell hysterical stories about a whiz-bang smoke with the Beatles in a Paris hotel elevator and how he'd shared his last cocaine with the Stones. Maybe it was true; maybe it was not. It didn't matter.

He'd come to impersonate Dennis Weaver in order to seduce a chick, a woolly blonde Village figure who made leather pouches that tied onto the belt loops of blue jeans and who loved to fuck stars. One night he offered to drive her home to Brooklyn Heights. They had just met. She was glad of the ride because the walk from central Greenwich Village to her subway station was kind of hairy. She asked his name and he replied Dennis—yeah, well, he was an actor but down on his luck, his TV series was going off the air. "Dennis Weaver?" chirped Madeline, raising her eyebrows, pursing her lips, and unconsciously parting her knees (which was not lost on Sheldon).

"Sure," he replied broadly.

And from then on he elaborated the impersonation so well that there are many still around who believe him.

He and his old lady, Naomi, whom he'd met and married in an Orthodox ceremony on the kibbutz where he'd lost his leg in an accident, would make the scene every so often, dressed in full Arab garb, a pouch (which Madeline made him) under the folds of the robe, dealing right out in the open in coffeehouses and hangouts. He was so outrageous that nobody ever suspected, and he was welcomed as a colorful regular (the tourists loved to peer at off types when they slummed it in the Village; proprietors were hip to that, so Dennis and Naomi usually had a free tab anyplace they'd hang out regularly in drag).

The closest Dennis ever came to being busted was the time he was driving a friend and me down to the Village for some heavy hanging out after a movie and he went through a red light on Third Street. When he went through the light, a cop pulled him right over. There was about $1,500 worth of dope in the El Al bag on the floor. Dennis, with great and conspicuous effort, struggled out of the car and feigned clumsiness as he fumbled in his wallet for his license. His trouser leg hung miserably empty, fluttering in the breeze beneath the stump.

The cop, he just gulped, gave Dennis back the license and registration with a stammered rebuke, and waved him away. They sold most of hash that evening at Figaro's.

With the considerable profits from dealing and the spoils of a lawsuit against the Israeli government for the loss of his leg, Dennis eventually split for Switzerland to study the design and construction of prosthetic limbs in conjunction with paraplegic therapy, returning to the States once or twice a year with a design to sell and a huge cache of dope to give away.

Lila, a pale, emaciated waif from the East Village, was an easy connection for speed. What a drag she was. You could always tell when she had goods; she'd walk uncertainly into a room, shaky, eyes wide, rapping quickly and continuously and aggravating everyone around. Lila, no last name, a runaway, probably underage, always dirty, incessantly whining. Nobody was particularly distressed to learn she was busted holding amphetamine crystals, morphine, and several hundred Seconals.

She was truly dangerous, neither an efficient nor a cool dealer. Her own state of constant physical anxiety was enough to turn anyone off speeding. Getting high was cool; destruction, of self or otherwise, was not. To live out on the edge you had to be strong; if you fell to danger from the outside, everyone was too afraid or too revolted to come to the rescue. Blues, tragedies, crises of the heart we could and did handle with a sense of community that saw us through them. But speed from Lila? Only as a last resort. If you needed some pure crystal or a set of works to get you through a second rewrite, or gigs on the road that crisscrossed time zones, if there was absolutely nowhere else to score, Lila was always there.

The good acid came from San Francisco, where the kings of LSD manufacturing lived and distributed. The most famous mother of all was a brilliant and totally crazed light and staging man that worked for the groups developing there. He'd give it out by the fistfuls to and through musicians and road crews, sell it on the street for about 75 cents a tab (a good dose, about 500 mgs) through a kind of ad hoc distribution network that floated about Haight Street.

In his time he made literally millions of tablets, each batch a different color or shape to distinguish it from the dull-colored street dope. In New York the tablets would sell for as much as $5 to $7 through dealers. Hired runners would fly the acid across the country for airfare, a fee, and some dope.

There were two enemies: cops and the Mafia. The Mafia was being circumvented and underpriced by amateur grass dealing so eventually they gave up the downtown market. It was bulky (a compressed kilo of grass is about the size of a small shoebox), troublesome, and unprofitable to compete with street price. But with acid, a potent, colorless, tasteless substance, a test tube of which would dose tens of thousands of tablets, an interesting territory was being developed. As the legend goes, organized criminal interests cornered the market on Swedish ergot, a vital ingredient, and proceeded to manufacture lookalike tablets resembling the San Francisco prize product, selling it for $2 a tab on Haight Street.

The San Francisco manufacturer found out about it instantly and took about ten thousand tablets to Golden Gate Park the following Sunday and gave them out free. In one day the bottom fell out of the Mafia acid market and the manufacturer and his happy tribe of disciples rode around in their laboratory truck making more, always on the move, one step ahead of the man, doing his highly esteemed light and staging work for groups on the side.

A comic that worked at the Playhouse invented a little pump for smoking grass. It shot a super hit of concentrated smoke down your throat and by the time you exhaled you were wiped out. *Non compos mentis.* On the floor wondering if you'd ever be able to get up, not really caring one way or the other.

In Los Angeles, some stony glassblower came up with a steamboat pipe, a glass funnel in which you'd place a lighted joint. There was a bulb in the center with a hole on the tip. Cover the hole, inhale, and fill the reservoir with smoke. Uncover the hole, inhale, and it would blow into your lungs. Every head in the village with access to tools would come up with some variety of handmade hash pipe, and head shops carried little screen discs to place in the bowl so no burning embers could come through the shaft.

Roach holders, which had humble origins as paper clips, bobby pins, hair clips, toothpicks, alligator clips, or split matchsticks, eventually became an art form. There were elaborately looped ones you could wear around your neck, arousing no suspicion because they were so decorative, and little handwrought pincer-type devices with amulets at the base. Surgical clamps worked beautifully and were so big they rarely got lost. Roach clips are used on the very end of the joint, to hold the roach so that every bit of grass could be smoked. The main trouble was that by the time you were ready to use one, you were so stoned you forgot where you put it, having been at least that stoned the last time you used it. Alligator clips were handy and had the added advantage of being a necessary piece of electrical equipment any road manager would have on supply.

There were imported stash boxes, lava lights, posters finely detailed for stoned examination, lovely small glass beads to string and wear or give away, and all manner of pretty toys to enjoy while stoned.

If Congress had any idea of the extent of the marijuana market, for both drugs and paraphernalia, it would legalize grass instantly.

Because of the increased sensual awareness that being high produces, artificial food tastes artificial. And because being high widens perspectives on physical as well as mental well-being, organic and genuinely nourishing food becomes more attractive, clean air becomes more important (smelling pollution stoned is immensely depressing), pure water is appealing, and a physically stimulating life becomes more attractive. Staying as high as possible under the most pure and comfortable (and uncomplicated) circumstances takes on a singular importance.

The drug scene grew geometrically. The first people into drugs were those with nothing to lose by it. Ghetto kids honestly believe that as the man kept indigenous peoples under control with fire water, he was keeping the blacks complacent with drugs. For us, hardly ghetto kids—except perhaps in an emotional sense—it was a way into ourselves, one of the first steps on a road that led to many fascinating journeys through the mind, that set the imagination roaming in hidden or forgotten corners and conjured up subliminal scenes that snaked surreally through the consciousness. Bob Dylan was the most talented artist to articulate these hallucinations that were not hallucinations at all: they were there, they fit, they moved and went off into a blackness resolving deep in a moist mysterious level of thinking. He had a hold on our minds that was religious and he'd set them afire with kaleidoscopic chain reactions to his visions, which were always precise and revealing.

Defiance of the law, or any kind of authority for that matter, was merely a byproduct of what we were doing when we got into drugs. True, the surreptitious nature of obtaining and using drugs was a part of the romance, but the real point was getting high. "If it feels this good, it can't be all bad," we reasoned; either we're crazy or the law is, and between us, it was working out quite all right. We lived beyond the law, above it, just out of reach of it. It was obvious after a while that millions were turning on with soft drugs, that dealing (*pushing* is a rather irrelevant term because the demand, without exception, always exceeded the supply) was an honorable way of life. By sheer force of the quantity and stature of the people that were turning on, the law would be overpowered. It was just a matter of time during which one had to be particularly careful and develop a keen intuitive sense of trouble about to happen. Keeping the grass coming while avoiding a bust stimulated our inventiveness about survival and kept us sharp. We would stick it out.

Heads came out of the woodwork. Young lawyers (Lenny Bruce always said grass would eventually be legalized because all the law students he'd ever met were heads) who smoked grass became specialists in defending pot busts, which were usually carried out with a plethora of errors and torts; druggie doctors would straighten out medical facts and squelch widely publicized rumors about drug complications such as the relationship of acid to chromosome damage, about which there is an overwhelming amount of doubt. Heads would open head shops with psychedelic merchandise, some would open health food restaurants (no cigarettes allowed inside), freaks would invent toys to play with while stoned.

Attire gradually became exhibitionism of the most generous sort; to be a thing of beauty for stoners to groove on was a concern of audience and performer alike, and the music became a language of heads. Whether or not the lyrics were specifically (however surreptitiously) about drugs, it was head music, music to turn on to, music to fill new spaces in one's mind that drugs unlocked.

But not everything was going down roses. There was always a tight bunch of junkies around. They seemed to attach themselves like cancer cells to the connective tissue of every good scene that developed and eat away at its goals. Some of them were musicians—mostly jazz leftovers—and they were terrifying. They seemed amiable enough, but if you turned your back on one of them he'd steal you blind. It was wretched to see it fester in our midst.

Nobody liked the junk scene. And as songs were written that appealed to the marijuana consciousness, a lot of songs, like Tom Paxton's "Cindy's Crying," were written despising junk and what it did to people's lives.

> *Cindy's cryin' but it ain't no use—*
> *She's got a habit and she can't get loose.*
> *Stoppin' each and ev'ry man she meets,*
> *Gonna be a hooker on Bleecker Street.*

Once, when the girls' room in the Dugout was out of order, I went into the men's for a pitstop and there was one of the most beloved musicians around sitting on the toilet, his jeans hanging around his knees, his belt wrapped around his arm, his eyes buggy, his mouth hanging open in a dullish smile and a bloody spot on the inside of his arm. I slammed the door, fought back nausea, and ran for help. I didn't know whether he was dead or alive.

But there was fire, constructive crackling fire, going down in the music. There were jug bands, happy hick sounds of the Kweskin band, and Dave Van Ronk's Ragtime Jug Stampers. Jim McGuinn, an accomplished sideman who played with Judy Collins and Bobby Darin, all natty with a goatee, was singing folksongs in between sessions. David Crosby sang with Les Baxter's Balladeers. Dino Valenti made the coffeehouse rounds, singing in a coarse, intense howl powerful enough to put people through a wall.

John Sebastian's father was a classical harmonica virtuoso, his mother worked at Carnegie Hall (you had to be on Mrs. Sebastian's good side to get into the good concerts free). He'd grown up on Long Island and his family later moved to Greenwich Village. At nineteen he hit the streets and rarely went home even for a meal. He was chubby and forlorn looking, he wore his harps slung round his body in a holster. At the Playhouse, with the encouragement of Joey Stevens, its young manager, Sebastian found a place to get himself musically established. Stevens invited him to come and play whenever he wanted. "If we have bread, we'll give you bread," he offered. "I don't know how much or even if we can pay you but we can always give you a place to play."

Mississippi John Hurt was playing the Gaslight when John Sebastian found him. A weathered black septuagenarian, he had a lifetime of blues and beauty to offer the kids on the street. His face had the years and tears of life in the South etched in it, his huge bony hands held a beat-up guitar with the affect of a mother holding her child. He sang with a sweetness, humility, and authenticity that set a room softly charged with feeling. His guitar playing, a double-thumbing style he developed, was unique, his lines so musically facile and rhythmically intricate that he affected the approach of every guitarist who heard him. "'Sippi John," Sebastian called him, and he sat at the old man's feet like a fan, learning songs, licks, and a tenderness of delivery. Eventually 'Sippi John had Sebastian play harmonica with him. Sebastian was beside himself with delight. He became inspired, ingenuous, enchanted; the puppy sadness that hung in his face disappeared.

Everyone seemed to adopt John Sebastian as people were adopting Dylan. He played harmonica and, for that matter, any instrument needed at any given time. ("Sure I can play bass, Bobby!")

Paul Rothchild, who produced records for Elektra, had him come in and play harp on Freddy Neil and Vince Martin's album, *Tear Down the Walls*. They got along so famously that Rothchild would have him in on every session possible, each a $51 union scale date. Rothchild and Sebastian got together a group and a recording called the Even Dozen Jug Band, one of the most historically interesting bands recorded, containing quite a number of individuals who later became well known for other musical contributions. There was Steve Katz (later of the Blues Project and still later of Blood, Sweat and Tears) on washboard, Joshua Rifkin (an outstanding young classical composer later to gain pop fame for arrangements on Judy Collins albums), Peter Siegel, who later became a producer, and Stefan Grossman, who requested that John Sebastian not sing because he didn't like his voice.

Manuel (Manny) Greenhill, a small, fortyish, very cooled-out man, had been running hoots around Cambridge, charging half a dollar for admission and managing to keep it afloat on that. In 1958 Greenhill produced Pete Seeger's first commercial concert as a solo artist. Along with "Tom Dooley," it was one of the single most decisive events that started the folk boom avalanche rolling.

Pete Seeger was at the very heart of it all. If you talk to anyone out of the folk scene, every one of them would mention Pete Seeger as a seminal influence and inspiration. His presence on the folk scene was as loving as it was significant and, as he taught many a boy to be an artist at his craft, he showed all of them how to be a man. He'd been a voice for justice and simple sanity in every struggle of his time, and the young musicians he inspired would take his torch further than he could ever travel, even though, as it eventually turned out, he was not enthusiastic about some of their means.

It was Greenhill's profound attachment to Seeger that led him to work with young talent. "If it were purely a matter of music," he admitted years later, "I probably wouldn't have gotten that involved. It was this crusade aspect that involved me, getting Pete recognized as a solo artist." Seeger had his own crusade going: to humanize a society in which he saw so much good turning in on itself and decaying. They called him a Commie and a subvert, but his mission had never been anything less or more than humanity itself. It was peculiar that it made American institutions so uptight.

Seeger was hassled to the fury and frustration of everyone around him, but Pete, he just stayed cool and kept singing, living his music, making everyone within earshot just a little bit more human, more compassionate, less uptight, and less alone. At the second concert Greenhill organized, an FBI man came around asking questions.

Joan Baez's parents, in to see the young Boston co-ed, were furious that she was living with her boyfriend, and when they left Boston for California they asked Greenhill to look after their wayward girl. He did, and eventually became her manager, building a string of young folk artists around her and a management company, Folklore Productions.

While Greenhill was working with Baez he heard about several benefits in the South for Martin Luther King, Jr. He suggested they help the King people out. Joan was added to one of the programs and a concert was set up. A slightly embarrassing problem developed, however. The concert was on a white campus and blacks were terrified to attend. They literally had to capture (Joan's word) blacks to integrate the audience.

Deep in the heart of Dixie, the new folk music—the coalition of youth, music, and social movement—was forged. The sit-ins, freedom rides, demonstrations, and civil rights marches went into full swing and entertainment provided by folksingers was one of the prime attractions of these events. Not only were the young folksingers selling their art, they were promoting their conscience, and a contemporary audience responded. Whether it was the mission or the music was an irrelevant inquiry. They were inseparable.

There was something beyond the causes for which these actions were mobilized; they were as social as they were political. It was the feeling of being together in numbers unafraid and united in purpose, and to the great majority of people in attendance it was something new and attractive. It was the first real music-fueled rush of power since mobbing *Love Me Tender*.

There was always something just a bit duplicitous, a hint of dilettantism, about the linkage of folk artists and fans and civil action. The movement really had very little to do with the black community. What we were really searching for— and finding—was our own liberation. It was not completely or even primarily about racism; racism was only an isolated symptom, albeit a pressing one. It was just a part of the creeping malaise, it was just a part of hitting out at it and for so many reasons it was going to turn out to be a burn, just another disillusionment. What the civil rights movement promoted was akin to inviting the black people to the ranks of the white; there was always the faint stench of elitism about it. Black people, though interested in making crucial legislative changes, weren't having any white chauvinism; and that resentment, together with infighting among various organizing groups within the civil rights movement, diluted its effectiveness as time went on. Eventually the black kids took over SNCC (Student Nonviolent Coordinating Committee) and threw all the white kids out over differing attitudes about militancy.

A growing feeling of irrelevancy gradually eased the music scene out of the center of the beginnings of radical politics with both sides feeling a little used. Still, they would exist symbiotically and with various degrees of unease from then on.

We lived in this world of our own, self-proclaimed social exiles. Black people didn't have that particular choice. Anyone out of our past was gravely censorious of everything we were doing. If they didn't take us seriously they questioned our sense of responsibility. If they did take us seriously they'd say *why rock the boat?* They'd allow as to how the world had had its problems always and we'd just best adapt to them. But we were into something a little more inquisitive than all that.

We were managing to get someplace, not really knowing where, but it felt right, together, as a group, as a generation, as a culture. There was absolutely no reason to accept less than the best we could envision. We'd had a taste of the freedom of being; it had spoiled us for anything less.

Our experiences had been broadened and our consciousness had been raided. A personal insight was thought of in terms of the planet, of something shared with all peoples. We could understand conflicts and solutions in dimensions. It was something that as a generation we shared, it was something that set us apart from our past and the people who represented it. And they were in power. Worse, we had absolutely no idea what the practical applications of our enlightenment might be.

It wasn't as if anyone knew what we were doing or why. On one level, it seemed like the best idea at the time. On the other hand, there was a tangible sense of things getting better, if only, for the time being, among those people into it. It was inevitable that it should spread.

We'd had our senses stripped by what we'd grown up into. The stuff we'd been taught before we hit the streets didn't even begin to enlighten us. The present demanded more of our balance than we'd ever been prepared for. Anyone born before World War II, it seemed, had already stopped questioning out of the necessity of getting along. Anyone who lived through the Depression never really was free from a desire for material security. We could see that security, real security, wasn't possible anymore. Our security had to do with what we could accomplish ourselves, with available hardware, in our heads, in our work, in our world. We'd sit around and bullshit about it for hours. Why were we here? What's to be done?

What had brought us together? What were we doing? Mostly there was no other place for anyone among us. All of us had something in common. At one point in our lives we'd discovered that the only way to get by was to wing it, an ad hoc lifestyle. It had brought each of us to the same table at the Dugout at the same time. It would keep us together, too; in the years that followed that crowd of street people became a mobile underground, congregating in every city where there was music happening. No organization, no plans, just winging it. And the process of it all was slowly becoming clear.

It was Pete Seeger's savvy and soul that the Village scene fed on, and Woody Guthrie's style. The folksinger was the migrant worker, the countrified philosopher, the irate hick with a global consciousness. All the citybillies developed drawls to bolster their authenticity. Ragtag boys with guitars and autoharps roamed the streets with fistfuls of songbooks, composing paper, scraps of lyric to swap, share, and try out. Everybody scuffled. There was talk that one young folksinger, a delicately beautiful boy who sang fragile poetic songs, the son of a wealthy Buffalo family, was out hopping freight trains with a credit card in his pocket. All things being equal, which they certainly were not, everyone can't be poor all the time. We understood that.

In the early days that scene was quite inbred, basically because major radio stations didn't respond significantly to folk music. There were odd small segments of ethnic-music programming on specialty stations, but a steady stream of folk music reflected the nucleus of what was becoming pop music, developed almost at the very tail end of the street music scene's lifespan. Most of the music of the times was heard firsthand at concerts or in coffeehouses. Its real strength was that it was a person-to-person phenomenon and within that kind of framework the shatteringly intimate stage presence, the ability of musicians to cut right through barriers between themselves and the audience, developed. It would be the single most dynamic factor contributing to the explosive reciprocity rock bands (in which many of these same musicians would later be) could catalyze.

Just as clubs developed a steady stream of "regulars," so each performer generated a cult of followers, a situation attended by no small degree of smugness about being in on it all; a sort of parochialism developed that would be a limiting factor later on.

The folk scene had been documented all along by a little magazine called *Sing Out!*, which since 1950 (the year the Weavers had a pop hit with "Irene, Goodnight") had been publishing articles, songs, and position papers on the state of the art. Their editorial policy strongly endorsed the concept of "people's" music (as opposed to commercial music), but they were never above confronting hypocrisy in their own ranks. After the first Newport Folk Festival, folklorist Alan Lomax called it a publicity stunt; *Sing Out!* reported an observer had commented that Lomax's statement was a publicity stunt.

The Newport festivals each summer were acknowledged culmination points. They were a codification of what had developed over the year in the folk world, a meeting of the movement, and an indication of the future. They began as a commercial event in 1959, at which Joan Baez made a major and widely publicized debut, brought in as a guest of folksinger Bob Gibson, before a huge crowd. Later they became the main venture of a nonprofit foundation for the preservation and exposure of ethnic folk music, past and current, and an encouragement to contemporary folk performers. The roiling division of loyalties between traditional and composed folk music never ceased to interfere with festival politics.

Audiences for the Newport festivals consisted, quite naturally, of young people who came to be a part of something. There were programs in the evenings and the days would be broken down into workshops where artists and audiences could meet and exchange music and ideas. It was always the friendliest and most egalitarian of gatherings, but very subtly a star system began to form. The clique of folk performers, centered on Joan Baez and Bobby Dylan, was generating most of the excitement and energy of the festival and was responsible for the biggest audience draw.

Kids were less interested in the last dying voice of Mutton Hollow because, though they identified with the traditional aspect of folk music, they were not really a part of it. They belonged to their contemporaries and were held there by ties that hadn't even existed when Elizabeth Cotten was a youngster. The singers and poets of their peculiar age were translating the thing that held us all together into art. It was a matter of communicating our fears while celebrating that communion. It held the promise of a beginning of a time when we would know what we could do to make it better among humans; it carried a shred of hope that in the space of hours hope would snowball into confidence and then affirmation. It compared to an empowering religion, the idols were the performers and their pronouncements expressed that the gods were ourselves, each one.

This fanaticism was generally misinterpreted as a shallow sense of esthetics by traditionalists in the foundation and the politics of factions would determine an eventually unpleasant fate of the Newport festivals: insensitively mixed programs, crowd violence, and, for a time, cessation of the event altogether. But for the moment they were ripe with promise, in full swing, cauldrons of social and artistic change.

Until 1963 the festivals had been the biggest folk events regularly scheduled. What with folksongs on the hit parade and the festivals receiving national press coverage, television decided to cash in. On April 6, 1963, a folk-variety show called *Hootenanny* debuted on ABC. From the start it was a pretty lame excuse for a television show supposed to represent the artistic vanguard and the sentiments of the young. The producers' insensitivity was dramatically illustrated by their policy from the very beginning of blacklisting Pete Seeger and the Weavers. The conspicuous absence of certain performers from the series was roundly blasted by *Sing Out!*, and Nat Hentoff, on investigation, found out about the blacklist. The issue started a raging controversy about the show among the inner circle of folk artists and commentators. Joan Baez publicly announced that she would not appear on the show unless Seeger, the real progenitor of the movement (the Weavers actually were largely responsible for the popularization of the word *hootenanny* itself), were included on the program. Other performers followed suit. More significantly, many didn't, and the dichotomy in the creative community of the culture of the new awareness began to show its seamy side.

The blacklist was common knowledge, but some performers felt the exposure folk music in general and their own careers in particular would receive was in itself a valid reason to participate. As movements always do, this one had come beyond. It was showbiz. Everyone was out to make it. Where personal advancement came up against moral commitment it was really interesting to see who made what out of the conflict. Before you can live by something, you have to survive—nothing has ever changed that hard reality.

A young artist with something to say had to say it on whatever terms were available until he became so important he could have it on his own terms. For the performers, these were the dues. *Hootenanny* was a bitter pill to swallow. But for anyone who was interested, when it came time, it was easy to see who was where.

Life was a scuffle but it was part of the trip of being out of the polluted mainstream. Most of us were searching for viable alternatives and what we found was that the answer was the search itself. People on the street were mostly white, middle class, and educated. We were not runaways; it was a wholly mutual rejection. Until artists, poets, writers, musicians, and hustlers of our element became famous, nobody wanted us around but ourselves. That was just fine with us.

Our lives would be affected by a selective series of events to which we would react in unison. It was as if we were all extensions of a peculiar way of thinking and a conscious sense of this unity moved into our sphere of awareness. When most of the music was topical it was a development of current experience by artists; they were songs composed often just for the year of the event or the day. By the time most of the folksingers had records out, the material took on a more permanent aspect, and it had happened simultaneously on campuses, in cities, and small towns, wherever kids were aware, listening, feeling, and laying their hands on guitars. In trains and bus stations, in barracks and parks, young people would get together and make music.

The journalistic exponent of the folk movement was going strong. In Minneapolis, in 1959, two young folk enthusiasts, Paul Nelson and Jon Pankake, started the *Little Sandy Review*, an outrageously refreshing controversial journal of folkstuff. They would review records and suggest that those to their distaste be used as coasters. It was one of the most delightful little publications around. In 1962 *Broadside*, a mimeographed newsletter type of paper, began publishing under the aegis of two folksingers, Sis Cunningham and Gil Turner. Pete Seeger put up some money to get the publication going. It was published in and of Greenwich Village and was the most vital of the magazines, containing handwrought articles by contributing editors, among whom were Bobby Dylan and Phil Ochs. *Broadside* was the first magazine to publish Dylan and recognize his talents. The book became a clearinghouse for new material and movement news during the time when they were trying to unify the folk movement, find out where everyone was at and where *they* were.

Joan Baez, far and away the most successful folksinger of the time, met Bob Dylan in California in 1963. She was singing of lilies and ladies and wayfaring chords; he was singing his damn guts out, making more money from Peter, Paul and Mary's versions of his songs than from his own records. He'd been scheduled to appear on *The Ed Sullivan Show* but refused to go on when they wouldn't let him sing "Talking John Birch Society Blues."

Dylan had been signed to Columbia Records by John Hammond, Sr., a gentleman described as one of the very few men who could inspire anyone with soul to work in the music business. Dylan was Columbia's first artist whose consciousness was in effect his appeal, a rather nebulous concept for such an organization to grasp, and it was some time before even they became dimly aware of what kind of time bomb they were holding.

When he heard that Dylan had been signed to Columbia, Jim McGuinn was openly astonished. "I didn't think he was that good," said McGuinn. Columbia, it might be noted, was its corporate self a little bewildered. The entire record business was so completely unprepared for this explosive tousle-headed singer-bard that his success and the cultural tidal wave it generated caught them off guard. Here they had to deal with artists who weren't going to deal with them on traditional music business terms.

Almost everyone else was recording for Vanguard, Elektra, Folkways, Riverside, or Tradition—all small independent companies whose principals were folk enthusiasts with a genuine feel for, and involvement with, the music of the times. Peter, Paul and Mary, signed to Warner Brothers, where they were a huge commercial success, had given some inkling to the larger companies that the streets of Greenwich Village were littered with gold. Dylan's manager, Albert Grossman (also a principal producer of the Newport Folk Festival), went after a large contract with a large company for Dylan. Association with Grossman at the time was synonymous with fabulous success.

Billy James, a scrawny, slow-talking young man, was hired by Columbia the same year they signed Dylan. His job was writing press releases. Soon after he'd been hired he got an inside telephone call, was invited to go uptown and hear this new kid, Bobby Dylan, in the studio.

Dylan was recording "See That My Grave Is Kept Clean," and James was utterly stunned. "It was incredible!" he enthused. "Aside from being a moving performer, I was struck with the age that seemed to be contained in this kid." From then on, James was Dylan's inside man at the record company. It was not the most comfortable of choices, but James was as evangelistic as a convert where Bobby Dylan was concerned.

Dylan had been invited to a Columbia sales convention in Puerto Rico and he sang "The Lonesome Death of Hattie Carroll," a song about a black maid in the South being caned to death by a white assailant for the entertainment of his houseguests, and the attacker's subsequent acquittal. Oh, boy! The southern Columbia sales representatives and distributors didn't like that one at all. When they complained to the home office James defended Dylan's position and his right as an artist to confront any audience on his terms. A reply, in the form of a memo, according to Billy James, said: "Why don't you tell Dylan to save his best material for himself. If it's in the grooves, we'll sell it."

"Then," as James remembers it, "we all went back to selling Ray Coniff records."

Bleecker Street Revisited
Village Voice/April 7, 1969

Buckskinned Jimmy Fielder, Blood, Sweat and Tears bassist, slouched lazily against the wall in the Cafe Au Go Go. "Hey, congratulations, cowboy, the album's number one *this* week!" "Mmmm," grinned the kid. "It went gold last week."

Inside, proprietor Howard Solomon's voice came out over the P.A. introducing Ed McCurdy. "Let's go in and see the show," said Jimmy and disappeared, in a flap of fringe, into the bowels of the venerable coffeehouse for an evening of the folk scene of the early Sixties revisited.

An impromptu hoot had erupted to welcome Bob Gibson back on the scene. He'd been away and Ed McCurdy had been ill. And the others, the hanging-out-strung-out crew from the late Fifties and early Sixties—some who never made it and returned to the wilds of someplace to be homesick for to keep their music and visions alive, some who made it and went on to influence the rock revolution in any number of ways: as members of groups, vital sidemen, or producers. The Village had died in their absence, burnt out with hippie-gyp button and poster shops where the music used to haunt. Figaro's was gone, replaced with a Blimpie Base, and plastic sandwiches had to substitute for cappuccino.

The previous evening Fred Neil and I reminisced into cups of Tin Angel coffee. "Can you imagine!" he shook his head and dug his fingers into his brow, "Seven years from now the kids who are here are gonna come by and the Blimpie Base will be gone and they'll say, oh, wow, the Blimpie Base, what next! Where is that gonna be at!"

Tonight it was right back where it started. Ed McCurdy always did hold hoots worth sneaking past the ticket taker to see and Bob Gibson's baritone was gaining, his twelve-string picking as fine as ever. Newcomer Billy Mitchell, a reminder of many young men who came before him to hit the street with guitar, was developing into a fine stylist and David Cohen—oh, right, now David Blue—*sans* paunch and jowly belligerence, had it all together in beautiful voice. The Greenbriar Boys, rearranged and renamed Frank Wakefield's Country Classics, played a spectacular bluegrass set and damned if the half a houseful lucky enough to be around didn't clap and stomp along and damned well sang along, too.

Incredible. All those back-when people together on Bleecker Street for a revival. It wasn't planned or scheduled; it just happened. Somehow it sort of had to. It had started in the prophetic flurries of last week when Tim Hardin was closing his return engagement at Cafe Go Go, getting his chops together. All of a sudden Fred Neil is really in town, Nick Venet wasn't shitting us again. Vince Martin showed up, Bob Gibson was, of course, expected, and all of a sudden a rogues' gallery of remember-whens from the basket house days were all there.

A throng of people in the back, remnants from the old Folklore Center, the boys with long hair and glasses, the melancholy long-haired girls looking like Baez, squealed with recognition as they all arrived. John Sebastian! Shel Silverstein! Felix Pappalardi! Dino Valenti! Harvey Brooks!

A venerable Village-folk-music-era crowd poured in from the street above: Karen Dalton, Dave Van Ronk, Charley Jones, and John Bassette among them. While a set was onstage, others went in back, swapped axes, and wailed. Fingerpicking sprinkled from every corner of the house. In the office, somebody's baby slept happily through the night.

Shel Silverstein (he really exists, said McCurdy in his introduction) sang a priceless set of rheumy satire, Dino Valenti blew everyone into the backs of their seats. Vince Martin played all those jasmine songs he wrote in Florida "when I was horny." Judging from the number of songs he had, he doesn't get it off too often down there. Hamilton Face, the house rock band, did a set for contrast. Ed McCurdy presided with funky dignity, introducing each act off a sheet of paper.

The evening culminated with Fred Neil's set, a rumored event, which was what brought a lot of us down there in the first place. His sidemen were Felix Pappalardi on bass, John Sebastian on harp, Harvey Brooks on drums, Daniel Natoga on conga, and Monte Dunn on lead. They eased into the gentle chordings of "Other Side of This: Life," "The Dolphin," and "Everybody's Talkin'." Fred Neil was the musician who influenced an enormous number of singers and players on the rock/folk-rock scene. And Fred Neil still has it all together, beautifully under control. "You sing and I'll break your head," he said to Pappalardi.

Dino and Freddy howled "Look Over Yonder," a refrain-and-response work song, from opposite ends of the Go Go. They wailed to each other, trading parts, calling out from years ago out of the dark. At the end of it Fred Neil leaped over the stage, tear-assed to the other side of the room, dragging Dino backstage in an enormous tearful embrace.

Bob Gibson dedicated the last number to everyone who played, one last tune called "I Like Your Song." Gibson would be playing the Go Go through that week and said he'd continue to do Monday night hoots "with fairly infrequent regularity," said Howard Solomon.

It was close to 5 a.m. when it was all over. Solomon roamed the backstage area bawling, "Out, *out*, OUT!" I walked up the stairs to the street and everyone was hanging out in the doorway, hesitant to cross the street back into 1969. I stepped into the concrete reality, wondering if I'd see Bob Dylan or Phil Ochs barreling around the corner, with those quirky hats on, or at the very least, an apparition of Paul Clayton.

MacDougal Street Revisited
Belfast, Maine/2018

Charles Laurier Dufour, a Bob Dylan aficionado in his late fifties, heard that the Gaslight Café, a venue vital to the folk scene of the early Sixties, the café where Bob Dylan first performed, had reopened as a café in 2010 (after changing hands many times). Charlie, in New York City to browse rare record stores for obscure Bob Dylan recordings, located 116 MacDougal Street.

"I walked down the stairs and walked in and it was exactly as everything I had read, so I knew that this was the place. The small stage was only a foot off the floor. The bar was up ahead to the left and beyond the bar, up against that wall, everything is brick and stone. You really do feel like you are in a cave."

Dufour, a part-time professor of psychology at the University of Maine, has been broadcasting a robust all–Bob Dylan radio program, *Highway 61*, for over twenty-five years, first at a college radio station and then an independent public Maine radio station. It was/is among the most popular shows either station ever aired, and, through the internet, has an ardent worldwide following.

He'd almost met Bob Dylan in 1997, when one of Dylan's musicians, through a mutual friend, got him a backstage pass for a concert Dufour was attending in Erie, Pennsylvania. The backstage pass was waiting for Dufour at the box office when he and his date picked up their front-row tickets. But when he went to the stage entrance before the show, a bouncer refused to let them in. Charlie enjoyed the show anyway, one of scores of Dylan concerts he's seen, most of them from the front row, and came away with one of Bob Dylan's harmonicas that practically fell in his lap during a scuffle that ensued when a rowdy fan jumped onstage and approached Bob Dylan.

In 2007 a Boston craftsperson, who was creating some furniture for another of Bob Dylan's tour musicians, was in one of Dufour's classes in Maine and had heard *Highway 61* on the radio. When the student told his client about it, the musician asked for a tape of the show to play on the tour bus. Charlie happily supplied a tape and they did play it on the tour bus. The musician made sure it got back to Dufour that Bob Dylan himself very much enjoyed *Highway 61*, that he appreciated Charlie playing uncommon cuts and duets and that his commentary on each song was so informed.

A few years later, Charlie Dufour stood in the reopened Gaslight. "It was about two or three in the afternoon. I approached the owner of the place, who was the bartender, who was cleaning up and doing things. I told her why I was there, that it was an important moment for me, to touch the past when Dylan was right there up on that very stage." He asked her, "Do you mind if I go up on that stage?"

She told him to go ahead. "So I stood there on that stage looking out at what [Bob Dylan] would have seen. I've got his eyes on and I'm looking at how small the place was. I ordered a beer, and I walked around the place, looking around. I went to the bathroom, because he would have used the bathroom. I sat at the tables. I had that moment. I was where he was when he was twenty-one, twenty-two."

After a little while, Dufour walked back up the stairs to the street and the twenty-first century in Greenwich Village, New York. The reopened Gaslight didn't even last a year.

It is impossible to overestimate the breadth and depth of Bob Dylan and his works. This is just one of the uncountable lives and creative paths he's inspired. He is, and always has been, our bard. He broke the sentence, not to mention the mold, and shattered beyond recognition the language of susceptibility.

New Ports

Newport Folk Festival, 1963. Peter, Paul and Mary's recording of Dylan's "Blowin' in the Wind" was a gigantic commercial hit. The trio introduced that song during their set, saying it had been written by the strongest songwriter in America. Their hit was in full swing and Dylan's own album hadn't begun to move. Peter, Paul and Mary, Joan Baez, Theodore Bikel, Pete Seeger, the Freedom Singers, Odetta, and Dylan himself—now the darling of the festival—gave a tumultuous finale to the evening's performance, singing "Blowin' in the Wind," then joining hands and singing "We Shall Overcome." It sounded like a barnyard gone berserk, but the crowd ate it up. Dylan was, with Baez, the star of the festival that year, which was attended by a completely turned-on folk audience, music business heavies, and the national press. When Billy James got back to his office the following Monday he wrote a memo to the sales department, pointing out that there were only forty Bob Dylan albums in the entire city of Newport, Rhode Island, should anyone have wanted to buy some. Hits, it turns out, don't come from heaven after all.

Independent record companies resulted from the production of the 33⅓ LP in 1948. Until then the record business had been dominated by large companies with a lot of money because only they could afford pressing plants and depots to distribute the highly breakable shellac 78s. After the LP was invented, the pressing plants could manufacture many times as much actual recorded content in less time with essentially the same equipment and were able to take orders from outside companies. Hundreds of little labels specializing in jazz, spoken word, folk, and novelty records could sell through independent distributors, who in turn would reach retail outlets. Rhythm and blues and rock 'n' roll had an outlet with these new conduits of distribution, and new forms of musical merchandising began to take over with new styles of doing business.

A lot of little labels went out of business as fast as they came in. It was very easy to be screwed by a distributor. If a small company released a record and it didn't hit, it had to eat the overage returned. If it did hit, the distributor could withhold payment until the next hit, tying up enough capital to put a little business under. One way or another, hundreds of independent labels vanished. A handful survived to become major independents.

Caedmon, Vanguard, and Elektra were three independents specializing in folk music that survived into the late Fifties when folk music was just about to bloom commercially.

Jac Holzman started Elektra in 1950 with a few hundred borrowed dollars and a tape recorder. He had been studying at St. John's University for three years (actually for about a year and a half; the rest of the time had been spent messing around in the electronics lab). A fellow student down the dorm hall was palsied and Holzman would help him out by stacking records on his turntable for him. It was largely a folk music collection and Holzman usually stayed around to listen, becoming fascinated with the pure, unaffected sound he heard. He started his record company shortly thereafter with the first record, an album of lieder music that cost about $20 to record (two hours in a studio for which Holzman had to bring his own recording tape). The album sold about forty copies.

Holzman went back to New York, set up shop in Greenwich Village, eventually running a record store and making records on the side. He hung out on the street just as the young folkies were all coming in and signed a number of them, developing a knack for merchandising that type of material and playing a significant role in the popularization of young folk artists and their material.

Nesuhi and Ahmet Ertegun, sons of Turkey's ambassador to the United States, grew up in Washington, D.C., hanging out with Ralph J. Gleason. The Ertegun brothers were powerfully attracted to native American black music, old jazz, rhythm and blues, stuff recorded on little fly-by-night labels. Those records were original and irreplaceable, usually discontinued discs that had been remaindered. They found rare old records selling for spare change in all kinds of odd stores.

They'd go through stacks of them, knowingly pick out masterpieces, buy them for pennies, and sell them to collectors for as much as $25. Right away you could tell these guys were destined for the music business.

Nesuhi, a gentleman of calculating mind and disarmingly formal demeanor, was the stable element of the duo; Ahmet was the character—a music wizard, a renegade, a fast thinker with an outrageous sense of humor and timing. Ahmet was such a bullshitter that his dentist couldn't get him to shut up long enough to drill his teeth. At one point he was telling stories of his success in picking and reselling those rare old 78s and the dentist got talked into lending him some money to start Atlantic Records. Nesuhi later joined the company as vice president and head of the foreign division.

In the late Fifties Jerry Wexler—a former journalist, an immensely intelligent, sensitive, warm man with a love for music—joined the Erteguns as a partner. Above everything else the principals of Atlantic were music people, producing the music they released, and having a sense of dignity about, and a joyous appreciation of, Negro music. Atlantic occupied a single office in New York, a crowded room in which Jerry and Ahmet worked, desks facing each other during the day. At night they'd move the desks back against the wall and bring in the recording equipment. In 1954 Joe Turner's version of "Shake, Rattle and Roll" was recorded that way. The song needed a chorus, backup voices going "Shake, rattle, and roll" at intervals to fill out the vocal. Since the budget did not allow for backup singers, Ahmet and Jerry hung in there and wailed right behind Joe Turner.

Years later, when both Atlantic and Elektra were major independents, Ahmet Ertegun approached Jac Holzman to purchase Elektra. Holzman would have none of it and Ertegun took the rejection of his offer kindly as the two talked genially about the independent record company business. There were a lot of ways to make just as much or more money, Ertegun observed, but not too many ways to have more fun. By 1970 both companies had been bought out and had become part of a huge conglomerate, Kinney Leisure Services, which also owned Warner Brothers.

Holzman had been on the Village scene all during the folk years and somewhere early in 1965 was feeling restless. The Byrds' emergence, the Stones' excitement, and the Beatles' vast sophistication were stirring something up. During this time Holzman checked out the Night Owl, where the Lovin' Spoonful were playing, and his head snapped. While most record company presidents were lawyers, Atlantic and Elektra's presidents were producers, talent scouts, writers, and generally music people. Holzman approached the Spoonful for a recording deal. Things seemed so right. Paul Rothchild, Elektra's most prominent producer, had been working with Sebastian for years by then, and Sebastian and Holzman were friends. The empathy for a spectacular combination of talents was all there. Bob Cavallo, manager of the Spoonful, agreed. Congratulations and joyful hugs were exchanged.

For reasons never believed or fully understood, the next day the deal was off and the Spoons were signed to an independent production with a label deal, later bought out by a large entertainment company. The Spoonful went on to become hugely successful but the hitches showed. Under their business arrangement they ended up four times removed from their money and Sebastian was committed to publishing contracts that would plague his later career with litigation hassles.

Nonetheless, Sebastian's friendship with Holzman and Rothchild never faltered. The Spoonful had a hectic career; they made good music. With the antic outspokenness of Zally Yanovsky, a big-faced nice Jewish boy, and the delicate gentility of John Sebastian, a nice Italian boy, the group had a spectrum of ethnic and emotional characteristics that catalyzed their impact. When John Sebastian married a Jewish girl, Zally—with the Jewish guests on one side of the chapel and the Italian relatives on the other—threw spaghetti at the wedding.

Holzman had to wait for Elektra's first rock group and they emerged in 1965: a group named Love under the direction of a madman leader named Arthur Lee. Love, magnificent though they were, somehow never made it big during that time. They had their problems, which resulted in a constant change in personnel compounded by Lee's reluctance to leave California for promotional touring. Love was, and remained, a predominantly West Coast sensation, living reasonably well on local business, a throwback to the days a few years before when both East and West Coast markets were insular, different, chauvinistic, and self-contained.

In 1966 Elektra released an album called *What's Shakin'*, a compendium of blues featuring Ginger Baker, Jack Bruce, and Stevie Winwood, who was listed as Stevie Anglo. A companion album titled *The Blues Project* was released featuring, among others, a musician billed anagrammatically as Bob Landy, who was in fact Bob Dylan.

The label was growing, and in 1967 hit a pot of gold with the Doors, a local Los Angeles group that burst nationally into one of the most profoundly successful phenomena in the music business. They were the top, the most controversial and most provocative group of their time. Elektra grew geometrically at that point, opening a West Coast office and studios and functioning as a major independent company.

Atlantic, too, had grown; it had a large and diversified catalogue of great artists and great albums and a reputation for breaking out soul hits, expanding the musical breadth of pop in the marketplace.

As the music developed and became intensely humanized, it affected the music business on all levels. In their own sphere of professional influence the musicians revolutionized the industry. For one thing they turned the executives on. One major West Coast studio subsequently began allotting funds for smoke in the budget, several thousand dollars a year disguised on the books as "garden supplies." Companies whose principals were not particularly hip hired what came to be known as company freaks, easygoing ombudsmen to facilitate communications between artists and company functionaries.

Ahmet Ertegun's antics became legendary gossip on the grapevine. He produced great music, wrote successful songs, gave great parties, and talked the best game in town. When he hit Hollywood with his Rolls-Royce the whole street knew about it. He had a talent for having a different game going with everyone, each littered with practical jokes and alive with personality. In the early Seventies, courting the Rolling Stones' label deal (which was successfully consummated), he spent weeks hanging out with Mick Jagger, winning his confidence, entertaining him, wheeling, dealing, negotiating, and cooking up schemes. It came to the point where Jagger was about to make a decision but was holding out for time. Ertegun placed a telephone call from his suite at the Dorchester Hotel in London. Reaching Jagger, he asked for a commitment. Jagger replied that he had decided to talk to the president of Columbia Records to see what he would come up with. Ertegun hung up the telephone, baffled. A frown creased his face, then his eyes lit up as he dialed Jagger's number again. "Look," he demanded with an air of finality, "I've got to know your decision soon because I've a decision of my own to make. It's either you or Paul Revere and the Raiders." Without waiting for Jagger's astonished reply, Ertegun smoothly and gently hung up the telephone.

When the Apple label, the Beatles' recording venture, first came out, Stan Gortikov was president of Capitol Records, which distributed Apple. Gortikov had always been pestered by one certain retailer in Los Angeles, who always insisted that he didn't mind the implications of pop music per se, but his was a family store and he had to keep it clean. Every so often this retailer would complain that one or another record was too sexy, had drug references—any complaint at all calculated to keep Gortikov beholden to his business. When this retailer took a good look at the Apple label (the front side of which was a green apple, the flip side of which was an apple sliced to reveal the core), he saw something very strange and upsetting. Immediately he was on the phone to Gortikov, livid with indignation. How could Capitol do such a thing, he demanded. The flip side of the Apple label disguised as an apple core distinctly resembled a vagina!

Gortikov held the phone away from his ear in amazement as the dealer carried on.

"You think it looks like a cunt?" Gortikov demanded. "Then go fuck it!"

Artists, with producers, make records. Record companies foot the bills and coordinate promotion. The actual manufacture of the record is either contracted to an outside pressing plant or one owned by the record company complex itself. From there it goes to a network of distributors to the dealers, the retail stores. It is the distribution factor that is the critical point of failure for the most part, for the distributor neither identifies with nor cares about the product he handles, nor does he make any effort to improve the situation. It's a constant hustle. Somebody must sit on the record company to hustle the record to the distributors. The record company must sit on the distributors to get the record into stores. Promotion people must sit on radio stations to air the records. Coordinated, these processes, given the right product, make for commercial hits. But on the way to heaven, a snag could occur at any of those points.

It's the thin, often-crossed line between cooperation and competition that kept folk music and later rock 'n' roll so mutually satisfying for artists and audience. Other artists pitched in for Dylan, knowing full well he would surpass them all. Those who sang his songs made audiences aware of his presence as a performer as well as of his talent as a writer. Baez squired him around, sharing stages on which she was the sole billed star, introducing him and giving him a portion of her program. Dylan was irrepressible. And the scene was growing incredibly fast, soon to connect across the Atlantic with something quite unpredictable, as unpredictable as the next few months after Newport '63 would be for all of us who were to watch in horror, to see and feel the beginning of the end and the end of the beginning.

Still, when I think back, trying to see shape in what we've become and what we will be, I miss John Kennedy badly. For a while it seemed like something was really happening; while we were realizing our lives, our dreams, might be born as more than something only we could manifest. In those days it seemed everyone was part of the same movement. The man smiled, glowed with health and humor, laughed at himself, loved his kids, and took fierce stands. He seemed to embody the heroics of a pioneer and the cavalier offhandedness of a new statesman, all with a kind of easy grace we'd given up on. He was young and we felt close to him. We believed it was a mutual feeling. When the president took time for himself, he went to the sea.

We were talking late at night, sometime later, some friends of mine and I, about revolution, paranoia, drugs, counterculture, and the problematical distinction between them and us, when one of us suggested that Jack Kennedy was shot because he seemed so happy. It's a long, long time to let it bleed.

We got it in the neck when they put JFK away. Marches and folksongs and festivals notwithstanding, the despair was worse than when we started. We'd been existing on a plane of our own, and the hope we were experiencing suddenly seemed to have no relation to reality. Kennedy's murder proved it.

I remember believing in something before the assassination. With a tinge of some cynicism I'd acquired in self-defense I thought back to freedom rides and how we thought they were really going to do it. There was nothing a nonviolent demonstration couldn't solve—we really believed it. Nonviolence was the ultimate tactic and we were going to see in a new age of peace. David Brinkley once called it the time when our national innocence was still intact.

Revelation came in a spasm of pain, growing up came in a crackling split second, an unbearable moment of fear, anger, humiliation, and pain that wouldn't stop. Sometimes I wondered if I really wanted to live in America. But it's mine, goddammit, it's mine.

And we sat, chin in hands over many a cappuccino, contemplating, pessimistic, brought down. We took it personally. We couldn't comprehend it. We were in shock. And we might never have come out of it, but across the Atlantic, unbeknownst and unsuspected, another street was happening and the first ones up off of it were the Beatles.

At the Playhouse, on the bill with Fred Neil, Vince Martin, Felix Pappalardi, and the Holy Modal Rounders, was Jim McGuinn and his twelve-string guitar, doing what was billed on a sign outside the house as "Beatle Impressions." He could get out about three harmonies at once and so much sound from his instrument that it contained a good deal of what the Beatles would eventually bring. No matter how the folkies tried to discount it as *ausländische* music, it fascinated all of them.

The house was packed with musicians: Cass Elliot, the enormous mothersinger broken away from the Mugwumps and the Big Three; Peter Thorkelson (Tork), a street elf who sang out of tune; David Crosby, in from boats and wanderings; Stephen Stills, and others, almost everyone who would eventually become a vital part of seminal American rock groups to be formed over the following year. It sounded different but it felt peculiarly right. It had come by a different route to the same place in a good deal better shape than we were in at the time.

Liverpool, London, Hamburg. Young English musicians inspired not by Woody or Pete but by the previous teenism era burst of pop: Chuck Berry, Little Richard, and the blackest blues from the American South, and with it they were making real, gritty, rhythmic rock 'n' roll again!

They'd tour the European circuit with reckless abandon. "It was like being in a motorcycle gang without brakes, in an army unit, or on your first school bus trip," grinned Eric Burdon, whose group, the Animals, was the first to follow the Beatles across the pond to tour the U.S. "Medieval strolling minstrels. We were on the road in Germany, young, completely free, no responsibility, grabbing every chick we laid eyes on if they didn't grab us first."

So wild. Taking anything that would get them high. Burdon lived above a club in Liverpool where all the London groups played. He, Zoot Money, Georgie Fame, Chris Farlowe, the Who, John, Ringo, and Mick Jagger all hung out there—drinking, playing, shooting the bull, and getting each other fired up to play. Eric used to fall out of bed, hit the club, hang out, play, get wrecked, and stumble upstairs into bed again.

They'd make weekend raids on Hamburg, mess around in strip joints, and raise hell in the great English custom of raving. From the sounds of skiffle bands to the crackerbuck American rock 'n' roll of the Fifties, the black rhythm and soul sounds they'd assimilated and interpreted, they'd get a sound with an irresistible beat and the wild abandon of being young, horny, stark loony and backstreet British boys making street muffin music—very loud, lowdown, funky, and real.

Less than three months after Kennedy was buried the Beatles arrived in America and took every last one of us on a ride we'd never know the likes of.

Somehow, with the change in focus the Beatles exerted on our lives, the malignant depression of the Kennedy assassination didn't hurt so much anymore. Whether or not any of it was a valid distraction is not the point. Beatlemania gave us back our enthusiasm, parted the tangles so the hope could work its way back through again; it bought us time to feel and begin to think again.

It was too real to ignore, impossible to explain but easy to accept. It felt so right, so undeniably right. It was quick and magical, almost complete, painless, and fast moving. Who could argue with ecstasy at a time like the mid-Sixties when nothing else seemed right? There was something to live with, if not for, and it was during that time it seemed everyone in great multiplying numbers started getting high.

From that point on it happened fast, colorfully, outrageously. The Beatles had kicked down a door and we all in our own ways rushed it, made it through. When the Beatles had come and gone the first time around everyone in earshot from the streets to the penthouses was somehow irrevocably changed.

By 1963, John Sebastian, tired of being the house harmonica player for every house on the street, left town for some seaside town in Massachusetts to become a sailmaker. He was fascinated with the idea of a career for which he could carry all the tools in the palm of his hand. If he hadn't developed a violent allergic reaction to the paint they used on the bottom of boats he might have quit the scene altogether. But within a few weeks he was back on the street with a new idea.

He got some friends together to form a jug band, the Lovin' Spoonful. Electric good-time music they wanted to play, removed from the dirge and protest of the folk scene, which was beginning to feel a bit stiff. The Lovin' Spoonful lived together at the Albert, a great white elephant of a Greenwich Village hotel, held together with a lick and a prayer, straining in good-natured filthiness at its very seams to stand up to what was going on inside.

A going riff on the street was a movie we'd make, *Fire Drill at the Albert*. Pull the alarm and watch creatures of every description teem out the doors, windows, and cracks, ancient weird unholy people, a Fellini collection of humanity's fringe followed by the Lovin' Spoonful, four kind of goofy boys who made music in their room.

The good-time music coming through the door was giving the hotel a bad time. The building was old, the acoustics about as good as those of your average latrine. The assistant manager, a sweet lady with a measure of forbearance above and beyond the call of duty, one evening found it necessary to storm the room and put it to them. No rehearsing in the room. "Practice on the street, practice in the basement, but not in this room or you're out of the hotel!"

The hotel bill was a long way from being paid and the boys were broke and anxious. The Albert had taught them to be terrified of being chronically poor. The street was not the answer (no electricity or surely they would have tried it) but the basement was. Nice Miss Feldman at the desk was quite amazed one night to hear rock 'n' roll clomping out of the basement. The band had moved into the cellar, drums and amps and retinue, and when they turned on the juice, roaches you wouldn't believe—thousands upon thousands of them—streamed out of the cracks. Rats sat up and listened, traumatized by the sound. Alligators in the sewer went into a coma. If you walked on the west side of the Albert, you could hear it coming up through the grating in the sidewalk.

And while all this was going on, literally underground, they all went to hear Jim McGuinn's Beatle Impressions and were enthused and encouraged that somewhere four other guys were into the same thing hard and they were doing quite all right.

Whammo! The heavies evacuated the Village and split for California. Folk had become too commercial to be comfortable; tourists jamming every coffeehouse were degenerating the scene, cover charges and minimums every place we used to hang out for free were a drag, the stars of the folk world were off the streets and on the road or in secluded, exclusive enclaves.

The Spoonful played in the Night Owl to hundreds of teenyboppers in from the boroughs. *Time, Newsweek, Life,* and *Look* were discovering and exposing, exploiting the Village Underground, and things had laid low for about a year. The English invasion was on, group after group came, sang, and conquered and the American boys were getting shown up but good. You had to love them, those English groups, they were such rakes, such loud, irrepressible, funky rakes. They certainly shook things up.

Songs of discontent were still happening, but other music was germinating, a wild breed off from folk, infused with rhythm and electricity, and they were songs of affirmation, of joy and renewal. They felt much better; they spun us around to the good side again.

It had been a restless year. Late in 1964, prophetically, ABC TV dropped *Hootenanny.* Newport '64 had been overcrowded, and a lot of the intimacy was lost. It was a beautiful festival, so much going on in the workshops and stage shows, but, well, the Newport city mothers and fathers were beginning to get a little nervous about so many unkempt people with guitars. An item in the *Newport News* read:

> I wonder if anyone listened to the lyrics of the songs sung at this festival? Some of the lyrics advocated the overthrow of all parental, church and police authority . . . making seditious remarks. I don't think the city should give these people a pulpit to speak from.

Dylan in workshop at Newport
Photo by Jac Holzman

The heat was catching on; they were beginning to smell dope.

Though folk music was enjoying the highest degree of commercial success, something was being lost. It gained momentum and lost vitality. All those rock 'n' roll boys from England were showing the American dudes their heels. And American musicians, in the good old gunslinger tradition, were going to give them a run for their (our!) money.

In the early spring of 1965 Dylan had released *Bringing It All Back Home*. A shrill, pealing guitar note in the first bar of the first song, "Subterranean Homesick Blues," pierced all precedents in the direction of folk music and Dylan's musical progress. The album had a frothing beat, an electric backup band, and did it ever cook. The songs were contagious. "She Belongs to Me," a compelling saga of a strong woman breaking a strong man's will; "Maggie's Farm," scathing and vivid; the beguiling "Love Minus Zero/No

Limit." "Mr. Tambourine Man" sparkled with lyrical grace and metric momentum. "Bob Dylan's 115th Dream" opened with a false start, Dylan laughing idiotically, collecting himself to do the song again, that manic giggling hanging like a ghost over the album's presence. It was as if he had a vision of what the album would do to warp the heads that eventually heard it. "I accept chaos," he wrote in the liner notes; "I wonder if it accepts me."

There had been a forewarning. Dylan's previous album, *Another Side of Bob Dylan*, released late the previous year, had hinted at some kind of transfiguration in Dylan's creative ego. It contained "My Back Pages" and the revealing and prophetic line: "But I was so much older then, I'm younger than that now." Younger indeed. He'd been mainlining rock 'n' roll like everyone else.

It was obvious he was feeling changes in the tide. He was also going through massive personality shocks—now famous, now obscure, now a remote phantom presence on minds and ambitions and the language of the time. His stimulus had to work its way through veils of fame, flattery, and riches he'd accumulated in accelerating doses over the last two years, and his career was breaking through to unimaginable success.

It was Newport Folk Festival time, 1965. Everything was riding high. The Beatles had made progress in their music and pop consciousness was changing fast. In San Francisco, bands were getting together; in Los Angeles, rock 'n' roll was rampant, eating up the street like a great phosphorescent glob from inner space.

The stars of Newport that year were the stars of the world, and everything crackled with a special stellar flash of excitement. It was a celebration somehow extraordinary even for these folk festivals we'd come to look forward to so much each year. The very air shimmered.

Never before had the antagonism between folk purists and young folk stars been more venal. The stuffed shirts of folkdom despised the coat of many colors the young ones wore, insisted that real folk music came from and strictly adhered to traditional sources. The political people, too, were incensed that this music had turned back to songs of changes people go through with themselves, with one another, leaving protest music to seed itself. The new music to hit this festival was treated by the traditionalists as a Judas lamb and the venom was rife.

At one afternoon workshop for which Alan Lomax was the emcee, he introduced the Butterfield Blues Band with some stupid remarks about, well, they're white and young and use electric guitars, but for what they're worth . . . with the implication being not much—and like that. Mind you, here was a band whose key organizer had hung around the south side of Chicago for years, sitting in with Muddy Waters, hanging out with James Cotton, absorbing the blues as directly as he felt and identified with them. Paul Butterfield had paid his emotional and musical dues night after night in crappy little bars at the feet of blues masters whose essence, talent, and musical profundity he recognized, respected, and emulated with honor, dignity, and rare inspiration, not to mention an infectious enthusiasm that turned many a white kid on to Chicago black blues who wouldn't have come around to it any other way. Perhaps that's what stung Lomax and his like the hardest, that Butterfield would go a long way toward getting those old blues masters recognition and commercial support long past due.

Albert Grossman (who managed the Butterfield Blues Band), himself a refugee from Chicago's folk and blues scene where he'd once run a club, was mottled with rage. Since his association with Dylan he'd grown his hair long; it fell around his full face knotty and white like seaweed transfixed by the Ajax white knight. He looked for all the world like Ben Franklin on acid, and being on the Dylan trip had given him a kind of smug obscurity he wore like a banner and a shield. He was a hulking porterhouse of a man with an aura of sternness about him which broke right on the brink of some amazing private scheme the music-biz monarch always seemed to be concocting. But when Grossman heard Lomax's introduction for the Butterfield Blues Band, he blew his ever-loving cool.

As Lomax turned to leave the stage, Grossman strode over toward the steps to meet him and he was fit to be tied. "That was the *dumbest* introduction I have ever heard!" he reportedly said, glaring at Lomax with blood in his eye.

Somebody always seems to yell "sellout" when someone else is getting the good end of the bargain. The people and publications who carried the news and muses of traditional folk music before and after it was recognized critically and commercially contributed a great deal to our education, musical enjoyment, the proliferation of topical songwriting, and, most importantly, to our social and political consciousness.

So it was somewhat disillusioning how righteously indignant they became at the prospect of young talented performers carrying the torch further than any country fiddler could have. They could not see the new music as folk with different instruments. Electronics. Millions of teenagers and college students who probably never would have thought of questioning the system into which they'd been born turned on to contemporary folk music made by their contemporaries with instruments that reflected the contemporary technology they lived with, and with that began an examination of their own values regarding the society in which they lived. With that came the beginning of an increasing awareness among the young of their position, their potential, and finally their power.

Times had changed and changes affected artists as well as audiences. They affected one another so vitally, profoundly, and rapidly that what emerged was unrecognizable compared to anything that had gone down before. We were sailing on uncharted waters as far as we were concerned; our futures belonged to our choices.

Music developed along these lines, probing the inner depths of conscience as well as its outer manifestations. *Bringing It All Back Home* was just the tip of the iceberg. Nestled into those syncopated harmonies of Peter, Paul and Mary were songs of questions, of war, of integration. "We Shall Overcome" had become an anthem sung now with more conviction than hope. The Byrds' version of "Mr. Tambourine Man" had just been released with the changeling turns of sounds and minds growing together among us. The next few months would bring "Like a Rolling Stone," Dylan's first own mass market hit and it would bludgeon the concepts of commercial pop music, temper, fire, and remold them into something much stronger, much more a personal expression of an artist's vision and more soul-shattering than ever before. His two greatest albums, *Highway 61 Revisited* and *Blonde on Blonde* (the first ever double album in popular music) would follow in short order.

These sounds were counterpointed by Motown, the Supremes, the sexy, glossed-over rhythm and blues sound; Herman's Hermits' pop pastry, "Mrs. Brown, You've Got a Lovely Daughter," built around an infectiously persistent bluegrass banjo riff; the Beach Boys' "Help Me, Rhonda," with its gasping tempo and harmonic plumage; and Barry McGuire's "Eve of Destruction." The Beatles' *Rubber Soul* was a quantum leap in the sophistication of their work. The Rolling Stones had landed, rolled up their sleeves, and doused the scene with ruffian roulette music.

Music developed and the folk purists simply could not understand or abide it. They railed with the fury only those who were fast losing power could hurl. In the very heart of the birth of the new culture, its patriarchs were becoming staunchly conservative. What seemed like youthful folly to them was just the passage of some very loaded time and those that were so much of that time as to be above it and at the very edge of revolution were playing it to the hilt, seeing just how far beyond a new frontier they could push it.

Newport 1965 was being politicked away. The whole evening's performance built around festival headliner Bob Dylan's appearance. The tousled troubadour who started in the midst of this milieu returned now with the laurels of the continents on his shoulder, to say nothing of that pungent chip no one had ever knocked off. He came on, roaring down the turnpike of his multiplicity of minds and feeling his impact, his power, his presence as reflected and refracted by the crowd out there. His approach was ever so intensely felt.

The lights dimmed. Anxiety crackled through the audience and sparked around the stage area. A single spotlight picked out a small figure clad in black leather and a white shirt. He radiated tension and energy so fiercely it hung like a barrier between himself and the crowd that hailed him. With the backing of the Butterfield Blues Band, a red electric guitar slung from his shoulder, he played "Maggie's Farm" and "Like a Rolling Stone." He flaunted the forbidden and made it sacred. He pulled his deepest defenses down, stretched them unrelentingly, and transformed them in front of thousands to strength, ferocious and determined. He was open and vulnerable, he was untouchable, with the ultimate weapon in his hands, an electric guitar: "How does it *feel!*" It had been flying around for a couple of years but at that very moment the shit hit the fan. The bewilderment and outrage were flaring.

People applauded—some dumbstruck, some heartily. People cheered, booed, people blanched. Pete Seeger was furious, outraged, disgusted. Backstage, it was said, somebody shouted, "Pull the plug!"

Fat chance.

Dylan walked offstage with his face down. Peter Yarrow, flustered and upset, jittered onto the stage and tried to revive the audience, which was reacting in all manner of stunned shock, wild joy, and everything in between. He urged them to clap rhythmically and bring Dylan back on and they responded. Crash, crash, crash—stomping, shouting. After what seemed like an agonizingly long wait, Dylan came back onstage, alone, eyes cast down, his mouth set firm. Without looking up, averting his face, he held a wooden guitar and strummed the opening chords. He bent forward into the microphone and sang "It's All Over Now, Baby Blue."

And it was, right then, that moment, that place in time, that song, that sound, that beginning and that end. Where there was fire there was now smoke. And something else had already begun to burn in California.

The Newport Folk Festival was also the first time Bob Dylan performed the blistering diatribe "Like a Rolling Stone" in public. The festival booked more and more rock acts as time went by, after floundering financially for a while, and now features a variety of contemporary music not strictly or even loosely considered folk. This policy is successful and the Newport Folk Festivals have sold out consistently since its fiftieth anniversary in 2009, some years selling out even before the lineup is announced.

The event of Bob Dylan going electric was commemorated with a well-publicized "65 Revisited" program in 2015. The festival lineup performed an extended Bob Dylan set, but Bob Dylan did not appear. I do believe he'd had enough.

Trips! Lights! Fantastic!

The action had shifted, dazed and rushing for a delirious raid on California. Westward ho to the Golden State with the golden people and their iron pyrite dreams. The Beatles were coming on like gangbusters, the English invasion was full blast, and the fans were in a constant state of sexual hysteria. People were charmed, enthused, involved, and rip-roaring through days to nights to days again. It wasn't a matter of seeking and finding anymore, it was happening, full of good changes and good times. We asked neither what we could do for our existence nor what it could do for us. It was just happening, and we lived the raving hell out of it.

L.A., a gangly town, forever in adolescence. Rock 'n' roll music, like a colored carnivorous bird, giant, oafish, and full of mischief, descended on its center. This town, this free, crazy town, where both freaks and the law ran wild.

It had always been the place for border souls. There are fire-worshiping cults, chanting sects, apostles all over Sunset Boulevard giving out amulets and karma. There are footloose wanderers in from all kinds of trips milling all over the Strip.

There are people driving around in Bentleys who own only the tires, plastic-and-pasteboard–furnished apartments lining the innards of some cross streets sheltering sequestered lovely stucco homes, gardens, balconies, flagstone, and trees all about oblivious to the tackiness of the surroundings. There are palaces, Grecian temples, gingerbready cathedrals, and huge stone castles in the hills, all for rent, to house the multitudes of extraordinaries who pass in and out of L.A. at that level.

Late at night for small change you can get cardboard tacos and shoeleather pizza and drink in the neon gloom, coming down. And there are moments, crazed charged flourishes of time, that can make the universe worthwhile.

Right off your first day, driving around you get the feeling— something's really—and it's about to—but it just *did* and isn't it, wasn't it—but nobody's . . .

And it just keeps happening. All the time.

They don't know what time is in California. It's the beautiful weather, always, the beautiful people always, and scenes lapse into rich intensities and cataclysmic bummers, merging, turning, metamorphosing, changing, always moving, forever still, caught frozen in the outer circle of a center spinning.

You can scan the basic inanities by the signs encountered in one day:

On a solemn marquee over a drycleaner: DRIVE CAREFULLY— BLOODSTAINS ARE HARD TO REMOVE.

In a hamburger hutch on the strip: LOST: 110 LB. LION CUB. CALL . . .

On a rubble pile in Laurel Canyon: FREE DIRT.

Uphill around a curl in the road on a stranded car wilting on the shoulder: HELP!

Even the restaurants go on a special-effects binge, as if the aura of unreality that permeates the city is not enough authentic weirdness. On a perfectly good wall in a Mexican restaurant they have painted cracks. A steakhouse put up a stained-glass window and backlit it with the most garish neon lighting believable. And there is, in actual reality, in the City of Los Angeles a Chinese restaurant called Gung Ho.

And what is this place? And why? It is America's kosmic backfire, where surface flash is preferable to solid substance, whatever glitters is a star, and everyone lives in Disneyland.

It is one of the more recently settled geographic areas of the planet. As if they take the cue for their lives from the shifting shale beneath them, the people of Los Angeles are always involved in some rapturous, spectacular earthquake. From the sky above this monster open land of united states proceeds west in taupe-tone flatbed slabs, crumples upward at the Rockies, lunges in all directions, changing colors and textures with increasing speed, and culminates in California. From the ground below, the San Andreas Fault keeps the energy in a state of suspended turmoil, hovering just this side of the ultimate trip. Now and then you get your visionaries, like one mangy pop producer, all braggadocio and no hits, with a brainstorm: in 1969 when rumors about California falling into the sea were rife, he tried to get a bunch of speculators to go in with him on a large parcel of land in Nevada, figuring that's where the oceanfront property would be when Los Angeles became the new Atlantis.

And to this scene the myths come to multiply and go forth.

Whether any of them realized it or not, when the English rock 'n' roll invaders, with their red guitars, wide eyes, and cubby suits, came over, this is where they were coming. All the mystique that beckoned them had originated there in America's P.R. department, Hollywood.

They knew about America from the way John Wayne could take a crack over the head with a bottle and still turn around and beat the ass off the attacker. James Dean, Marlon Brando, and youth had its head Stateside. One English musician remembers that he thought the moment he got off the plane in America, if he got cut he wouldn't bleed anymore. And what did they find?

They'd been taught about a great country on whose territory a world war had never been fought, as if divine order held it sacred. America, the country of refugees and outcasts working together to be the biggest motherfucker of them all. And they came, they saw. The dream had already been auctioned off to the highest bidder and made into a serial screenplay, pay as you go. And because they weren't from America, they could just observe, dig the excitement of the confusion. It turned them on and they showed us how to boogie again. They gave as they partook and they brought it home with them, leaving us with our energy refueled, our imaginations alight once more, and our enthusiasm restored. They gave us back the faith.

Los Angeles had always been a very special place for music and its rock 'n' roll contained so much of its magic. There had been the surfing music early in the Sixties, in that little pocket of inaction just before folk music began to steal the scene. There were the Beach Boys and the Surfaris, and that heavy chorded sound of the sea, the cars and the tans, the clear blue eyes, diamond droplets shining off beautiful shoulders, packs and packs of kids on the beach at sunrise surfing into the new morning. It was another world, this beautiful coastal paradise of extremes, and its children with sun-bleached eyebrows were growing up in never-never land, free, naked, long limbed, and beautiful, standing loose on a shaped fiberglass plank, riding the sea, walking on the water like Jesus, getting very high on the sun and the air and the tide and into such heavy emotional ties with the elements that all they could utter were epithets to express their exhilaration.

What a beautiful sound. It carried the magic and grace of the height of teenism in flower, torment forgotten, lost in the salty wind and shriek of zippy cars. Those harmonies, those Beachboy sound-twines, growing fuller and fuller, resonating, peaking, clearing, diving, wiping out. From that sound the rest of the nation's teens could just feel something happening over there out west in California.

You can hear the sound in the canyons and hills behind Hollywood. Laurel Canyon, a network of snaggled mini-mountain roads with cottages and chalets and all manner of quixotic compact architecture snuggled close to the hills that rise abruptly from Sunset Boulevard into a world nestled in greenery, cluttered with half-hidden houses where most of the Los Angeles pop musicians lived. A wind comes down the crease in the hill and it whistles up against the walls, maybe carrying music from a band rehearsing up the hill and now and again, on one of those timeless days, a jet flying overhead and, with the wind, hits a harmony for a brief instant, a quick sound that resonates through the canyon and lingers for a moment in the air before it fades.

Brian Wilson heard that sound and took it to the sea, the Mamas and the Papas heard it and took it to the studio, and Jim McGuinn back from MacDougal Street and Beatle Impressions heard it, put it back on a jet, and took it to the air again with the Byrds. Those three groups started a collective myth of their own: California good-time music. It was rock 'n' roll with surf, folk, and a special breed of West Coast infusion, touched with a special native familiarity. With the Lovin' Spoonful ("Do You Believe in Magic?" was their debut and the song was an affirmative answer to the question), they made rock 'n' roll new and American again.

It was not a simple transformation, or as mystical and natural an experience as encountering it from a surprised and delighted listener's advantage. There were personality hassles, the inanities of the time, the perspective and competence of the musicians, producers, working conditions, timing and, where neatness doesn't always count, there were the music business goniffs to contend with.

From the beginning it's a gut-busting trip—intense, filled with the most glorious heights and the most extreme, rude, soul-deteriorating shocks, demands, and humiliations. It's something on the very outer edge of experience, being in a rock 'n' roll group, and you have to be strong, flexible, wise, consistent, resilient, and determined to make it. So few, in their twenties in the Sixties, children of the assassination of the American dream, could get a grasp on it in the first place.

There was once a kiddie cartoon in which a bulldog was furiously chasing down two magpies who tormented him. They flew out a twenty-story window and he tore after them in rabid pursuit. He leaped over the windowsill and continued chasing them, hundreds of feet up in the air. All of a sudden he screeched to a stop, looked down, and growled, "This is impossible!"—at which point he went plummeting down to disaster. It's about like that with a rock 'n' roll group.

It might be the night after a mesmerizing concert where the music was so right, the current streaming back and forth from audience to stage, the evening synergistic and throbbing with emergent affirmation, and the next morning you find out that the promoter didn't pay you. There isn't enough money to get to the next engagement on the tour and they're going to sue if you don't make it. Management is conveniently unreachable for help. Maybe it was the time a group was renegotiating a record contract for a bigger royalty and discovered that on the existing contract the manager pocketed half the advance in collusion with a record company executive who was no longer employed there. The group is signed to the manager for another three years and he's going to have to be watched constantly so he doesn't do it again. Either that or they're going to have to sue him, which will cost again as much as what was lost, with recovery doubtful. With tricks in legal language most groups haven't the sophistication to understand, it might even have been a legal scam. Maybe the group has had it, they hate each other after twenty-one months together, recording is a drag, and they're starting to sound lousy. But if they do break up all future bookings will sue and they'll end up owing money. Each of these situations is authentic and has, with endless variations on the theme, been repeated countless times.

Jim McGuinn, Gene Clark, and David Crosby were singing individually at the Troubadour, one of L.A.'s most important folk houses at the time, in early 1965. David and Jim had been enemies from back in prep school but fate would keep them abrasively associated for some time. Jim and Gene started writing songs together—pretty, folksy, lovelorn things, melodic and sensitive, a lovely combination of writing and performing talents. David caught wind of them and wanted very badly to sing with them. McGuinn grudgingly agreed.

Jim Dickson, a gentle, perceptive man, sensitive to both music and the music business, had been working with David on solo things, doing tapes and demonstration material for possible commercial release, mainly out of friendship and interest. He was known and liked by both Jim and Gene so the triumvirate had a common focus in the personage of Dickson, who felt all along and advised David that he should try a group thing; his voice did not command the authority to be compelling as a solo vehicle yet.

David was fiery and full of soul and a hunger to get it on; he had an irrepressible sense of humor set off by an equally, if not more, irrepressible temper. Jim was a musical technician, experienced, calculating, with a finely developed song sense and a probing mind. Jim had an easy, quiet, and unapproachable sense of authority about him; David, a posture of challenge and belligerence.

McGuinn was the natural leader of any situation as a conditional aspect of his part in it. He was the director and he was a good one. Group consciousness was one thing, but decisions, musical decisions, were up to him. Gene was the tender ladies' man, a fine songster, very sweet. David found Michael Clark playing with Dino Valenti. He just had to be heavy, didn't he, playing with Dino? And Chris Hillman, a mandolin player with a group called the Hillmans, got wind of the convergence of the other four, bought himself a $40 Japanese electric bass guitar, put away his mandolin, and learned to play it. Nobody among them played drums so Michael did. There was a group but there wasn't a name. McGuinn wanted to call them Jimmy and the Jet Set, which was not what you would call typical of his unerring sense of correctness, and was quickly shouted down. There were Beatles with an "a" and they became Byrds with a "y." There was no pretense about it; they were out to challenge the Fab Four or at the very least cash in on it.

McGuinn played his Rickenbacker twelve-string guitar, which he picked out after seeing George Harrison play one in *A Hard Day's Night*. Crosby played rhythm guitar, chords, tone colors, to set off McGuinn's melodies. Chris played a melodic bass line, still hearing it through the mandolin. Michael followed around on the drums and Gene looked beatific.

Dickson rehearsed them and took them into a studio to make a record. They were working in World Pacific studios, where Ravi

Shankar had recorded. David Crosby, to whom undertones and harmonics are instinctive, became enamored of Indian music, totally enthralled with its intricacies and how lines snaked like silken threads through various tonalities of the drone that enveloped the sound, reaching through regions of the mind, touching each circuit and easing the flow.

The demonstration record the Byrds made was beautiful. It can be found as an album called *Preflyte* on Together Records. Dickson took it around, aiming at Columbia Records, which he felt was the firstest with the mostest.

But the pop field at Columbia was still a little too general. They had Dylan but still didn't relate to him as the kind of phenomenon he was. There were millions of people on the planet aware of Dylan's profundity and at the time only one of them worked for Columbia—Billy James, who by then had been transferred to Los Angeles.

Columbia and pop had a curious arm's-length love affair. When Mitch Miller was the head of Artists and Repertoire he'd banned rock 'n' roll records. Before the Byrds' first pop hit Columbia's most recent big hit was something like "Go Away, Little Girl" by Steve Lawrence.

The Byrds were signed to Columbia. Billy James, one would surmise, had no small hand in it. The moment they were signed to Columbia, they got kicked out of World Pacific studios, W.P. feeling they should have gotten the group. The group had to record at Columbia studios in Los Angeles.

There was only one Columbia studio, mostly for recording Percy Faith, military bands, and the like. Dickson and producer Terry Melcher went in there with five scroungy-looking, defensive, scared, and scrapping boys, and the engineers just turned up their noses. They were rude to the Byrds, gave them short time, and in odd snippets. Over great objections, partially due to the time situation and partially because McGuinn didn't have confidence in the band's musicianship, it was decided that the instrumental tracks, with the exception of McGuinn's guitar part, were to be done by hired studio musicians. Nobody, not even their own leader, would take a chance on them. Dylan had sold Dickson a song of his, "Mr. Tambourine Man," a song of trips and boots and streets and nights, of drugs and visions, people, scenes, and singing.

Dickson had McGuinn read Stanislavsky to train his delivery and McGuinn took the song, interpreted it, put it to a samba rhythm and it became mesmeric. It had everything of the moment in it, the structural ingredients of a hit single, sly druggy innuendos, and a vocal treatment extraordinary for an American group. The song churned through the airwaves, releasing its magic. It rolled in the spangled dust its sound set spinning, lighting up places where it fell, rushing into the air from some godstruck mechanical device, touching lives, hearts, and imaginations with infatuating impact. Not that it was a matter of sales; "Woolly Bully" was on the charts simultaneously and it outsold "Tambourine Man" two to one. But "Tambourine Man" had *it*. It came just at the right time at just the right angle with just the right sound. It was precisely what the Byrds had in mind. They felt a change coming and they were riding the prow of it, they knew it, they felt it, they often, however clumsily, expressed it, and miraculously they were able to translate it into the most powerful communicative tool of the time: a hit single.

The vehicle was off the ground and winging. Rock 'n' roll's audience increased geometrically. From underground both the music and its audience erupted. Over the next four years it would explode unimaginably in size and manifestation, but every single ingredient of what was to come was in the Byrds' "Mr. Tambourine Man."

It was late 1965 and we weren't observing ourselves as protectively as we did when we began reading about ourselves, and in that, there was a certain innocence to the revolution. Music seemed to fill our lives, our adventures, with experiences common to all of us. Rock was creating a continent of community whose prime emergence, whose sense of communication, revolved around the music.

A conceit set in. We were the ones, slim-hipped, slinky-eyed, birth-controlled, free. We had a music and a uniform, we were saturated in generational splendor. We had created and consumed, completely supported a contained context in which we could live and behave as we wanted, which we did, glowing with some kind of mysterious prescience we shared like a secret contract.

We were the ones, baby, we knew, we had it covered. We had a voice and we were catered to as a market. In America, that's real recognition. We were old enough to know better, young enough to know best, and blind enough not to give a damn about anything else. The pursuit of happiness was a justifiable vocation in and of itself and all of us were on something—acid, grass, hash, vibes, a little cocaine now and then (everybody at least knew someone rich enough to have a taste). Whatever floated to the top of our minds was the truth. What a bringdown. We had everything but the answer.

The Beatles had been through the U.S.A. from coast to coast touching the youth of entire cities with hysterical, irresistible, and unexplainable magic. They were oh-so-charming, glossy little scrubbed and tousled bunny boys with lovey smiles and cooey warbles. They were deliciously naughty but acceptably nice, and that's what turned on everyone on both sides of the generation gap. Their moptop haircuts titillated transatlantic columnists for millions of words. It's hard to believe but there was actually a time when it was agreed that the Beatles had long hair.

The Byrds had hair to their shoulders—manes, full and flying. They'd cruise Sunset Strip at night, puffed up to here, prowling, prancing, throwing their hair back into the wind of their walking. Afro bushes were growing, hair was free, wild, a symbol of the minds they adorned. Masculinity and the concept of what a desirable male was changed. Long hair was not sissy, it was sensual, softness; sentimentality and a flourishing strain of romanticism was in. The Beatles cast a shadow and a light into which all myths but Dylan's would follow, establishing their dominance of pop, a dominance that would remain unchallenged even after they'd broken up. But somewhere, a few years before, the Rolling Stones were being born and in a curious way a much more meaningful moment of truth was in the making.

From the beginning the Stones, with their blossoming notoriety, were cast as the real rebels of rock, the *ne plus ultra* of youth music, entertainment in revolt. They were gutterwauling, randy, slapdash dirty wailers, rough-cut outlaw bluesmen and they were mean! Their presence had an exciting tinge of wickedness to it, their music was blues-based, lowdown, hard-bitten, and the sting of their insults was, like Lenny Bruce's assaults on sacred cows, perversely satisfying. The Beatles were the sensation, no doubt about it, but the Stones were the shock. In pop, when you talk about the separation between the men and the boys, you mean the Rolling Stones.

In performance they had it all over the Beatles; in eminence, the Beatles would, for as long as they stayed together, surpass the Stones. They were jealously regarded by one another; Mick Jagger always wanted to write like John Lennon and John Lennon always wanted to perform with the *sturm und drang* of Mick, though he never really did, always trying, always lapsing into clownishness to save it.

The press would grudgingly abide by the Beatles, but the Stones were bitterly abused. The line was drawn by adult tastemakers desperately scrambling for credibility after the fact and youth crossed it gaily. This phenomenon precipitated the emergence of peer group rock critics. The rock 'n' roll press at the time consisted of anyone who was low enough on the staff totem pole to be sent out to cover a rock group. A handful of determined freelancers challenged all that, puddle jumping publications until the savvier periodicals took notice. We were that first wave.

At radio station WINS-New York, where Murray the K held swinging soirees of rock 'n' roll, that's what happened. There were, amazingly enough, no newsmen available to go to the airport to welcome the Beatles so Murray went out there himself, copped interviews with the lads, and appointed himself "Fifth Beatle," accompanying them for the rest of the tour. He just moved in. He had so much chutzpah, said the Beatles later, that none of them had the balls to stop him.

Brian Epstein had carefully groomed his fab four for presentation to the world at large, but the Stones—that was another story. Andrew Loog Oldham took great pride in having the mangiest group in Great Britain. Of course it was a ploy, a deliberate grab to win some attention by contrasting the Beatle image. It certainly worked. It appealed to something distant and animalistic lacking in pop at the time. The insinuating blackness of the Stones reincarnated what was always the most fearsome, hence, attractive about the black rhythm, blues, and rockabilly pop of the Fifties. They made smarting good music and put on the best show in the business. They were good, competitive, distinct for their out-front smuttiness. They never cooed about holding hands, these guys liked sex. Rock 'n' roll had come beyond puberty and the trouble was only just beginning.

"Satisfaction" hit the week after "Mr. Tambourine Man." What a song! If rock had become the anthem of youth's community of complaints, the Stones were the metaphor for all that was rock. "Satisfaction" would become the archetypical rock song. "Can't get no . . . can't get no SATISFACTION!" A roar in the wild, a plea, an encounter with the ultimate truth in the sum of experience: "An' I try, an' I try, an' I try, an' I try!" That was it, the epigraph of the millennium. Rock was defined. Some eras are described by wars, reigns, treaties, assassinations, or dictators. For the youth in the Sixties the era is described by that song.

"Mr. Tambourine Man" was released just as springtime settled in on San Francisco. One lovely Sunday afternoon when thousands of hippies were out in the park, all flowers and robes, flutes and tambourines, all dancing, someone had a radio on loud and the D.J. played "Mr. Tambourine Man." They were, most of them, high, soaring, colors wafting in among them, lighting their faces and shimmering down the stalks of their bodies to swirl glittering in a cloud around their dancing feet. About two hundred of them were so transported by the record they embarked on a pilgrimage to go down to Los Angeles to hear the Byrds, then playing at a club called Ciros, their first important gig.

It should be mentioned that San Francisco and L.A. have, for some strange reason, a heavy antagonism going on between them, which was not overcome by the love movement. San Francisco is too smug and self-centered for L.A. champions; L.A. is so bad that the worst implication you could put on something in or from San Francisco is to call it an L.A. trip.

But when the hippies from Golden Gate Park got down to the Strip in Hollywood they found a scene freakier than their own. The Byrds had changed the street, the Strip. Celebrities, Mary Travers, Odetta dancing with Jim Dickson, starlets, writers,

Michael Pollard, were all grooving. Dylan would sometimes stop by and play with them. Paul J. Robbins, one of Los Angeles's literary treasures, had hand-painted a design for flyers for the Byrds which said, "Listen to them Sing as you Dance," with the letters LSD in special colors.

There was Vito Paulekas, an ancient forever-young man, a sculptor who had been taking bunches of kids dancing for years, all in costumes. The Byrds had played a rent party for Vito and he came out to see them at Ciros with his retinue, a people salad that was as much an attraction there as the Byrds. Those nights brought L.A. out on the Strip and set them dancing in the streets, dancing in halls, wild and formless, arms, sleeves, fringe, hair, all airborne into this spiraling sound that didn't stop even after the music had. The Byrds were fast becoming the most potent early pop legend. Those nights at Ciros were the talk of both coasts' underground and they hadn't even hit the road yet.

Where dancing in L.A. was a phenomenon, bringing freaks out of the woodwork and onto the street, in San Francisco it was already the style. Dances were held periodically in huge halls with rock bands and they would be tribal congregations, the celebration of the emergence of these people as an entity.

There was actually a community in San Francisco, clusters of houses around Haight-Ashbury where people lived, dealt, and did nothing more important than learn to relate to one another on an immersion basis. Native Californians at first, then an influx of people from all over as the word spread. Sunday's bands would play from flatbed trucks in Golden Gate Park nearby and there was a powerful spirit rising out of these convocations, to say nothing of quite a few incredible rock 'n' roll bands.

Bands had formed to play a variety of coffeehouses in San Francisco and Berkeley. Jefferson Airplane would play these houses as an acoustic folk band until Jorma Kaukonen got an amplifier for his lead guitar. Paul Kantner got a bigger amp for his, at which point Jack Casady, intrepid bassist, went out and got two amps. *Thwannng!*

Across the Bay, in Berkeley, a radical kibitzer turned rock 'n' roll writer-singer, Joe McDonald, was forming Country Joe and the Fish for musical as well as political expression. Originally it was to be called Country Mao and the Fish but that name was ditched in a fit of capitalist practicality.

Within the workings of San Francisco's blossoming musical community there were musicians, technicians, poster artists, lightshow innovators, and management people trying to work out the logistics and economics of bringing music to people in an often naïve but totally charming way. Probably the most loving and valuable patriarch the burgeoning San Francisco scene ever had was in the person of Ralph J. Gleason, esteemed critic and columnist for the San Francisco *Chronicle*. The Family Dog, a loosely organized collection of community people, was trying to put together a dance with rock music, refreshments, and a lightshow in Longshoreman's Hall—and they wisely came to Gleason for consultation.

The dance was a huge success; thousands of freaks showed, the bands were monumental, and the evening was a historical landmark in rock 'n' roll history. Gleason wrote this and future dances up in his column and the protection of at least some kind of recognized approval kept the heat off for a short while. When some uptight San Franciscans tried to shut the dances down, Gleason rallied to their defense. It was significant enough to make the hippy events a *cause célèbre* for civil libertarians and to keep them going.

Eventually Bill Graham, a mercurial, ambitious man with nervous, thick-lipped, rough-hewn good looks, became a rock impresario and opened up the Fillmore in San Francisco as a regular place for rock 'n' roll dances.

And while all these scenes were brewing on the West Coast, the Byrds went on the road with a busload of friends and equipment people including Vito and his dancers, Carl Franzoni, a disciple of Vito's who had invented a rubber cunt (yes, a rubber cunt; he claimed he got loads of letters from priests and servicemen praising its authenticity), and other assorted people. The bus was off, freak flags flying from the far corners of Oshkosh to Spillville, Iowa, and their magic spread like milkweed on a windy autumn day.

All over they would set audiences dancing. Time and again on that first tour they would start cold, everyone sitting down, watching, listening, and all of a sudden the audience would get up and dance as if possessed. At one stop the Byrds met a copy band, a local group that had every lick on the first Byrds album down cold, even playing the mistakes perfectly. Everywhere, kids would lay gifts on them—dope, beads, love, parties, sex, rides, and worship.

Since the American tour and the first album were such a success, a tour of England was arranged, to be accompanied by Derek Taylor. Taylor was a master publicity man that the Byrds had inherited from the Beatles. When he worked for the Beatles, a more accurate title would have been "pandemonium overseer." He would preside over press conferences, executing them with such *savoir-faire* and implacable cool that he became as much a celebrity to communications people as the Beatles. When he came to L.A. to work for the Byrds, Beach Boys, the Mamas and the Papas (all the pop stars there were in L.A., but only the stars), he lent a presence to that city's publicity outpourings it never before had: class. Whether he wrote releases, liner notes, or articles, they were always done in dignified sonorous prose, he the prime purveyor of the gilded sentence and the purple paragraph, and in the very midst of this unimaginable fray he had the knack of making everyone see just how absurd and how beautiful it all was. It was impossible to be uptight around a man who surveyed that decade's most hysterical social upheaval and reacted with such bemused calm.

So it was arranged, right after the U.S. tour, for the Byrds to go straight to London. That was what every American rock 'n' roll band wanted, to get back at the Beatles. They were all Beatle fans, all wanting to poke a dent in the Beatles with their presence, which no band or musician has ever done. There were the Beatles and the rest of pop music in descending order. A great deal of the energy and sheer force of performance of American rock bands was simply the Beatles, burning ass.

As for the Byrds, it didn't work out quite that way either. They went to a little club in London, played a nervous, overtired set and afterward met the Beatles. John Lennon shook Jim McGuinn's hand grandly and pronounced, "Good set, man." The other Byrds lit up.

"Nah," replied Jim, "we played lousy." The other Byrds winced and cursed. Lennon was most highly insulted and remained aloof for the rest of the evening.

It would have been very difficult in 1966 to find someone who wasn't a Beatles fan, unless perhaps it was a Beatle. But there was always that reach for peerage among other rock groups, something the Beatles never allowed. And the Byrds, these "American Beatles," these charlatans, who couldn't even cut the club dates in England they booked with such braggadocio, they just didn't measure up.

So the Byrds returned to Los Angeles, knocked down. Minus Hollywood points. Hollywood is funny that way, these things count everywhere, in catty gossip and over the phone music-biz hype jobs, but in Hollywood it is an acknowledged and glorified fact of life.

No matter. The Byrds had started something that in retrospect would reveal more importance than any single American rock 'n' roll experience. They gave American youth the first direct identification with the soaring heights of the trip upon which they were about to embark.

They had somehow caught the conscience of the time, combined it with the technology of the age, lit it afire with imagination, and honed it with ambition. They catalyzed a whirlpool so unexpectedly powerful that they themselves would eventually be disintegrated by it.

Their first album carried the name and motif of their single "Mr. Tambourine Man," this time with the group actually playing their instruments on that title Bob Dylan cover. The polished version of "You Won't Have to Cry" by Gene Clark from their demo was on there, as were Dylan's "Spanish Harlem Incident" and Pete Seeger's "Bells of Rhymney." The songs had the timey, homogenized feeling of a group that was secure with its material and its sound. There was the chrome-clear ringing guitar sound, the infectious counter-rhythmic lines and harmonics that twined and changed in the air, perfect, full and up-close true. Even at this early stage, their own material stood up well compared even with the Dylan songs that they had such an uncanny knack of interpreting.

Moreover, their sound was undeniably American. It wasn't a matter of chauvinism; it was that as yet no rock group could catalyze the political paranoia, technological fascination, airborne heights, urgent expressionism, and folk homey-ness of the mid-Sixties in America. Beatles music, until that time, had been higher and louder than anything heard in pop; the Beatles, before *Rubber Soul*, were an anesthetic with pleasant, ebullient, if not particularly symbolic, side effects, but the Byrds came on strong, aware, closer to home. They were a physical and intellectual as well as an emotional life raft—with a party going on aboard. "Chimes of Freedom" was their cry in the wilderness—articulate, aroused, touched with a grace and staunch beauty that set minds and bodies moving in a cycle of awareness and sweet release. Their debut album closed with the trailer song from *Dr. Strangelove*, "We'll Meet Again," giving their posture a sinister, cynical edge, just enough to let you know that though they sounded airily beautiful, they knew whereof they sang.

Almost immediately after the Byrds' "Mr. Tambourine Man," Dylan took off on a mass commercial level. His time was bursting with overdues and the Byrds were merely the last in a series of "booster rockets," as McGuinn would later put it. Dylan's first massive hit single, "Like a Rolling Stone," was released and it clawed its way through the charts and airwaves. Its sheer power, its visceral intensity, was a frontal attack, echoing that memorable concert at Newport, that same year, where with that very song he had blown the scene apart. *Highway 61 Revisited*, his most significant and pivotal album until then, followed close on the heels of "Like a Rolling Stone," completely affirming the change.

The Stones came over in 1965 to tour, just after "Tambourine Man" hit and the Byrds were riding the wave. Dickson had managed to get the Byrds booked on a few Southern California dates with the Stones. At one engagement the Stones were later than usual; the concert was in a civic auditorium with the kind of idiotic driveway arrangement where you had to drive around and around to find your way in, and they got quite lost. The Byrds went on and captivated the audience, their largest to that time. By the time the Stones finally went on, the Byrds had not only prepared the crowd but had averted a major riot. Their reputation as a dynamic and effective live band had begun.

The Byrds would absorb and express the figures and figments of the time, and they began to attract them. Lenny Bruce would hang out at their sessions; Allen Ginsberg would be backstage at their concerts. Their second album was *Turn! Turn! Turn!* (titled for Pete Seeger's adaptation of verses from Ecclesiastes). McGuinn's thematic orientation was from Ecclesiastes to science fiction, from Seeger to Dylan, and his genius lay in juxtapositioning these diverse cultural elements. On *Turn! Turn! Turn!* the Byrds did Dylan's "The Times They Are A-Changin'" and "Oh! Susannah" on the same album (on the same side even) and made it work. But basically *Turn! Turn! Turn!* was an extension of their first album, a worthy one to be sure. Their sophistication would show most significantly on their next album, *Fifth Dimension*, which relieved the vague restlessness *Turn! Turn! Turn!* diffused.

They were a worldwide success, the Byrds, and in *Fifth Dimension* they took things their own way. Their arrangement of "Wild Mountain Thyme" floated on a subtle cushion of a string section, guitar lines audible just above the surface. Their harmonics had never been more sweetly lush or so tenderly compelling. It led into "Mr. Spaceman," their goofy hit with which they, believing that spacemen would naturally monitor all radio frequencies and hear the song, appealed to one to "please take me along for a ride." McGuinn privately complained about the inclusion of David Crosby's "What's Happening?!?!," grousing that David's unreasonable insistence on doing his own material far exceeded either his taste or his talent. The tension crackled between those two members of the group, each of whom was jockeying for power. McGuinn had the power in the group; there was no question but that he was the leader. But Crosby was the more colorful performer, the fire to McGuinn's cool calculating ice. During 1966 the first fuse to blow was when Gene Clark left the group. The announced reason was his fear of flying, which was, ironically, quite accurate, but McGuinn's later references to "the group ganging up on him" probably revealed more of the dynamics. Their success, the pressure of the road, and their own immaturity were wearing them down.

Fifth Dimension continued with "I Come and Stand at Every Door," one of their most underrated compositions. The tune was an adaptation of the achingly beautiful ancient Childe ballad, "The Silkie of Sule Skerry." The words, set in a soft undulating cadence, were words from the ghost of a seven-year-old child killed at Hiroshima begging the world to make peace. "Captain Soul," on side two, their first recorded instrumental track, was also, quite notably, the first time what would later become known as the San Francisco sound was ever heard on a phonograph record, semi-improvisational, solo-oriented, heavy on the bottom (in this case a prominent bass line as an anchor), comprising a heavily textured modal drive. There was "Eight Miles High," one of the first songs to earn the dubious honor of being banned from significant airplay because of its reputed drug associations. Now, really!

The album closed with the "Lear Jet Song," a montage of a rhythmic track and the sounds of a jet taking off. The album played on long after the record was over, refusing to land.

The year 1966 was on the wane and so were the Byrds. Their albums were spectacular, though they would never, in any form, surpass *Fifth Dimension*, but their live performances were a shambles. They never rehearsed, they hardly ever spoke to one another anymore. Animosity, jealousy, and competitiveness within the group were cracking it at the seams. It didn't take long before most people closely associated with them began to get fed up—from the girls who, for bus fare, answered fan mail by the stack, to the lady who had fronted them $5,000 for equipment before they had a record contract, to Jim Dickson, who stomped out on them after a punching fight and wasn't seen by the group for almost a year. There was never a dull moment except when they gave a concert. And it was going to get worse—disillusioning fans, press, critics, and each other.

Their next album, *Younger than Yesterday*, opened with the cynical "So You Want to Be a Rock and Roll Star," bitterly documenting their disappointment with the trip. "Plastic ware," they accused themselves. "La-la-la-la-la." It was nonetheless a brilliantly assembled record, named after the Dylan song of the same name. Their new space song was "CTA-102," appealing to life forms on that distant star. By then the Byrds' audience was so far-reaching that a noted scientific journal bristled and replied that theory notwithstanding, the possibilities raised by the Byrds' song "CTA-102" were quite slim. "Renaissance Fair" celebrated a love-in; "Time Between" was taken from a hexagram of the *I Ching*, an ancient Chinese oracle becoming quite popular with the underground mysto set, though the song was sort of a hillbilly love song. The Byrds were always dropping names, coding references, throwing bait. "Mind Gardens" was a track that McGuinn politicked hotly against, a David Crosby song Crosby himself would later admit was a lapse of taste.

On tour, the Byrds were the embodiment of synergism, energy, magic, and exhortation, bringing multitudes to their feet in dance. In those outlying towns that nobody gives a damn about but everybody has to play, they'd prowl about in their limousines, hair longer than anyone's around, conspicuously stoned, conspicuously happy, conspicuously making more money than the mayor. Great numbers of young minds became aware of the fact that there was indeed an alternative to continuing with Dad's accounting firm, another way to live, any number of ways. A child unaware that he has a choice has no choice at all. Rock groups, the procession of emblazoned singers and songs that would touch their lives so profoundly, were making them aware of the existence of choices and, more profoundly, their power to make them.

The change came in many forms, but at the heart it was the same and happening to many young people who had only themselves to turn to. The culmination of all those years of nameless longings came over them, feeding on the music that brought them to their feet and to their senses. It welled up in a regenerating self-love and self-confidence with determination to make it on their terms, the courage to discover just what that meant and what it took to pull it off. And, in one moment of pain and ecstasy, it was possible to just-let-go, completely and forever. All of what had gone before drifted into meaninglessness and what was then important was this something new, a movement of a lifestyle that danced, that grew, that continued until it seemed to envelop the world within its earshot. For young Americans, it was stronger than anything else happening, stronger than the insufficiencies of societies and the resulting hostility. Everybody seemed to hit the road in one way or another.

The big fight came while recording *Younger than Yesterday*, when Crosby wanted to sing a song he wrote called "Triad," about a *ménage à trois*, that totally upset McGuinn. For spite, Crosby refused to do a song called "Goin' Back," and the blowup led to his stomping out on the session, leaving the group. That album was called *The Notorious Byrd Brothers*, and the cover featured the three remaining Byrds looking out the windows of an old barn, a horse looking out of the fourth. And though McGuinn would keep the name and a group together, the Byrds, their inner harmonies and mythology, by late 1967, had crumbled.

When the Beatles returned to L.A. in 1965 they rang up the Byrds to do some heavy hanging out. The Strip had been bursting with life, music, and dancing, the Byrds had been in their prime, and the musicians were still bursting with the changes yet to be consummated.

The Beatles rented one of the Gabors' houses in Benedict Canyon and the Byrds came calling. They goofed together, took acid together, played guitar together in the bathroom, and talked all night long. Alone with his wife and George Harrison in the bedroom, McGuinn was puzzled when George asked him if the Byrds believed in God. Jim replied that he did but couldn't speak for the rest of the group. George said that the Beatles didn't know; they talked about it all the time but couldn't make up their collective mind.

It was on the street again in style, golliwogging around in limousines and Lear jets instead of boots and buses. David Crosby recollects a time when Dylan came to hear them play and after the set Crosby and Dylan drove around L.A. in Dylan's Rolls-Royce, smoking, sitting with their faces almost touching, saying very little but communicating deeply. Dylan was full of nonsense and word games when he did talk. "I looked into his eyes for a long time," said Crosby afterward, "and he was doing something in there!"

In 1966 youth airfare was initiated. Far as you wanted to go, standby at half-price. Seventy-some-odd dollars to California from the East Coast, one way, and hundreds of thousands of young people took the trip. Life was so different once you learned to fly and people under twenty-two began putting time and distance behind them, the terrestrial world below them, taking long-distance flights with less hesitation than their parents would have making a long-distance telephone call. It might be raining on the ground, raining all around, but up in the jetstream where the Byrds were singing, the clouds a frail carpet below, there was always pure air, sweet speed, clear skies, and shining sun. It's always lovely weather; you just have to get high enough.

Hitchhiking up and down the mental and geographical wilderness of the incredibly beautiful California coastline, hanging out on the Strip in L.A., communing in Big Sur, living collectively in San Francisco's Haight-Ashbury district. A mobile underground developed, encompassing so many artists, musicians, and kids who were on the road, that they learned that wherever you were, if there was rock 'n' roll music happening in any form nearby you could find friends, shelter, dope, adventure, and sex. Mentally and physically, America's turned-on youth flew as naturally as they walked. Distance, speed, time, all crisscrossing. Musicians on tour developed jet lag, a disorientation of the biological clock caused by ripping through time zones too quickly and too often. Before passenger jet travel, one didn't commonly travel far and fast enough to cause desynchronosis. The velocity was overbearing. It became all too easy to be stoned all the time, to talk to no one but other hippies, read nothing but underground press, and hear nothing else but the music. There was so much of all of it that little else need have existed. What for? It was such a consuming trip, one in which a single song could capture a mass movement.

In 1967 "San Francisco," an international hit by Scott McKenzie—"If you're going to San Francisco, be sure to wear some flowers in your hair"—came out and extended an invitation to millions, indicating, in that inexpressible way that songs can, what was going on in San Francisco. For two years kids from all over would pour through Haight-Ashbury in response to that song.

A hit song is on the air at every moment of the day at the time of its greatest impact, all over the world. It was the summer of 1967, the summer that went down as the Summer of Love, a most beautiful beginning, a most exquisite end. *Sergeant Pepper's Lonely Hearts Club Band* had been released. It was the first aroma of summer; it wafted over the horizon like sweet incense, and its permeation was so complete that everyone who heard it lived it, breathed it, and spoke of little else. You would hear it from cars, drifting out of windows where you walked, on the radio, in your friends' homes, and in your head, always. Its timing, the unequaled beauty of its contents, the pyrotechnical extravagance, the feeling of celebration and introspection, the powerful release of inspiration, the awe and hope it projected, made it the opus of the movement. On every level it was an event, from the highest bastions of critical legitimacy to the stoned epithets of the underground press. Richard Goldstein, the first and most important of peer group rock critics, singularly groused that it was not all it was cracked up to be, for which he was roundly blasted and never forgiven. For all its futuristic aspects, the rock scene and its communications network were essentially small-townish, parochial, and extremely jealous of its genius.

You don't hear the term "folk-rock" much anymore, but its importance as a bridge element in the development of rock can't be overstated. The term was first used to describe the sound of the Byrds. The 1965 Byrds further propelled Dylan's rocketing influence and popularity and introduced, for the moment, the rock consciousness.

For every core rock fan there is an album and a track that lit their fuse and changed their life with a detonation of inspiration, momentum, and transformed perspective. It wasn't "Mr.

Tambourine Man" for everyone in the mid-Sixties, but that track created a seismic shift in pop culture.

The single charted, year-end, at number twenty-five in a heady mix of rock, country, conventional pop, rock 'n' roll, and the California sound that was to figure so joyfully in the infiltration of rock.

It was, significantly, an American response to the British Invasion. "(I Can't Get No) Satisfaction" by the Rolling Stones charted at number three, the Beatles' "Help" charted at number seven, and the Byrds lodged their answer.

Monterey

It was the Sergeant Pepper summer, the summer of the Human Be-In, the summer when many came to the celebrations of the new age with a newfound innocence and were so enchanted by the sight, the sheer numbers of all of—us!—that they could keep the faith during the agonizing changes that were to follow. It was also the summer of the first (and, as it turned out, only) International Pop Festival at Monterey.

I met a gaggle of other writers on the jet from New York as we sat high in the sky en route to San Francisco, there to catch another plane to Monterey, and we talked about being transported. Sandy Pearlman was quiet and obscure, Richard Meltzer had a top hat with a Sergeant Pepper emblem on it, one from the cutout sheet that came with the album. We alighted from the stratosphere and made our way toward the fairgrounds to hunt down some press passes. Even as we neared the gates, not knowing which entrance to go in, we could feel something happening. The arena inside those wooden fences was fairly vibrating. Cars, motorcycles, and campers lined the road for miles and a pilgrimage of long-haired beautiful people was making its way toward the grounds.

From the beginning it was evident that there was something special about the festival. It was the first ever; there had never been anything like it in the U.S.A., and the excitement was contagious. Never before had so much first-rate rock 'n' roll been assembled in the same place at the same time and—good Lord—fifty thousand, fifty thousand people! We were incredulous; it was beyond our wildest dreams, unheard of for the times. There was this feeling when you walked through the gates, the delight of seeing performers, spectators, even the cops with those silly bewildered grins on their faces, milling about, conversing easily, sharing sandwiches, fruit, shop talk, or nodding knowingly and happily to one another.

The energy level was high, almost everyone there was high, and there was a sense of peace that put everything to rest inside. Energy crackled through the people there, some of whom knew each other, most of whom didn't, but it didn't matter. By virtue of their just being there, there was a sense of internal connection, of being on the edge of something amazing happening. It happened to us, inundated us, washed over us like holy water, gushed through us like a mystic catharsis and left us trembling on the brink of something awesome. From the faces of the musicians on the stage the audiences could feel that it was happening to everyone there—a sign between them, a common bond, close to one another, close to the divinity within each one. That's what kind of hold rock had on people whose lives are intimately involved; that's what's so special about rock music and these people.

Ironically, most people in the music business were completely out of touch with what was happening. There were brilliant and beautiful exceptions, but for the most part the old daddies walked around a little bewildered by the vibrations, wondering only how their vested interests would make out and how quickly they could get to the famed nearby golf courses. For one thing all these music-biz guys realized in one great whiff of the pungent breeze that their oddball charges were really stoned out of their minds most of the time.

Stoned! Giggling-goofy-Marx Brothers bumping into one another, stoned! Laughing, rolling around on the grass with great whoops and yelps, sitting up against the fence dreamily inhaling incense and weaving with the sounds, staring meditatively into brightly imbroglioed posters, dancing until you couldn't feel your body anymore, stoned. There was acid in the punch and the musky smell of marijuana was everywhere.

Documentary filmmaker D. A. Pennebaker was doing a film and the film, like the festival, was supposed to be a nonprofit venture. Everybody performing was to have signed a release before he went on. Nobody had been paid for their appearance at the festival or in the film, except for expenses. The Country Joe and the Fish pack were so wiped out of their minds that they just forgot to sign the release, the whole business got lost in a colored sea of events that didn't have any relationship to signatures and paper. Their stony bungling later got them $5,000, when it became evident that Monterey Pop was a hot film property (Country Joe and the Fish gave the money to one of the Biafra funds). They were the only performers paid for the film, which made an awful lot of money and put a lot of nonprofit in somebody's pocket. The money from the festival itself suspiciously disappeared, it was revealed a few months later.

But nobody was thinking about money at the festival. For there in the arena the monster egos were rubbing up against one another and the lovable monstrosity of the music blared through the space.

Laura Nyro prowled the festival grounds softly, as she does, like a feline with mice on its mind, spooking shadows, pouncing on imaginary attackers. She caught sight of Paul Simon, all five-feet-three of him strutting around like a little bookie in a big town and she chased him down, inserted her soft hand with incredibly long purple nails in his and began to pump it gently. "I'm Laura Nyro," she fluttered, "I really love your album." Simon looked at this large grandmotherly girl with masses of dark hair falling around her black-shawled shoulders and paled. "Well, it's okay," he said and abruptly walked away.

Laura was stunned. She stood there for an instant and immediately scampered after him and spun him around again. She had had a hit on the West Coast with "Wedding Bell Blues" and had sufficiently impressed the festival board (of which Paul Simon was a member) that they invited this newcomer to perform. Hardly anyone knew she had an album out, but that didn't faze her. She glared at Simon like a mother at a naughty boy. "When people tell me they like *my* album," she admonished haughtily, "I thank them!"

She didn't give Simon a chance to reply. She turned in a swirl of skirt and flounced away.

The concerts were exhausting for musicians and audience alike. At times, if your seat was far from the stage, no matter how you rushed the aisles, everyone in front of and behind you was on his feet, on the chairs, screaming, laughing, rejoicing, and dancing. You couldn't see the stage or even hear unless the sound system was so finely tuned it deafened everything. It was the order of the occasion just to be inside this squirming howling rapturous beast, feeling its pulse in yours, feeling the sound of its voice resonate in your chest, urging your heart onward.

Acid, grass, rock 'n' roll, this whole new life—any single part of the combination was something that left attitudes forever changed, with new heights and depths open wide. It touched an ancient lost connection with tribalism; it beckoned toward a vision of a future worth celebrating at every excuse, a once and future now.

It had gotten to be beyond a show. The performances were almost impossible to assess singularly. Rock was presented proudly, for the first time with the dignity of art as entertainment, a development of unquestionable talent, popularity, and the first wave of an unstemmable tide.

There were many magic, vital moments that were metaphors of the movement, like when David Crosby, during the Byrds' set, confronted the audience with: "JFK was shot from several sides by many guns. Witnesses have been killed and evidence is being suppressed. And this is your country, ladies and gentlemen." The Byrds sang "He Was a Friend of Mine" for the slain president. Jim McGuinn was furious with Crosby; the outburst had embarrassed him and the incident was one of the last straws leading to Crosby's separation from the group.

A lot of people were hit hard in the credibility gap. Danny Kalb, then of the Blues Project, a sensitive, scholarly, deliciously melodic blues guitarist, spoke of this "dirty disgusting war." Country Joe and the Fish did an acid commercial. In the chronology of the movement, the Monterey Pop Festival was a historical culmination that began earlier that year, with the first Human Be-In in San Francisco. It was the coming-out party for the people who had dropped out in the Bay Area, and it was the first time any of them had any indication of how many of them there were. From there on in, a dropout society ceased to be an underground phenomenon. They knew who they were, and they knew there were many, and moreover they knew it was significant and growing.

At Monterey a lot went down besides a festival, its repercussions and implications. There were a lot of wondering people out there looking for a sign, hearing this music, waking up to the fact that they'd been short-changed on America. At the festival, the massive power of so much of it together was almost overwhelming. It was as if the whole festival were one band playing together, portions of which would fragment and spread out all over the country and beyond, spreading its seeds. Some of the seeds would sprout and flower, some would mutate. Some would wither and die. Most would take root and grow wild.

Otis Redding, following Jefferson Airplane, introduced by Tommy Smothers, backed up by Booker T. and the M.G.s, closed the show with a searing R&B set that emptied the performers' backstage area, as stars and producers surged out to watch, fists pumping, his joyfully turbulent performance.

The last concert was Sunday evening and it was a concert beyond comprehension. The audience leaned forward in hushed expectation, letting the music wash over them, sitting in utter disbelief and ecstasy over the magnitude of the talent performing. The excitement level rose precariously as rumors of the Beatles' arrival spread. Derek Taylor had announced earlier in the day, tongue-in-cheek, at a press conference: "They are here, but they are disguised as hippies."

But with or without the Beatles the evening was earth-shaking (though it shook only a small portion of the earth, it shook it so mightily that Mayor Minnie Coyle complained—to cheers—that residents in Carmel Valley could hear the music when it came on really loud). There was a triplicate of sets where it almost exploded.

The Who came on, their first major American appearance since a Murray the K tour, and they started the rock 'n' roll rumble.

Members of the press at the festival had to fend for themselves. By Sunday the credential system was so fucked up that there were three hundred press people in the section reserved for eighty of them, right in front of the stage. I was clinging to the proscenium, one of the smallest ones there and about the only girl in the throng, my feet braced on a loose plank, my chin thrust over the rim of the stage, my arms hanging on so hard they were sore for a week, but at the time I didn't feel a thing. There was a pit nearby from which the movie cameramen were operating and every so often a joint or a cup of clear tea would be passed by anonymous hands out toward me. At one point a boy's head and shoulders appeared out of the pit and he held me and kissed me for an entire intermission, then receded wordlessly back into the pit and I never saw him again in my life.

It was as though I had my head up against the hollow of a scream; the stage vibrated with every beat and I couldn't have been pried loose with a crowbar. I vaguely remember Wally Heider, an engineer who donated the sound equipment to the festival, saying that if things got too crazy the crew should keep out of the way. I had absolutely no idea, at the time, what he meant, though it would be clear very soon.

I couldn't even tell what I was high on, but I was roaring. The Who were racy and wild, pounding out that ferocious rock for which they have since become notorious. They jumped and howled and raved and looned and it was a spectacle beyond what any American band had or would display. This was the band that inspired the bust-up rock 'n' roll scene in Antonioni's *Blow-Up*, the band that in England was synonymous with pop in music. The explosion started when Peter Townshend, at the end of a supercharged song, raped an amplifier with the neck of his guitar, tearing the grille, sending its fizzling entrails spilling out onto the stage. Keith Moon, the most violent drummer in rock, threw all the drums around the stage, chasing them down as they rolled, kicking them in. Wally Heider scurried about the stage rescuing microphones as the cameramen followed him about at a safe distance.

The faces of the Who were contorted, the veins on their necks stood out like bright blue wires reaching toward their demented skulls. Moon was beet-red, screaming his head off. Red lights seemed to create the illusion of blood pouring out of his mouth. I had never seen anything resembling it and in a moment, hysteria turned to terror. I thought it was a genuine freakout and that the Who were actually trying to destroy the stage. The smoke pouring out of the amplifiers seemed to encompass the area. I broke loose from the stage, scampering under the structure in full panic, trembling and clinging to a wooden support and praying tearfully. Somebody came after me, laughing and trying to tell me it was all part of the act, but I could not be convinced. For the duration of the evening I was known as "chicken delight," and there are people around who are never going to let me forget it.

When I finally could be coaxed out of hiding, my rescuer identified himself as part of the crew with the Grateful Dead and boosted me up on the stage to watch the rest of the show from the wings. During intermission, when the stage crew swept up the remains of the Who's finale, he entertained everybody with details of my lapse. I was given some fruit, another joint, and a lot of attention.

From the stage, I could see the audience's agitation. The Who had left them crazed and nobody would sit down. A shiver of apprehension snaked through the air. There was a feeling of something uncontrollable, with all its good and frightening implications. Later festivals would stand or fall on that moment.

Momentarily the Grateful Dead came on and urged everyone to dance, much to the dismay of the already exhausted security force. There's a delicate balance between security and freedom at any rock event, and the dynamics of that balance are the deciding factor of its outcome. For this particular festival, the fire department insisted that the aisles be kept clear or they would close it down.

Reports reached the stage that people in back of the arena were ripping out the fences to get in. "Let 'em in!" demanded the Dead, "Let 'em *all* in!" (The city of Monterey demanded such an outrageous bond against damage insurance for future pop festivals that it never happened again at Monterey.)

After the Dead came Jimi Hendrix, making his American debut. In sartorial splendor, with shamanic deliberation, he snaked through music nobody had heard the likes of, enchanting the audience and boggling other musicians. He had turned the electric guitar into a uniquely electronic instrument; he pulled sounds from it no musician had conceived of and it was all musically intact, all rock 'n' roll. He was in a hypnotic fever when he placed his guitar on the stage, kneeled over it, kissed it, humped it, and set it afire, beckoning the flames upward with long bony fingers.

The audience was in an uproar and things seemed just about to ignite. It was beginning to hit the limits, but it was just about to end.

The Mamas and the Papas brought the evening and the festival to a level, intimate close, their cool shimmering sound soothing like spiritual balm. As the last harmonies faded into the foggy night, a collective sigh of satisfaction was heaved, then the most irrepressible ovation for American rock ever, until Woodstock, boomed through the sky.

The declaration had been made, the music revolution had a marked point of reference, the California dream was a national reality.

An hour later in the backstage performers' area, a feeling of pride and relief was in the air. There was none of the usual cast-party rowdiness, back slapping, and phony heartiness. To watch them was a joy, the feeling of being in it together; betting our hopes and ambitions against our futures was beautiful. Tiny Tim, then the house freak at the Scene, a small rock club on West Forty-Sixth Street in New York City, was strumming his ukulele off to the side and a small crowd was digging him and his delight at being a part of it. I sat quietly, watching, reflecting, my cheapo camera hanging by its strap, my notepad away, my pen lost somewhere, it didn't matter.

John and Michelle Phillips, a sculpture-perfect couple, all ethereal in robes and gowns and angelic presence, were sitting off at a table by themselves. They'd worked hard on this festival, it was pretty much a performers' show. The festival board of directors included such pop luminaries as Paul McCartney, Mick Jagger, Brian Jones, Brian Wilson, Donovan, John Phillips, Johnny Rivers, Smokey Robinson, and others.

John held Michelle's hand. She was leaning forward over a table, her head down, long blonde hair spilling over the top of her head. He smiled very softly. They were the mood of the moment, the consummation of a farfetched plan, hard workers in an incredibly successful event.

Something fierce and gentle had taken hold.

Laura Nyro, Delores and Juliet (her backup singers, the Hi Fashions), and I were supposed to go on to San Francisco together after the Monterey Pop Festival, but I was bumped off my flight from Monterey, it being oversold with rock performers and festival luminaries. I enjoyed the extra night in Monterey, a quiet time to reflect on how my life would change. I was from that weekend inculcated and forever infused with the emergence of rock as a serious, ecstatic cultural force. It shook me to the core. I felt bonded to whatever grew out of this force of nature that rock had become. I knew it was what I was going to be doing before I went to the festival, but now it was going to be all I was doing. The

festival was a legitimizing, affirming, enlivening event in the U.S.;
it decidedly elevated rock into the cultural panoply.

I arrived in San Francisco late the next afternoon and
had a message from Laura waiting for me. The pleasure of my
company was requested (Laura loved formality) for Chinese
takeout with the Fifth Dimension in her suite. I threw my
suitcase into my room and knocked on Laura's door. Members
of the Fifth Dimension were chatting genially with Delores and
Juliet about the festival and munching spring rolls and mu-shu.
Laura listened to them pensively for a little while and then said,
"I'm just realizing how bad it really was." The festival "house
band" had played her charts inconsistently, throwing off their
timing. "Artie paid them $100 to do a good job for us," she
said ruefully. She stood up and breathed herself full. "Girls,
let's sing the album!" The Hi Fashions positioned themselves
on either side of her and began clapping off time rhythmically.
Laura threw open the balcony French doors behind them and
they began to sing. They sang continuously for almost half an
hour, and when they were done, the nods between members of
the Fifth Dimension would turn out to mean they would cover
"Wedding Bell Blues," "Sweet Blindness," and "Stoned Soul
Picnic."

The following week a ceremonial horn sounded from the top of
a mountain. It was the Summer Solstice Be-In in Golden Gate
Park, San Francisco, a huge picnic with rock bands all over the
place playing from flatbed generator trucks. Thousands of people,
Bay Area hippies and people in from the festival, milled about,
distributing beads, strawberries, flowers, and grass, smoking it
openly all over the park.

It had been going on for some time, San Francisco's local
scene, the Sunday in the park, free people, free music, free

dope. Bells tinkled from wrists and ankles as people danced and tambourines sounded in the air. The cops just watched; there was nothing else they could do. Smiles, children, trees, lovers, and loners all being-in. Feeling their peculiar power—the ultimate power over their own lives and lifestyles, affirming its strength and rejoicing in its almost newfound existence.

At the smaller pop festivals and be-ins that peppered the coming year, thousands, hundreds of thousands of hippies captured the imagination of television and the national press. Instantly, as is the geometric growth effect of mass media, there were millions of these quixotic, searching freaks. Rock bands toured the country on the big-time, big-money circuit—L.A., San Francisco, Chicago, New York, and, to a lesser extent, Philadelphia, Boston, Phoenix, and Minneapolis—and found a constituency waiting. With the access of burgeoning underground media, radio and papers, a huge and vociferous rock audience was a predictable feature of any major metropolitan area or suburb. But it was those freaks in the boondocks and hinterlands who astonished everyone: Fort Lauderdale, Newark, Oshkosh, Sioux Falls, Rome (Georgia), Virginia City, Gary, Freeport, Wichita, and Spillville (the actual itinerary of the Byrds' first tour), all full of freaks flashing on rock. This music, this movement, it was fully evident, was the communications network of the turned-on revolution.

And the beat went on:

Saturday night at a rock concert—a live one, anywhere, in a university gym, a civic center, or a rock emporium. A group is spinning a web of music, shimmering guitar lines, racy, relentless bass, the organ flinging a sonic swarm around the frenetic, machine-gunning percussion figures. The song fights its way through the vocalist's throat, the harmonies wash over the faces in the first twenty rows like a tonal bath. There's that special balance of sound, rhythm, energy, and reciprocation and the night is alive with music.

In the audience people trounce around in their seats, jog their heads, and clap their hands in time. The light show rages with bursting colored forms, incense wafts down from the balcony. The entire house is high—high on the music, high on the milieu, high, most importantly, on each other. The crowd is littered with fringe and spangle, lights and lore. It's freaks' night out; they bought their tickets to see and be seen, to surrender. They arrive in droves to find each other, they come to celebrate the music and perpetuate the mythology. Star-struck fantasy surrounds them like a coat of many colors, rock 'n' roll beats the rhythm of their lives. The group is onstage making magic but the real rock 'n' roll stars are the audiences, their faces falling open, their hearts leaping into the light.

The final ovation is a flash flood of noise, deafening, pulsating, thunderous. An ovation no symphony could hope to expect, one no monarch would take for granted. It's the house's turn to wail and the walls heave to contain the sound and the joy. And when it finally ends and the lights go up, the audience goes out to the street, to the parking lot, to hang together for a while before fragmenting into the parts of its sum, meandering softly around, speechlessly sharing the afterglow of a collective orgasm of mind, body, soul, and aspiration.

And the musicians go back to the hotel, indulging as a matter of course in whatever festivities and girls were prepared for them and the next morning, perhaps it's only two or three hours of sleep away, after some vending machine breakfast, they plod out the hotel lobby at the urging of an attentive road manager and into whatever plane, bus, camper, limousine that will get them to the next place to play.

The Monterey Pop Festival was the first American rock festival, a defining moment. It was also, with the Human Be-In the previous January, the beginning of the Summer of Love, a massive upsurge of hippies converging on the Haight-Ashbury neighborhood of San Francisco.

"Can I Borrow Your Razor in Minneapolis?"

The road turns them into ravers, a byproduct of the inside rock scene that will someday be recognized as an art form. By the time American bands went on the road they'd learned all about raving from the English lads who'd been through and around it years before them.

There was a BBC TV show called *Ready Steady Go*, a madcap footloose display of British bands loose in civilization. The director was hung very loose and just let the show run wild.

Beatles, Stones, Animals, and others would come on and play live to live audiences. By the time the show came on they'd all been through the scene of breaking up instruments for a finale and more than once the stage was completely decimated. There were also shows that radiated the beauty and intimacy of the scene, like the one right after the Beatles came home from America and they sang to their original champions: so happy, satisfied, glowing with a closeness telecast to thousands so they might feel how much love could be motivated by the trip from which they returned.

The Animals were just revving up. They'd all pop amyl nitrate capsules, according to Eric Burdon, before they went onstage, and turn their amps on full. The music would grind them down until Eric Burdon was flattened on the stage, weeping, gasping out the song and screaming for mercy.

Once when the Stones came back from America they did a *Ready Steady Go* with the Animals. At the time, everyone was a camera freak; Ringo had gotten a camera—monkey see, monkey do. Backstage with the Animals, Mick Jagger and Charlie Watts were clicking shutters and dials, bullshitting f-stops and ASA ratings because none of them really knew the first thing about their newly acquired equipment. The loudspeaker crackled in the dressing room: "Rolling Stones to the stage," and the Stones split, leaving their cameras behind with the Animals. Eric grabbed Mick's camera and gave it to Chas Chandler, who in fact knew how to work it. Burdon dropped his pants and Chas snapped a picture of his . . . ah . . . *private pahts*, perfectly exposed, and then replaced the camera in Mick's pile of clothes and accoutrement.

Several days later Jagger caught up with Burdon and he was hopping mad! He had given the roll of film to Crissy Shrimpton, Jean's younger sister, whom Mick had been seeing, and she'd taken it in for processing only to be confronted by a leering clerk when she went to pick it up. She'd really dressed Mick down for it and he was furious. It didn't take him a second to figure it was Burdon's handiwork. Burdon just laughed and laughed. It wasn't the first time and it certainly wouldn't be the last.

Another time, when the Animals were playing a set with Georgie Fame and the Blue Flames, the Animals scampered onstage just as the curtain was going up on Fame and the others and stuck some amies up their noses. The Blue Flames went crazy, running into one another, howling and falling down, and a few minutes later there was nothing left of the stage, the sound system was all over the floor, and it was only the beginning of their set. They vowed revenge on the Animals, but Eric and his boys were only cooking up the next one.

The next time the two groups played the same bill the Animals started early, capturing a stray dog and starving him. While Georgie Fame and the Blue Flames were onstage, in the middle of a heavy ballad the Animals threw a piece of meat across the stage and the poor dog trotted out after it with a sign hung across his body: "Eric Burdon and the Animals Coming On Next!" Fame had his eyes closed and his glottis open when suddenly the audience went wild. He opened his eyes in the midst of his reverie to find total hysteria had erupted for apparently no reason. The dog got terrified and pissed all over the stage as he ran yowling away.

In 1965 when the Animals were in America they had the dubious fortune to be booked for a concert in Birmingham, Alabama. Although enforced integration of hotels was in effect there, the front desk was just not prepared for this load of freaks (who would earn more money that night than they would put together all month) and their black roadie.

At first the hotel refused to register them but relented when the roadie threatened to call the law. Later, when the group got to the concert, for which all tickets had been sold out, the house was only one-third full. Word had gotten around that they were traveling with a "ni**er" and folks kept their kids home. After the concert, all upset, the group went back to the hotel and found the place crawling with cops (the virginity squad). What a bringdown. Birmingham, Alabama, and no girls after a bad gig.

Next morning the airport was empty, whereas on their arrival, thousands of screeching fans had turned out to welcome the Animals. The place had been cleared by the cops well before the group got there and they snickered as the group filed past them through the gates. "Y'all come back and see us again, now," one of Birmingham's finest grinned as they passed him. Eric and the black roadie, walking side by side, burst out laughing and replied, "Sure!" in unison. "Not you, yuh black motherfucker," the cop retorted, this time meaning business. "You stay back in New Yawk where yo' belongs!"

All the bands in England were at one time trying to outmaneuver each other for an opportunity to tour with Chuck Berry, idol and inspiration to each and every one of them. Somehow the Animals won out and took off for a tour with the master. It turned out to be painfully embarrassing. Carl Perkins was also on the tour, and, while he and the Animals got along fine, Chuck Berry was removed and silent the whole trip, which made for a certain amount of discomfort for all involved. Berry, for whatever reason, had just shut himself off.

At the end of their last date together, Burdon approached Berry and tried somehow to communicate his admiration for the man and his music. "Even though you kept apart from us, you're still my hero," said the young white rocker to the black veteran. "We learned so much from you."

Berry softened briefly, his face relaxed into a smile, the folds and hollows of his gaunt visage turned kind and flashy, the way he shone onstage. "Thanks," he said, "our paths will cross again." That was all. Berry turned and left without another word or backward glance.

A year later, after trips and gigs and hits and flops and crushes of girls, in total exhaustion, the Animals were making their way out of the airport in Salt Lake City, Utah, when a thin black figure streaked past them, pausing only long enough to say, "See, I told you I'd see you again!" Chuck Berry kept going and Eric Burdon stood there in amazement.

Those are the memories of an international rock 'n' roller turned loose on Middle America to find his market and his way. The road gets pretty weird.

In those days it was so new. There were no precedents for these rock 'n' roll groups to follow, not in booking, not in playing, not touring, not behavior on the road. It was all new in every way and they just lived it to the hilt.

Keith Moon may have been the chief raver. He was known to go completely berserk on the road. Once he blew out a door in the Gorham Hotel in New York City with cherry bombs. It wasn't enough, dropping cherry bombs out a fourth-story window. But when he blew the door out, they'd had it. The Who were unceremoniously evicted at 3:00 a.m. and were requested not to return to the Gorham.

On an early Who tour, when they were kind of broke and traveling by bus, they were booked into a convention hall in Asbury Park, New Jersey, a huge concert spot located at the end of a pier. There had been a fast rule on the trip: no girls allowed on the bus. Absolutely none, no exception. This had been agreed to after some girls the group picked up somewhere in the Midwest had made off with a few thousand dollars left lying around a hotel room in the midst of some great stoned scene. It was a time when they couldn't afford to lose that much money and everyone was pretty sore about it. So the word went down: no girls on the bus.

Well, Moonie had picked himself a pretty one that night in Asbury Park, New Jersey, and he wanted to take her on the bus. After the show there was a huge fight about it, up in the dressing room of the concert hall. Some schmuck had given the group a dressing room right over the ocean.

Moonie was furious, riled incoherent, and he jumped up on the windowsill and shrieked, "She comes with me or I jump!" And before anyone could grab his ass off of there he *jumped*!

The group and roadies flew to the window and looked down at the waves crashing over the rocks. He'd really done it. No sign of him anywhere.

They spent hours searching, calling, begging forgiveness, and finally they called the Coast Guard, who came with lights and dredging equipment, and there were cops all over the place looking for Keith Moon.

And from under the pier in the freezing water through the rotting creaking timbers came a lone soulful voice: "Thought I'd never do it, did yoooooooooou. . . ."

Some years later, a group called Led Zeppelin came to America to make it, taking a highly calculated risk. The group had been put together around Jimmy Page, who had a heavy personal following from his previous work with the Yardbirds, an immensely popular, brilliant, spirited, and seminal British blues group that generated a great deal of charisma in the States. They got a singer from another group, a knockabout band on the English club circuit, a raw ferocious gutter singer, Robert Plant.

John Paul Jones joined next, one of the foremost young sessions bass players in London, then drummer John Bonham, who had been working on a construction job to earn enough money to feed his family when he was asked to join the group. Jimmy Page and his guitar virtuosity, together with Peter Grant—a burly ex-wrestler, ex-bouncer, a manager who knew the business from the tough side in—set out to put together the top group in the world. It is every musician's and manager's intention, but this band pulled it off. In 1970 they would knock the Beatles off the top of the Melody Maker popularity chart in England and would be the top touring group in the United States. It was a carefully laid-out strategy involving carefully chosen people, carefully made deals, carefully contrived music, all of which worked. A little luck, timing, and experience and a lot of talent, not to mention some outstanding original songs, pulled the troupe all the way to the undisputed top of the heap.

In the beginning they barely played England at all. The real money, they knew, was in the States. They had put together a first album, *Led Zeppelin*, a spirited, crisp breath of freshness at a time when rock 'n' roll was really getting bogged down. They released it in England, then in the U.S.A., in January 1969, and followed it over the Atlantic to tour it into legend.

The first tour just about broke even, a typical first tour; actually many first tours lose money. Jimmy and John Paul were stars starting all over again as relative unknowns with the new group, and the generational leap in rock bands had yet to be proven. Bands had broken up and their key members re-formed that year (1969) and all the heavy blues musicians from London had a new group to tour with. This pattern would repeat itself with American musicians, but only months later.

With Led Zeppelin's first date at the Fillmore East in New York, they scored. The album had only been out a few weeks and the audience displayed a great deal of familiarity with the material. The reputation of Jimmy Page's blues affiliations and guitar wizardry was enough to bring a full house out to hear the new band.

They began a second album back in England when they returned, rushing it a bit because they had no hit single, the express ticket to higher concert prices. Rock 'n' roll fans are easily distracted and were notoriously fickle in those days, with so much to choose from. Before the second album was even finished, it was time for another tour. They packed their gear and the unfinished tapes and set off for another five and a half weeks in America.

They opened in San Francisco, playing and drawing well for four consecutive days. Before the tour was over they would travel fourteen thousand miles, playing thirteen engagements to hundreds of thousands of people. They arrived healthy, rested, and well-rehearsed. From San Francisco it was down to L.A. for almost two weeks of concerts, interviews, and raving. San Francisco had gone exceptionally well; concerts in L.A. were selling out.

They made such an impact on Los Angeles that the ringside clique of pop cognoscenti couldn't stop talking about it for weeks. Not that their performances were that overwhelming; the reviews had been quite mixed, a fact they hotly resented over the following weeks. It was their carryings-on that set the popvine aghast.

John Bonham had dressed up as a waiter and served little Jimmy Page up on a room service cart to a flock of girls. When the fracas was over in L.A., they traveled to British Columbia for two concerts. When they arrived there they found the venues to be five hundred miles and only one day apart. They had to drive the distance overnight. From B.C. they went down to Seattle and from there to Honolulu, where even a few days of sunshine and rest after a concert didn't get them back in good physical shape.

But it's *make it, get there, play, and go on.* The rock business is volatile, rapid, and dangerous. There's no backing out of a concert contract. If a musician gets sick, they shoot him up like a racehorse and send him on. If he gets crazy, they slap him into line long enough to finish the tour before they dump him. For alien dopers a bust is legal ostracism, deportation—locked out of the money pile in America for a rock group aiming determinedly for the top. (Donovan had been invited to perform at the Monterey Pop Festival, but couldn't because of a 1966 drug bust for which he was refused a visa to enter the United States.) Tours were a tumult of exhaustion, anxiety, release, sex, drugs, traveling, and trying against incredible odds with their bare hearts and whatever managerial leverage they could muster.

At 7:00 a.m., having flown all night, the group straggled into a Detroit motel and walked right into the aftermath of a murder. The body had been removed only moments before and steam was still rising from the blood on the floor. Nobody asked who, what, where, why, or when. "I only knew I'd spew if I looked at it another second," said Robert Plant, and he grabbed his baggage and his room key, and stumbled into his second floor room for some sleep.

For a rock 'n' roll band on the road in this raw naked land, the trip is not entirely a barrel of yuks. They lived and worked and struggled to survive from day to day, from place to place, through unspeakable nightmares just to play music. It was loud, hard, gutsy rock, violent and executed with a great deal of virtuosity. Robert Plant, woolly, handsome in an obscenely rugged way, sang as if the songs had to fight their way out of his throat. Jimmy Page, ethereal, effeminate, pale and frail, played physically melodic guitar, bowing it at times, augmenting it with electronic devices, completely energizing the peak of the ensemble's lead sound. John Bonham played ferocious drums, often shirtless and sweating like some gorilla on a rampage. John Paul Jones held the sound together at the bass with lines so surprising, tight, and facile but always recessive, leaving the dramatics to the other three who competed to outdo one another for the audience's favor.

No matter how miserably the group failed to keep their behavior up to a basic human level, they played well almost every night of the tour. If they were only one of the many British rock 'n' roll groups touring at the time, they were also one of the finest. The stamina they found each night at curtain time was amazing, in the face of every conceivable kind of foul-up with equipment, timing, transportation, and organization at almost every date. They had that fire and musicianship going for them and a big burst of incentive; this time around, on their second tour, from the very beginning, they were almost stars.

While fans and the business staff were overjoyed, others were grudging. One of the managers of a rock 'n' roll emporium they played was downright bitter. "They [Led Zeppelin] played here the first time around when they were nothing and we bent over backward to put them on. Now they're back for ten times the price and put on half the show. This isn't the sort of place where we make everyone leave after the first set, the kids are used to staying till we close." Because the group received a percentage of the gate receipts as part of their fee, their contract required the management to turn over the house after each set. "We're the ones the kids hold it against," complained the manager of the hall. "Now that they're getting big, they're getting away with it."

The group awoke to Detroit late afternoon and munched on grilled cheese sandwiches in the motel snack shop, blocking out the next few hours before they'd have to play. Robert split for a brief walk and some shopping. As he crossed the street a motorist screeched to a stop beside him and spat in his face. He returned to the motel for a ride, all upset. "I'm white," he mused; "I can imagine how a spade feels here."

Detroit. The lowest.

He returned from the drugstore with shampoo, a comb, and some creme rinse for his copious mane, but no deodorant, which he needed regularly and badly.

During that evening's performance at the Grande Ballroom, a converted mattress warehouse which was one of the country's oldest established rock halls, equipment failures plagued their music. The house was packed and restless, warmly appreciative, and relentlessly demanding. The vibes were heavy; the audience and crowd were infested with armed police who took a grim view of the scene. Even the groupies crowding the large dingy dressing room seemed particularly gross.

A pair of grotesquely painted, greasy-cheeked, overweight sex bombs in their late twenties pushed their way through the young things to Robert Plant. One placed her hand on his thigh and brassily declared, "You're spending tonight with me." Robert grimaced and exploded. "Hey, wot, you bloody tart, old Robert's a married man!" The others tittered as he squirmed away, pausing to shoot them a leering wink.

The girls talked among themselves. The pair who had just accosted Robert bragged that they made their living boosting: shoplifting and selling the merchandise off. They claimed to make between two and three hundred dollars a week from their efforts, a story their sleazy apparel belied.

The band huddled together and commiserated, discussing the girl situation. The two in question were dubbed the "ugly sisters," cursed down, and a scheme was cooked up to get them later on. The plot was to bring them back to the motel and pelt them with some cream-filled donuts, then gang bang them.

They seemed particularly delighted with the aspect of abuse in almost any situation regarding girls who sought them out. "Girls come around and pose like starlets, teasing and acting haughty," said Jimmy Page—by way of explanation, not excuse. "If you humiliate them a bit they tend to come on all right after that. Everybody knows what they come for and when they get here they act so special. I haven't got time to deal with it."

John Paul Jones appeared at the door, looked into the dressing room full of girls and hangers-on, and closed it. He sulked miserably outside where fans badgered him constantly. Jimmy Page, inside, with that febrile, forlorn look that brought out perversity in fifteen-year-olds, sat inside, chatting occasionally and quietly to whoever spoke to him, neither receiving nor giving any invitations.

Robert and John, Cockney sports at heart, continued to turn their uproariously vulgar sense of humor on the situation. Detroit was unquestionably the low point of the tour, a town as foul as exhaust fumes and as hard as cement.

The following morning, as they met outside the motel before leaving, Robert was livid. Apparently he'd had one of the ugly sisters, despite the fact that the donut scheme fell through (late at night on the way home there was nary a donut shop open, it seems). He ranted and railed, cursing the girl out because she hadn't come once all night. "Can you believe that?" he fumed. "I was embarrassed!"

They were leaving for a concert at Ohio University on a two-stop flight from Detroit to Columbus. The sixty-mile drive from the airport to the campus in Athens, Ohio, was beautiful, lush in the height of springtime, but the group was too disoriented to enjoy it. Geography had been ripped past them at an unbelievable rate, so many time zones had been crossed and double-crossed that the date, even the time, became irrelevant. The road manager kept it all together in between his own schedule of sexual sorties. He arranged reservations, arrival times, picking up money, waking the lads up in time. An equipment man was responsible for the thousands of pounds of instruments and sound equipment which had to be shipped, trucked, expressed, driven, or otherwise transported from place to place intact. "How much time till the gig?" was the only question the group ever cared about at that point. Everything else was too fast, too complicated, or too troublesome to deal with. It got to the point by the time they got to Boston—where they asked a local disc jockey they knew to get girls for them—that they didn't even want to bother wending their way through the groupies' come-hither games anymore.

Check into the hotel. A quick swim in the springtime chill. A bit of a drink at the hotel bar, crawling with conventioneers who pointed at them and guffawed. A sound check at the auditorium. Another nip at the bar. No supper.

They played a set, an encore, another. They were tired, keyed up, not knowing whether to shit or go blind, and they tumbled back to the hotel where they had to take pills to get to sleep. In the morning there was a mad, almost-missed-the-plane dash to the airport. It was a rainy Sunday morning in Hocking County, Ohio, as the cars hissed along the highway, skidding around wild curves on unfamiliar roads. The country music played soft. God's great word washed over God's great Midwest as country gospel quavered from the rental car radio and the lads slumped in sleepy stupor through the careening drive, not knowing how dangerously fast the road manager was driving, seeming not to care. As the caravan of three cars turned into the airport the radio reported that John Wesley Smith had been shot in a fight in an eastside Cleveland bar.

Robert was first onto the plane, galloping down the aisle like a demented ape, his armpit hair hanging from his sleeveless open-knit shirt, yelling at the top of his lungs, "Toilets, TOILETS! Toilets for old Robert!" The passengers went into a state of mild shock.

Nerves frayed when they reached Minneapolis and the driver kept losing his way to the Guthrie Memorial Theatre. They arrived somewhat late; the performance nonetheless was spectacular, the audience laughing in polite embarrassment at Robert's orgasm sequence onstage, and applauding lustily afterward. It was a sit-down crowd, all natty and urban, country-club hip. Part of this particular engagement, it turned out, was the obligation to attend a party at the lady promoter's country house, full of young locals in blazers and party dresses who gaped at the group for several unbearably dull hours. Comparing notes afterward, other groups who had been through Minneapolis said that every group playing there had to go through the same lame scene.

The road manager called a meeting the next day. There was a decision to be made. There were four days until Led Zeppelin were due to play in Chicago. Nobody liked Minneapolis very much so it was decided by Jimmy Page and the road manager that the group would fly to New York for a few days of rehearsals and interviews by day, recording sessions (the second album was only partially finished) by night. They were reminded that the second album should be out by their third tour to stack the cards in favor of their success.

Their success was built on a well-engineered promotional strategy. Recordings, airplay, personal appearances, and publicity have to be coordinated for the greatest impact. A constant flow of albums, the release of a new one timed with the denouement of the current one, is desirable. Their names must appear somewhere at all times in some sort of press—columns, fan magazines, critical journals, underground papers—no possible exposure is left untried. Their English manager, American lawyer, road manager, and publicity agency, one of Hollywood's heaviest, conspired to pack the heaviest possible punch.

European performers are allowed only six months' working time in the States, for tax reasons. There is constant pressure to make every day, literally, pay. Little time for peace of mind or rest; play is nabbed on the run. Working into the early morning hours is the rule rather than the exception. Recording sessions in New York last until exhaustion overtakes each man by turn.

Groupies dropped in on the session to check out the music and make sandwich runs. These were the accomplished groupies, the ones with the savvy to check the studio out during the day and get the particulars as to time and location of Led Zeppelin's sessions. Much to the group's dismay the girls simply showed up, everywhere, as if informed by some freak's celebrity service of their every move. These are the socialite groupies, the *grandes dames* of the grapevine. Soon the word gets out (half of grouping is gossip) and the scuzzy second-stringers arrive in unmanageable numbers, just when the group really wants to work.

The girls chat among themselves, catty, bragging, doing one another in. The group's reputation is ripe and they are by now considered heavy scores on the groupie roster. None of them luck into an invitation to come along on the tour, though. There is a fresh crop in every city and the group is getting blasé and annoyed with these girls; their nerves are about shot and they are exhausted, too tired to care and too bored to resist.

Once an outraged bridegroom followed his wife to a motel where she'd come to see Led Zeppelin. He beat her up on the street outside while the group ate dinner in the restaurant, completely unaware of the scene. Furious parents have broken down hotel doors to wrench their daughters from musicians' beds. A groupie following a group from city to city, bearing dope as they are wont to do, is an extremely dangerous situation. Often groupies plague performers with their neurotic fantasies. Once, in New York, Grace Slick opened the door to her hotel room to find a man in her bed hysterically claiming to be the father of the child she was at the time pregnant with. But for better or for worse, groupies provide most of the companionship and all of the sex on tour.

Hardly anyone provides a good meal. At 3:00 a.m. the cruise around town for an open diner is often fruitless. Parties offer only crackers and cheese and such. With strange girls in the car, in a strange city, both the hunger and the loneliness are gripping.

There was one groupie in New York, about the biggest absurdity on anyone's list. Well into her thirties, she was an ex-wife of a legendary producer. She had dyed her hair pixie blonde (the roots showed only a little) and she wore high boots, a leather miniskirt, and a cowboy hat, the skirt just short enough to reveal a pair of well-shaped legs getting a little crepe-y at the thighs. She sauntered up to Jimmy Page, so in the know—dropping names, telling stories, talking English automobiles and pronouncing it *Jag-you-are*. She was cloying, enchanted with Jimmy—a fellow Capricorn, brilliant, rich, ambitious, creative, just like her. And don't you know how Capricorns are vastly attracted to one another? And, she confided to the room at large (that being the control room of the recording studio), he was marvelous in bed last night, and in doing so, informed the mere teenage amateurs that Jimmy Page was her sexual territory. None of the other girls seemed particularly intimidated.

She had somehow, being a music business insider, gotten hold of the tour itinerary and she rang him up at weird hours of the morning to check him out on the road. When the group got back to New York, she appeared at the Fillmore East dressing room, hovering over him. He'd scowl and move away but she was always there with some pretense at conversation with whoever would occupy her time and keep her from realizing that she was just beginning to be, generously speaking, unwanted. At one point Jimmy left the room and came back cuddling the worst-looking girl, all sooty eyes, smeared lip gloss, and rotting teeth. He protectively led her over to the old babe and asked her to give the little wretch her seat. The woman clenched her teeth and finally left, standing up straight, her face crumpling under that tight mask. The following night she was out prowling for new blood at the Scene.

Led Zeppelin was on the way to Chicago. By that time word of their success on the tour was well circulated and they were very much in demand. The room was enormous, cavernous, packed; the enthusiasm was genuine and deafening. Members of the other band on the bill were old friends and everyone was happy before the show. Fired by the crowd the group outdid itself and the ovation was monumental. Ardent fans in Chicago, heavy Yardbirds' territory, were familiar with the group from a previous appearance. Jimmy Page was given a boisterous, long and loving hero's welcome.

Fans attended the tour by the tens of thousands, flamboyantly dressed and outrageously mannered. Call them hippies, heads, longhairs, freaks, praise or punish them, they alone knew who they were and why they were there. That same Chicago audience that cheered rock 'n' roll into the night would have just as gleefully torn Mayor Richard J. Daley limb from limb had he been there. Being a rock fan in 1969 was riding that edge.

There in Chicago, in the crucible of discontent, the city that became a metaphor for violent confrontation, these kids sought out a music that to them represented their desperation, anger, fear, and, more than anything, hope. Led Zeppelin is by no stretch of the imagination a politically oriented band, but what they do and how they catalyze their audience into a joyous, merging mass makes them a center for the mobilization of a power politicians haven't even found a name for. It is significant that the heroes of rock's golden age have not been statesmen or industrialists, scientists or generals, but poets, philosophers, satirists, and rock 'n' roll stars who created out of their own personal torment the temper of the Sixties. They expressed their release through their art and embroiled their audience, who expressed their release through their lives.

Led Zeppelin were happy with their music. Jimmy Page fell seriously ill twice on the tour but played every night. "That's how you know you're a pro," he chirped on the plane.

Two nights in Chicago and one night in Columbia, Maryland. A day off? No, Atlantic Records was throwing them a party at the Plaza in New York. At the party they were informed that their album had to be ready in time for a marketing convention during the next few weeks. That meant another session that very night and they dutifully trooped off to the studio.

Jimmy Page was getting snappy, ragged, and pathologically work oriented. John Paul Jones seemed to let the bedlam bounce off a carefully cultivated hard shell. John Bonham was often bitterly silent and horribly homesick. Robert Plant who, much to the pique of Jimmy Page, was emerging as the star of the group, talked constantly about buying a christening gown for his infant daughter back home. Slugging down a glass of imitation orange drink one morning after a night of clowning around so loud the motel manager checked out his room to see what was happening, he sighed, "God, I miss my wife," to no one in particular.

But the depression never lasted very long. Conversations were livened by riotous accounts of the previous night's misadventures and the group developed a remarkable flair for irritating waitresses and airline hostesses who ogled over them. In flight, they would collapse in their seats, their eyes dull, faces slack, finally falling into uncomfortable sleep. They were upcoming stars, but they looked like something the cat dragged in.

Everyone was wrecked, drained, moody, jet-shocked, and almost sick. They were advised that the tour was going extraordinarily well, better than even expected, but it did not seem to affect them, or perhaps they didn't realize the implications of what they'd been through. But each time they faced an audience (and they never disappointed an audience the whole time) they knew. This music they played, these people who loved them, no matter how gut-bustingly horrible that tour was, made it all worthwhile. In those few hours the boys would be transformed from tired carping brats into radiant gods. Whatever happened, it never took the joy out of playing and playing well.

The tour came off in the black that time around. In a fairly typical arrangement, the group traveled with a paid road crew. The money they earned had to support those salaries, transportation, lodging, food, repair or loss of equipment, and every other road expense incurred. They retained a publicity firm, lawyers in both countries, a manager, and an accountant. Managers' and booking agents' fees are deducted from the gross, and by the time the accounting was done they might have gotten to divide among themselves one-third of the more than $150,000 that tour grossed. The fees they were able to get, from a flat $5,000 a night to over $15,000 for the particularly successful two-day Chicago engagement, were good, but not top money in the field.

The scheme had worked. That tour was a setup for the next one, the superstar tour, where they would gross $350,000 to $400,000 for less time, fewer dates, and much more comfortable living and traveling arrangements.

When Herman's Hermits, for instance, were at the height of their career, they chartered a private jet for a month at a time, stocked it with their favorite food, and played poker with their agent, often betting their evening's earnings in the game. From airports they would charter helicopters to the city and limousines to the gigs, never rumpling their soft teddy suits on the way, always sending the road manager out to cull and deliver the right kinds of girls. For more sophisticated groups there are the world's finest hotels, chauffeurs, managers, agents, and local bigwigs to squire them around town through pesky crowds of clawing fans into the most lavish of private homes with all their needs provided for. Past all this scuffle, if a band gets past it—and many don't—it's clear sailing for the duration of rock 'n' roll stardom. Get it while you can, pop is fast and fickle, the press is capricious, and scorn for fallen stars is merciless.

"In this business," commented John Paul Jones, "it's not so much making it as fast as you can but making it fast while you can. The average life of a successful group is three years. You just have to get past that initial ordeal. The touring makes you into a different person. I realize that when I get home. It takes me weeks to recover after living like an animal for so long."

"But playing makes up for it," chimed in John Bonham. He had overheard the conversation and responded to the sadness in John Paul's voice. "Wait 'til we get to Boston," he enthused, as much for his own sagging spirits as for John Paul's. "That's the place! Remember when we were there the last time? They were banging their heads on the stage!"

The Boston Tea Party was alive with anticipation. The house was oversold; the group had broken the second attendance record of the tour. Grist for the press mill, ammunition sending future dates skyrocketing in price. Glee for the businessmen, all of whom flew up from New York to be with them. For the boys it was sweet justice. All those dues on the road the last tour and these last five weeks seemed to be coming in that night. It was beginning to really dawn on them just how big they had gotten. The magic of Led Zeppelin had culminated with this Boston stopover and everyone was there just to enjoy it, wallow in it, drink it in.

More importantly there was Tina, a twenty-year-old art student who shivered with excitement. There was Rusty, who drove all the way from Providence to see them. Jody said he'd drive all day to see Jimi Hendrix and Linda emphatically declared she would spend her last cent on a Jefferson Airplane album. Colored lights flashed on wall-to-wall people who cheered each member of the group as he stepped onto the stage.

The Tea Party was formerly a synagogue; the stage sat in front of what was once the altar. Out of reverence or love or just plain joy, the words "Praise Ye the Lord" were left on the altar wall and the celebration of togetherness buzzing through the room like current did the benediction justice. In its own funky way the Boston Tea Party and its counterparts around the country were houses of holy worship.

The room was jammed, dancing impossible, the music so loud that ovations were as much relief as they were appreciation. Long fluid notes pealed from Jimmy Page's guitar. John Bonham ripped into dazzling percussion acrobatics. John Paul Jones kept a bass line running through like a keel, stabilizing the music. Robert sang in an erotic howl and fans writhed with the changes in sound, interjecting hoots, groans, and whistles at each lull in the sound. The floor resounded with pounding feet when the set was over and the entire building shook rhythmically to its foundations. Three encores and they were still yelling for more. "Let's give 'em another," urged Robert backstage. "We don't know any others!" croaked Jimmy Page in a desperate whisper, laughing, gasping, sweating, heaving, totally overcome by delight.

Robert marched out to the stage anyway. The audience exploded in gratitude and approval. The group launched into a medley of Beatles and Rolling Stones songs to the crowd's delight. They were ecstatic, insatiable, and merciless. But the concert was over, there was just nothing left.

Afterward the dressing room was full of admirers, all competing for the group's attention. Though they sensed they themselves were the substance of the magic that transpired, these people wanted to touch the source. John gulped a warm beer. Jimmy collapsed in a corner. John Paul Jones wiped sweat from his face and his electric bass with the same towel, then tucked the towel and the instrument carefully into a plush-lined case, gazing down at it a moment before he folded the top down and clipped the locks closed. Robert fumed, totally outraged because his favorite T-shirt was stolen from the backstage area. "That's what it is," he spluttered; "they love you and applaud you, you give them everything in your heart and they nick me T-shirt!"

Exhaustion, elation, and pride were all over the faces of Led Zeppelin. They exchanged congratulatory looks. It was late, very late. They had to play New York the next evening, the Fillmore East, the last date before going home. Everyone knew it was going to be a letdown after tonight but it was the last date. After Saturday, home to England. Praise Ye the Lord.

I had been covering this tour on assignment from *Life* magazine, living through the last three weeks of it with them, through the miles of exhaustion and undernourishment, suffering the company of the whiny groupies they attracted, the frazzled rush of arriving and departing, the uptightness at the airports, and the advances of their greasy road manager. I had been keeping a journal of our discomfort to document this unbelievably wearing and astoundingly exciting slice of professional life so germane to the rock 'n' roll Sixties.

At the Fillmore East, on the last date of the tour, I stopped in to say good-bye and Godspeed. Two members of the group attacked me, shrieking and grabbing at my clothes, totally over the edge. I fought them off until Peter Grant rescued me but not before they managed to tear my dress down the back. My young man of the evening took me home in a limousine borrowed from an agent friend and I trembled in exhaustion, anger, and bitterness all the way. Over the next week I tried to write the story. It was not about to happen. It took a whole year just to get back to my notes again with any kind of objectivity.

If you walk inside the cages of the zoo you get to see the animals close up, stroke the captive pelts, and mingle with

the energy behind the mystique. You also get to smell the
shit firsthand.

*The latter part of this chapter, the Led Zeppelin tour, particularly
the portion about the assault, has been anthologized, cited, quoted,
clucked over, referenced, and used for classroom purposes many
times. Although Richard Cole, Zep's road manager, attempted
to deny it or blame it on me, alleging I'd been flirtatious, he was
eventually overridden by guitarist Jimmy Page (who did not himself
take part in the attack). According to Mick Wall, author of the Led
Zeppelin biography* When Giants Walked the Earth, *when Jimmy
Page was asked about the tour as described in* Trips, *and "her
story," he admitted, "That's not a false picture."*

*I want it known that in my professional and personal contact
with rock artists, from the Stones to the unknowns, I was always,
except for a very few incidents, treated with enormous respect,
affection, curiosity, and cooperation. There were a very few awkward
situations. The Led Zeppelin incident was the only extreme one.*

The Plaster Casters
of Chicago

The chords come flooding out of the amplifiers like a tonal wave, swelling to an impossible amplitude, blaring, ringing, pounding. A broad beam of noise is shot beating into the swarming crowd with great resonant thrusts and throbs. The amplifiers are complaining.

They press up against the stage, the young ones, their faces bathed in delight or clenched in crumpled ecstatic agony. They lean over the edge of the platform, clutching gifts and beads or notes or the group's latest album. And some reach, reach out, squirm on their bellies trying to get up over the edge of the stage, just maybe to-touch-one-of-them . . . once.

> *And when it was over*
> *The lights turned on and the curtain fell down*
> *They stood at the stage door and begged for a scream*
> *The agents had paid for the black limousine*
> *That waited outside in the rain. Did you see them?*
> *Did you seeeeeee them?*
> — "Broken Arrow," Neil Young,
> Buffalo Springfield

"Did you see them, did you *seeeee* them, oh, Cathy, they're so *beautiful!* Look at that hair, that blonde hair—ooooh, those faces, Cathy, look at those *faces!* Oh, wow, the drummer, Cathy, the *bass player!* Let's go in back to the stage door, Cathy, Cathy, maybe we can meet them, talk to them, *something,* Cathy, let's go outside and see if we can catch them on their way out! Maybe we can meet them, talk to them, *anything!* Cathy, come *on!!!*"

Groupies. Their legions, bless their little rock 'n' roll hearts. are growing geometrically. Often they work in pairs, sometimes in gangs. Their techniques for getting backstage, which run from bribing, fucking, or knocking down security guards, and their methods of tracking a group down would put a private dick to shame.

("You call all the better hotels in town. If you're looking for the Stones, ask for a Mr. Jones, *not* Mr. Jagger, because that way it's less suspicious.")

When I have the opportunity to watch them in action, it is not without a genuine sense of admiration that I note their acuity. And rarely can I refuse a trembling, pleading teeny when she begs me to take her with me as I flash my press card at the security men that guard the dressing room areas at rock concerts.

Cops and security men are a fixture at rock concerts. They belong there as much as do the fans and the group and the rock 'n' roll press entourage. They personify the balance of tensions between rock and conservative society. They try to stop the kids from scaling the stage and causing riots. Occasionally they succeed.

But when they try to keep the groupies from their prey, they haven't got much of a chance. For the groupies are girlchild guerillas with a missionary zeal. They'll cooperate with each other to outfox whatever stands between them and the rock 'n' roll boys—but only to a point. That is, they'll gang a door to get inside, but once it's broken in, it's every girl for herself, unless there's been a previous agreement.

When the Buffalo Springfield first came to New York a crowd of groupies stood in the back of the house and divvied the boys up. If more than one girl wanted a certain Springfield they had it out as to *which* manner of lovemaking *each* would apply *to what* and *to whom*, right *then and there* so there'd be no squabbles when they *got* to him.

Some girls are specialists. The lead-singer-fuckers are a particularly strong contingent, and lead singers who write are considered a *tour de force* by any groupie's measure. They dress like creatures out of some glorious romantic drama, scrawl gross amounts of black around their eyes and wear the biggest, most gaudy baubles they can find, so maybe, *maybe* he'll see me.

The great ones, the super groupies, have real class. There's one beautiful long lithe black girl from New York. Lilly, with her enormous dyed bubble head and enormous dark glasses, who's been to Los Angeles to visit the Doors and been to London to live with the Stones. There's Cindy and Morgan, who live in San Francisco and make clothing for the groups—and don't you know those fittings get pretty intimate.

In L.A. there are the GTOs: Misses Christine, Lucy, Pamela, Sandy, Sparkie, Cynderella, and Mercy, a gaggle of groupies who have had a card printed up that they give to groups. They are said to have written torrid poetry about their rock 'n' roll conquests, which Frank Zappa may set to music for an album.

The level of involvement with today's music is quite amazing. One example: Groupies. These girls, who devote their lives to pop music, feel they owe something to it, so they make the ultimate gesture of worship, human sacrifice. They offer their bodies to the music or its nearest personal representative, the pop musician. These girls are everywhere. It is one of the amazingly beautiful products of the sexual revolution.

—Frank Zappa, the Mothers of
Invention, in *Life* magazine

Zappa knows. I'm very close to believing that Zappa knows where it's *all* at. When I first heard about the Plaster Casters of Chicago via the pop grapevine, which claimed Zappa as the source, I honestly didn't believe it. Yo-ho, another calculating Zappa fantasy unleashed on the unsuspecting great unwashed.

Some weeks later I was rapping late at night with Marshall Efron when this friend of his, the road manager from the Pacific Gas and Electric Company, comes in and oh, how's everything and the group is going great, one chick handed Frank Cook a note after a set which said "Dear Fuzzy, I came five times during your drum solo," and aren't these chicks outasite?

And I threw in the tidbit I'd heard about these groupies in Chicago, wow, I heard they make plaster casts of the groups' cocks, Zappa is spreading the word and who knows, maybe it's true.

And the road manager, he laughs and whips out this business card that reads "The Plaster Casters of Chicago, Life-Like Models of Hampton Wicks—Rennie and Lisa" . . . with phone numbers.

"Fly Jefferson Airplane, Get You There on Time," from *The Fat Angel* —Donovan

In Chicago's Aragon Ballroom, Jefferson Airplane and Blue Cheer and the Fraternity of Man are playing and it's Friday night. What's left of the Steve Miller Blues Band is in town and Terry

Reid is expected any day. Chicago, long renowned as a music town, could that weekend be called a Groupie Happy Hunting Ground. A stocked pond, in fact.

The Plaster Casters weren't hard to find. I chose the Aragon Ballroom because Jefferson Airplane was there for one night only. My escort was a local record company executive who kept looking in mirrors and running his fingers over his dried lips throughout the whole adventure. In less than an hour a stagehand brought them to me.

I take them upstairs. They are thrilled that I came all the way from New York to find them. They are both draped in black antique-y looking capes and shawls and whenever and whatever they move, something—hair, fringe, cape sleeve, or skirt bottom—is hanging, fluttering, swaying.

Rennie is twenty-one, pretty in a round, soft kind of way. She has expressive, animated eyes, a petulant mouth, and her dark hair falls like a protective curtain around her face. By day she's an IBM keypunch operator and her father works in civil service.

Lisa is seventeen, chubby and very young looking, almost innocent. She has one of those millions of expressionless midwestern faces that nobody gives a damn about. She still goes to school and her father is a Chicago cop.

They've both been grouping for almost five years, and they told me rather proudly that all of their sexual experiences have been with groups.

They started working as a team because both of them are very shy and they share a penchant for English groups. Being very shy girls, even now, who don't converse easily with boys they don't know, they walk up to them and ask, "How's your rig?"

Rig?

"Rig. It's cockney slang for dick. There are a lot of those slang words. Rennie learned most of them from the Hollies. *Up the stairs* means take a shit. *Bristol cities* are titties, *daisy roots* are boots, *chopper, rig,* and *hampton wick,* they all mean cock, and *charva* means fuck. *Eye* magazine printed it 'charver.' *Eye* magazine. So un*hip!*"

In those early days, before they were Plaster Casters, they would use the cockney slang in their letters to groups. It was the sort of in thing that none of the other Chicago groupies were hip to.

To the Hollies:
Rig Men,

Are your hampton wicks looking for some Chicago Charva? If so, look no further. Your two Barclays bankers from the Chicago Charva Chapter have arrived. We'd love to satisfy any needs you may have. For appointment or more info, call . . .

To the Beatles:
Dear Beatles,

We happen to know that you hold the record for charva championship around the world. We suppose that's why you've got such healthy looking hampton wicks. Tight pants tell a lot of stories, you know. And from the way yours project at the zipper we can tell you've got four rocks of Gibraltar stashed away. Maybe this is the secret behind your success. If your rigs get nervous from being cramped up and need a little exercise when you're in Chicago, we are the girls for you. We're two Barclays bankers, our bank has convenient night hours and you can make all the deposits you like . . .

To the Rolling Stones:
Dear Keith (Richards),

We watched you on teevee the other night and the first thing that grabbed our eyes was your hampton wick. After that we did a little besides studying it. We're not kidding, you've got a very fine *tool. And the way your pants project themselves at the zipper, we figure you've got a beauty of a rig. Sometimes we hope you'd whip it out or something, but they don't have cameras that would televise anything that large, do they? Hey, tell Mick (Jagger) he doesn't have to worry about the size of his, either: we noticed that (really, who could help, <u>but</u>?).*

Keith, we're serious. We judge boys primarily by their hamptons because they're so exciting to look at and contribute so much to a healthy relationship. We can hardly wait until you come to Chicago in November: maybe then we can find out more about what's inside your pants . . .

"I'd like to cast Jagger," flashed Rennie defiantly. "I'd like to see about *this!*" And she whips out her wallet and thumbs through the plastic-encased memorabilia until she comes to this picture of Mick Jagger's crotch she clipped out of *Tiger Beat*. There is a hypertrophic bulge outlined by his pants. Wow, it looks like a *tumor!*

"I think it looks like a bar of Sweetheart Soap. I heard that he was once caught in the men's room before a TV appearance, stuffing paper towels into his pants. They told him to take it out and he wouldn't so they got even with him by not shooting 'im from the waist down."

Dear Brian:

I am in one of "your" moods at the moment. I was looking at your picture and what a pity your rig wasn't so noticeable. I saw it once on telly and what a grand thing it was!! Well, I can't help it, I'm in a hampton bag and I just can't climb out of it. Only Andrew's hot one is as creamy as yours . . . here goes:

Your televised body is something to pant on
Above all else sticks out your hampton
I know it seems a lot of much

but in your eyes I see a toosh
I'm not the type whose eyes first goes
To long blonde hair or delicate nose.
At the art institute I studied perspective
To ignore the way yours projects would be disrespective
Pointing downward like a lance
Pounding hard inside the pants
Extraordinary is your rig
Is a fact that cinches.
Pray tell, Brian, how many inches?

It all started when the Beatles came to Chicago, lo those many years ago. There they were in the third row, Lisa in her early teens, and shrewd; Rennie so fetching in a dark lowcut dress, black lace nylons and big round glasses. They were screaming and laughing and crying while John, Paul, George, and Ringo were singing "Please Please Me" and Lisa was getting violently restless.

"Let's go downstairs," she urged. "Maybe we can meet them."

And they went downstairs and outside and there was the Beatles' limousine, and a cluster of girls with the same idea were already there. Lisa grabbed Rennie's arm and yelled "*Run!*" and they ran down the block to be there when the car passed them.

Rennie hurriedly scrawled a sign that said "*Charva*" and held it up as the astonished four rode past. "McCartney just kept staring and staring at us—he couldn't believe his *eyes!*"

For the Who, their acronymous sign read, "Welcome Hamptons Outstanding."

And for the Raiders, the first sign read: "HAIL—the Conquering *RIG!*"

That was before they learned the Paul Revere and the Raiders word for rig: *lanoola*. And at the next Raiders concert, with due respect, they held up a sign which gloated: LANOOLA. The Raiders, they dug *that*.

After the set—it was a Catholic high school dance, and there were all these nuns around—one of the Raiders stepped to the front of the stage and thanked everyone for being such a great audience and thanks especially to (lickerish wink) Lanoola.

The next day a review of the concert appeared in the *Chicago Tribune*, which contained the following paragraph:

> *The Raiders . . . left after wishing a special thanks to Lanoola who went limp on the sidelines where she was standing holding a name sign.*

The paragraph title was:

LANOOLA GOES LIMP!

Oh, they laughed about that one. That was far out. Reading about yourselves in the *Chicago Tribune*. Too much.

How did they graduate from super groupies to Plaster Casters? Oh, it was very respectable and with the highest artistic intentions. It was about two years ago and Rennie was an art major at the University of Illinois, Chicago Circle Campus. They started doing plaster casts in class and the assignment was to cast something—anything—and bring it in.

Rennie, now very much the experienced lady and not at all inhibited about such things, thought: Why not a rig? Why not, indeed? So a fellow student became the first plaster cast.

Lisa's part of the job was to "plate" him (i.e., fellate him) so that he'd get hard: "That's the way to look at a rig, right?"

Then they lubricated him with Vaseline.

Rennie jammed a vase full of casting material over his rig, let it set and removed it. They poured plaster into the impression and made a near perfect cast.

"We didn't get all of it, just about half—it looks like a salt shaker."

Before that they tested some poor quaking little neighborhood boy and he was so terrified that it got soft. "It turned out like a *bas relief*. We didn't know to go straight in at the time."

"The first popstar we tried was da-da-da-da from the Procol Harum but please don't mention his name. See, the mold failed and it didn't come out at all and he begged us not to tell anyone because he didn't want people to think his rig failed. Then we got Hendrix. Oh, and don't forget Ogilvie. Ogilvie, he was the road manager for the Mandala—mmm—one of the *worst* groups. We got him right in this very room!" (Which was a dressing room, upstairs in the Aragon Ballroom. A little narrow and a little drafty.)

Ogilvie is the road manager. "That's what a lot of groups do, set their road managers on us. They're afraid of losing their precious rigs."

There's this story going around, I tell them, that Hendrix almost *did* lose his because the mold material got so hard they couldn't remove it. "Oh. Nooooooo." And they convulse with laughter.

"What happened," they gasp, "is a few of his pubic hairs got stuck in the mold. Otherwise it would have just slipped out as soon as it got soft. We were frantic. Fifteen minutes he was in there. We just picked the hairs out of it, carefully, so we wouldn't hurt him. I was frantic. I thought he'd hate us or kill us. He was so—*impressive*—and I was so *nervous*. And I'm going, 'I'm sorry, it never happened this way before' and he's going, 'No, it's all right.' Fifteen minutes he was in there and he said he *liked it,* he said it felt like a *cunt!* And you heard that the plaster got stuck on his rig? Oh, no. Ohnononono—it just shows you how things get *twisted!*"

And the process? "You mix the mold material. We use dental alginates, it's wonderful—it gets all the little veins and crevices and indentations and everything. While I (Rennie) mix, Lisa does the plating. Then we get the rig down into (the alginates) straight. The guy has to help, he has to reach back and push his balls into the mixture. He has to keep his rig hard, too. After a few seconds the alginates harden, the rig gets soft and falls out."

Then they got Noel Redding, Rennie's ultimate best favorite popstar, the one that got her started on bass players. She's had a thing for bass players ever since that day last March when she casted Noel.

Tonight she is here at the Aragon to *talk to* Spencer Dryden of the Airplane. A serious discussion, you know, he's a friend of Zappa's and all that. But the Steve Miller Blues Band is in town and that bass player—but that's tomorrow night. Tonight it's the Airplane and though they're as sick as dogs they're in rare musical form.

They grind out that clumsy sweet and violent San Francisco rock, and evangelical harmonies wash over the room like a caress. The audience is transfixed. Blue Cheer and the Fraternity of Man are here also, but the Plaster Casters of Chicago don't want *them*, nosiree, no. They're—uggggg, no—Blue *Cheer* . . . Yahhh. You've got to have *some* sense of distinction.

"Have You Seen Your Mother, Baby, Standing in the Shadow," from *Between the Buttons*—The Rolling Stones

There was a fateful day for the Plaster Casters, one day in April, 1963, shortly after they casted Noel Redding, Noel, lovely Noel. The Cream were in town and Lisa found out where they were staying. They rang up Eric Clapton and he said sure, come on up and talk to me.

They went upstairs and told him about the castings. No, no, Clapton said, not tonight. Tomorrow for sure. And I have this friend who probably wants to meet you, they'd both do casts then, he promised.

And, since life truly moves in concentric cycles, the friend was of course Frank Zappa and Rennie thought, oh, no, that ugly, gross thing. But Zappa flipped out, *flipped out* he did, when he talked to them and they all became extremely close friends. But both of them, Zappa and Clapton, copped out when it came to the castings, and Rennie is still a little bitter about *that*.

They call Zappa their "sponsor" now; he tries to protect them from any derogation. He confiscated their diaries and plans to publish them along with the diaries of the GTOs. "It's an important sociological document," he told me. And he wants to have a Plaster Caster exhibit in an art show or museum as soon as the collection is ready.

He has ideas, like playing the cockstar's music behind the exhibition of his plaster casted rig. Cock-Rock. Why not? I suggested a tool kit, but Zappa just laughed. Zappa's manager, Herb Cohen (says Rennie) came up with the idea of making lollipops out of the casts and selling them under the slogan "Suck your favorite star." Haw haw. What a capitalist!

Rennie is an artist; she don't look back. She feels if her collection were put in the hands of somebody who believed in it, it would be a significant thing, a tribute to and reflection of the sexual revolution, a radical change in morality.

Lisa, on the other hand—she's only seventeen—is not so sure she wants to continue to be a Plaster Caster. She did officially resign but she's going to keep helping Rennie until she finds someone else.

For one thing, it's Rennie telling all the boys in the bands that Lisa is the best plater in the world. "Suppose I plate them and they don't *like* it?"

And also some people are grimly censorious of the whole idea of plaster castings and it's beginning to bring her down. "It's okay for Rennie, she only lives for the moment, but I want a heavy thing with a guy someday and I'm afraid this would prevent it."

"Nothing's perfect," Rennie snaps, "everyone can't like you. You've got to make up your mind that you're a pioneer."

The Plaster Casters are, by now, legend. They have fans. They are frequent *dramatis personae* of the rock grapevine. And recently they discovered two imposters: Alice and Candy are copping their thing! Getting to groups by saying *they're* the Plaster Casters!

Rennie, whose dedication is a joy bordering on abandon, hopes they don't learn how to plaster cast—it would spoil her exclusivity. Because they're getting more famous by the moment. Spencer Dryden told them that Friday night that groups in San Francisco were writing tunes about them. And they're still reading about themselves, though the coverage has been somewhat tangential.

The *Chicago Tribune*: "The Yardbirds were in high spirits. They had just seen about 300 girls at the Civic Opera House to receive gifts and sign autographs. They received everything from imported caviar and kumquats to instant psychiatric kits, 69 sweatshirts (*Rennie gave him that*), stuffed animals, and incense. One girl was on crutches and took moving pictures. Another brought along her plaster kit to get a mold of Jeff Beck's leg forever!"

His *leg*, indeed!

Playboy: "Roland Ginzel, whose paintings have unfailingly captured the existential spirit of the famed author's work (Nabokov's *Despair*) . . . is currently teaching in Chicago and has works hanging in the permanent collection of the Art Institute in Chicago and the Dallas Museum of Fine Arts and has exhibited in the Metropolitan Museum of Art and the Museum of Modern Art in New York City."

But *Playboy* left out what must certainly be considered as Roland Ginzel's most significant contribution to contemporary art. Roland Ginzel, after all, was the professor who taught Rennie how to plaster cast.

And in the middle of a review of Jimi Hendrix's latest album, *Electric Ladyland*, published in the *Chicago Circle Focus*, all by itself, set off with asterisks:

****

Ask Jimi Hendrix about Plaster Casters
****

And the adventures, the grouping, the meetings, the chase and the casualties. There was that time in July '67 with the Monkees. Oh, those dumb Monkees. They were in the lobby of the hotel and there was a lot of security around. Getting upstairs was going to be a problem, they thought. But the Monkees had heard about the Plaster Casters and, oh, yes, wanted to see *this*, they did, and they sent down for them.

"We approached Davy Jones and he said yeh, it would be great, you could have duplicates made and sell them in stores." But Davy went into the other room and got Peter Tork, brought him out with nothing on, he did, and said, "Okay, here." And there were about thirty people around, some of the Buffalo Springfield were there and oh, it was a scene.

"*Bright* one over here," Rennie flips her hand toward Lisa, "takes hold of his rig and starts hand-jobbing him. They're all sitting around waiting for me to do something. I grabbed his rig, too. We both had our hands on it. Somebody got on the piano and started playing 'Lovely Rita Meter Maid.' It was—like a *movie*!

"Then Dewey Martin of the Springfield takes off his pants and drags me over to the couch—too much!"

Later Rennie got up and went into the kitchen. Opening the can of alginates she cut her hand severely on the metal strip. There was blood all over the place and they had to tourniquet her. Then they all got mad and went to bed. "They're so *stupid*. The *Mon*-keeees!"

Then there was that awful time with the Detroit Wheels, though it's funny when she thinks about it now. Rennie didn't particularly *like* that organ player who brought her to the hotel room, but she was nuts about his music. "He was kind of a turd," she recalls.

"There was another one in the group that I liked and I thought if the drummer took me back with him to the hotel, I'd get to see the other one." No such luck. Rennie was in the room, stuck there with the drummer.

"I wouldn't ball him. He had my clothes off and he threw me out of bed. He wouldn't give me my clothes back, he just said 'Okay, get out.' And I had just gotten this new outfit from my mother—she'd be sure to notice—not that I was nude, but that I didn't have my new outfit with me."

But that was back when they were very young and didn't really know who they wanted. It's different these days; more organized, more professional. Rennie is dieting like mad for next week when Hendrix will be back in town and she can get to Noel again. And Saturday night, tomorrow, there is the Steve Miller Band. . . .

It is now Saturday early evening and we are in Lisa's house in a flouncy girl's bedroom, all pink and white and precious. And there are posters and popstars' pictures and hundreds of albums—Traffic, Procol Harum, Rhinoceros, the Beatles, the

Stones—pretty good taste, I must confess, not a chickenshit album in the bunch.

And Rennie is assembling the plaster kit, putting all the paraphernalia in a little briefcase with a sign on it, "The Plaster Casters of Chicago." That briefcase has become their trademark, and a well-respected one at that. The underground radio station knows about them and so do all the club owners who let them into the clubs for free now. After all, they're celebrities in their own right.

They lovingly show me the casts and allow me to photograph them and other mementos, the signs, the apparatus in the plaster casting kit and all. And I read their letters and they proudly show me their clipping file. But it's getting late, you know; the Steve Miller Band goes on in an hour and the Cellar is all the way out in the suburbs so we'd just better hurry.

I *knew* they were going to be in Chicago that weekend. Their press agent, Mike Gershman, had called from L.A. to inform me of the activities of another client in New York. Did I want to do the story? No, no time, but who's going to be in Chicago this weekend? He was really in no position to refuse to help me, and I asked him would he ask Steve Miller to cooperate, I really wanted to witness a casting and I had a pretty good idea the Plaster Casters would go for him, such a pretty face. So I had called Miller earlier that day and I told him I'd already located the Plaster Casters and would be arriving at the club with them.

"Whew!" he answered. "I've just been sitting here writing a tune and now, this, wow, it makes it all so freaky." But Steve Miller already *knew* about the Plaster Casters—remember, they're legend in San Francisco, *legend*.

We arrive at this little asshole-of-a-club out in the Illinois sticks full of beery high school kids. They are generally noisy except for a small crowd of blues heads and girls three and four deep hanging glassy-eyed over the stage. The vibrations are fair to middling and I have a sinking feeling things are not going to work out.

The Miller Band is down to three—leader Steve Miller; Tim Davis, the drummer; and the bass player, Lonnie Turner. Rennie has her eyes on Lonnie, that girl doesn't miss a trick, she's-edging-toward-the-backstage-door-working-her-way-through-the-crowd.

But the set is over and—omigod, no!—there's *Lisa*, talking to *Lonnie*. And Rennie bristles and trembles and g-l-a-r-e-s at her. But Lisa doesn't see and Rennie, crestfallen, makes her way into the tiny dressing room in back of the stage where Miller is in a really weird mood.

"Did you see that kid give me a cheeseburger? A *cheeseburger*, he handed me a fucking cheeseburger!" ("Somebody give me a cheeseburger" is a line from Miller's song "Livin' in the USA.")

Miller is rapping to some friends, an ex-member of the band and his wife. And to distract Rennie, I point out a graffito on the dressing room wall. Someone has written *Whatever became of the plaster castors* (sic) and Rennie cracks up; that's very funny. She takes out a magic marker pen and corrects the spelling error. Very dignified.

I introduce Rennie to Miller. "How do I know you're the real plaster caster?" he demands, all too eagerly. Rennie is *not* prepared for *this*. She hands him the card. Very proper. But Rennie's mind is elsewhere, with Lonnie, the bass player who is maybe her very second best favorite popstar next to Noel Redding.

Lisa is still talking to Lonnie. "We usually divide them up between ourselves," Rennie complains miserably. "She *knows* I like him . . . what's she *doing* to me?"

And there is another complication. There's Gail, this grotesque, skinny, painted Henna redhead who knew the Miller band in San Francisco and she wants Lonnie too, oh, no!

And now Rennie is chastising Lisa for talking to Lonnie first and they're both upset and they're not sure they want to go to the Holiday Inn after all, but, well, we have a ride and everything, and Ron has to go look after the Blue Cheer and we don't want to do that, do we. So? Are we going—yes?—no?—Yes.

We get to the Holiday Inn in Elk Grove and walk into the room and there are Steve Miller and Tim Davis from the band and some company and—damn! Gail!—who somehow got there before us. And oh, there's going to be trouble. Groupies, even Plaster Casters, must deal with competition on some honorable level (like the Plaster Casters give out the GTOs cards and the GTOs return the favor) and there's Gail. Ahead of them. Entitled. What a bringdown.

Miller is still bitchy. "Let's hear this, girls, what is this about what you do?" But Rennie is in no mood to discuss it, no mood at all. Lonnie is in his room across the hall and Miller is badgering her mercilessly. Marie is there and Lisa is whining because after all, it's so uptight and she's all but retired from being a plaster caster and she just doesn't want to be there at all, not after how Rennie *bitched* at her for talking to Lonnie first. I resign myself that I'm not going to see a plaster casting tonight. Shit!

The girls are going into Lonnie's room because that's where they left the kit. I assume they'll gather it up and we'll all go home. Tim, the drummer, a swaggering randy tall black man, checks out Lonnie's room and comes back guffawing. "They chickened out! I was all ready but they don't wanna cast tonight. I told them if they had a change of heart, I'm ready—my jools will still be here!"

Where's Lisa? Someone comes out of the road manager's room and says she's in there if I'm looking for her. They're playing the new Beatles album and, yes, it's cool to go in there. I knock on the door but it's open and I walk in and there's the road manager lying on his back on the bed with nothing on, there's a towel under his ass and Lisa is fondling his rig and absently looking at the color TV where Abbie Hoffman is doing verbal jousting with Chicago City College Chancellor Shebat, Dizzy Gillespie, Robert Q. Lewis, Pete Seeger, and some others. It doesn't look as if Abbie's doing too well but the sound is off and I can't tell. The Beatles album is playing and there in the corner on a chair is Gail with her eyes glued hungrily on the bed scene.

I'm, ah—unsettled. I turn and stare at the TV pretending to be intrigued while I panic and try to figure out how to split the room fast without putting everyone on a bummer. I turn and leave all in one gasp, mumbling something about cigarettes.

I close the door behind me and across the hall Tim's door is opening. Steve Miller is gone. The guests and friends are leaving. Rennie, I correctly surmise, is with Lonnie. Lisa was with the road manager. And I'm standing here in the hall with my face hanging out. It's the middle of the night and I'm not even sure where the hell I am, what does "Elk Grove" mean to me? I don't know what cab company to call, the desk is closed and I forget the address of the place I'm staying and whatthefuckamigonnado? I stand there, that's what I do. I am hoping that Tim is, um, a gentleman. . . . (n.b. he was).

The morning after. The boys in the band are checking out of the hotel and everybody is saying good-bye and Steve Miller is really irritable. He's looking at me, half surprised to see me there. He knows Rennie was with Lonnie and Lisa was with the road manager and he's figuring I was with Tim, and boy, he's pretty crabby 'cause *he* spent the night alone. And in my mind I'm going hahahahah, eat your *heart* out you stupid garbagemouth, bugging the Plaster Casters like that, hahahahah.

We girls call a cab and eat breakfast in the dining room while we wait for it to arrive. When it comes we have to take a few minutes to pay the check, get the change, leave the tip. Meanwhile, the cab driver is trying to convince this prostitute to come in the cab with us; he'll take her along because her cab is late.

But I want to talk about plaster casting in the cab and I tell him I don't want another passenger in the car. The driver shrugs and casts the hooker an apologetic, maybe a disappointed, look and we walk outside. "They probably want to make love to each other," the hooker spits.

On the way back to the house I am made aware of another dynamic. Gail is very pissed. She wanted Lonnie, too. And that makes it almost certain that she'll go after Noel Redding when the Jimi Hendrix band gets into town the first week in December. It's sort of like defending her honor in groupie society. Rennie is so upset. . . .

I'm still disappointed I didn't get to see a plaster cast. Lisa gives me cherry-flavored cigarette papers and Rennie kisses me good-bye at the airport. I leave Chicago with my tapes and my photographs, but somehow without my favorite shirt, and I fly back to New York.

I've received a letter from Rennie.
Dear Ellen,

Here is your shirt (it is magnificent!). Ron drove me over to the hotel and I started getting scared when he started talking about, do we ever plate people without casting 'em, but I stared out the window the entire journey and he didn't pursue it further.

What groups do we want pictures of? Oh, goodness, almost everybody, if you'd really like to know. Well, Hendrix, Procol Harum, Traffic, Jeff Beck, the Who & Steppenwolf and Dianne's and my fave raves but could I get anything on the Bee Gees, Small Faces, Doors, or the Herd for my groupie compatriots. Oop—almost forgot—and Rhinoceros!

Only six more shopping days 'til Jimi Hendrix. Does my stomach ever know it! (For the week before Hendrix comes to town, my stomach always goes nuts.)

Maybe by the time you get this we will have casted Terry Reid. Oh, boy!!

When are you coming back to Chicago? When, when? I am already missing you, my dear Ellen. Do you have any pictures up there of yourself that you can send me? Send them along with a nice fat letter, would you? SOON!!!

Practically all my love (Noel's got the rest)

Rennie

On the envelope there is a design constructed out of the letters in "Ellen," and in the corner is this note: "Partially finished token of my love to you. Due to Terry Reid's road manager calling up and saying come on over (and NO ONE knows they're in town yet). So must cease this and hasten to get the kit ready."

On the back of the envelope, neatly lettered:

"TODAY TERRY REID, TOMORROW THE WORLD!"

Maybe by now they do indeed have Terry Reid casted. But then again, maybe not. Because Rennie is a true plaster caster, yes, an artist, a pioneer, right up there in the front lines of the new morality. But rock 'n' roll rigs, *objets d'art* or no, are rigs nonetheless and ever so, well, *distracting.*

And Rennie, bless her little rock 'n' roll heart, is first and foremost a super groupie. And that's a *very* high art in itself.

Editor's note (in *the Realist*): Originally, pseudonyms were used in this article. Now, however, the girls want not only their correct names published but also their photo, because of the increasing imposter problem. So, "Lisa" is actually Dianne and "Rennie" is Cynthia, who writes: "Here is the best of what we hastily scrounged up at 2 in the morning at the Oak Park Arms with my very old Polaroid. I'm even sticking this in the mailbox at an ungodly hour, I'm so anxious with our competitors closing in on us all the time."

Plaster Caster Update
The following update was published, in slightly different form, in the Summer 1993 issue of the Realist.

On April 27, 1993, Judge Lillian Stevens of the Superior Court of Los Angeles handed down a decision in favor of Miss Cynthia Plaster Caster. Our heroine was awarded the rightful possession of her plaster casts of famous and not so famous male mostly rock 'n' roll genitalia, and $10,000 in damages. What was actually returned to her were bronze replicas of the original plaster casts mounted on wooden pedestals. All the originals are lost, according to music businessman Herb Cohen, the defendant in the lawsuit.

Cynthia brought suit against her publisher, Herb Cohen, who after storing the plaster casts for fifteen years, refused to deliver them to her when she requested them in 1988. "Herb started calling me about it being time to exploit my diaries [for which Cohen bought the publication rights], but whenever I brought up the subject of returning the casts to me, he got very vague. When I learned there was going to be a problem, I was sick to my stomach. During the trial I got to inspect the casts. I got dizzy spells just looking at them after all those years."

Cynthia sought legal counsel in 1988 and brought suit in 1991. It took years to get a trial date. At the trial, my article (above) "The Case of the Cock-Sure Groupies" from *the Realist* dated November 1968—which was the first national report of the escapades of the Chicago groupies who made plaster casts of rock 'n' roll penises—was accepted as evidence to establish the extent and history of the Plaster Casters' notoriety.

The subject of the lawsuit was twenty-five casts, identified by the catalog number, date of casting as inscribed, and name of the subject. Among them were plaster casts of Jimi Hendrix, Harvey Mandel, Zal Yanovsky, and Anthony Newley.

Dianne Plaster Caster, one of the two originals chronicled in "The Case of the Cock-Sure Groupies," retired and moved to England sometime in the Seventies. Cynthia moved to L.A. for a while, where she pursued her now famous artistic endeavors, continuing her casting with local assistants named Harlow and Lixie.

One of the last castings Cynthia did in L.A. was of Aynsley Dunbar of the Mothers of Invention, and Cynthia remembers it well. When she first prepared the mold, he all of a sudden refused to be casted. "He would not put his dick into my mold," recalls Cynthia, "because he didn't think it was big enough. He said he could get it bigger." That really pissed Cynthia off: "It's a costly prep! When the alginates are ready, you have to stick something in there or it'll set right away." Cynthia made several attempts at a casting before finally succeeding.

"What we came up with was no bigger than the first time. It took several times and it never got any bigger. He's decent, not very huge. He kept thinking he was capable of biggerness. It's a nice cast, very good detail. Nice looking dick, I must say."

The years have not taken any of the wind out of Cynthia Plaster Caster's sails, although these days she prefers to work with a casted one's significant other rather than a dedicated assistant plaster caster. The assistant is responsible for preparing the subject to enter the casting material in a rectilinear condition. Good help, as always, is hard to find, so in-house production has sufficed for recent castings. It has, by all reports, worked out well.

"Mostly I like to work these days with the wives or girlfriends of the subject," said Cynthia. "I get to know them, and they trust me when they see I'm only in it for the artistic thing. Then, they can believe that if I have to put my hand on the balls for a second, it's just to make sure pubic hairs don't get stuck in the mold like Jimi Hendrix's did."

Cynthia left L.A. in 1972. A combination of other groupies getting married and the sexual revolution coming to a screeching halt with the specter of AIDS did not bode well for Cynthia's unique memorabilia, upstanding monuments to the raw power of rock 'n' roll. For the past thirteen years, Ms. Plaster Caster, under her given name, has been employed by a typesetting firm in Chicago. When she applied for the job they recognized her because they'd once typeset a local magazine story about the Plaster Casters. During the Eighties Cynthia was part of an MTV movie about groupies in the Sixties. Her employers were very supportive of her quest to get her missing masterpieces returned, particularly when she had to take so much time off work to testify at her trial in L.A.

Three casts are missing from the collection of about twenty being returned: one, of the late manager of Iron Butterfly, another of a roadie of the Young Rascals, and another of the bass player from Savoy Brown. "That was a cute twisted one, really a fave," she said wistfully. "It was one of two twisted ones. Noel Redding's was twisted, but this one was looped, like the hook on Captain Hook's hands. When I casted Ricky Fataar (who played George Harrison in *The Rutles*), his drooped in the mold and, as a result, I have to hang it on the wall because it can't be mounted."

"I'd like to cast other men besides rock musicians," she says. "I'd consider doing a modern superhero . . . like an honest politician, for instance."

Having taken her potshot of the day, Cynthia then huffed about her L.A. trial attorney, Geoffrey Glass, for going around saying that he wasn't really impressed with the Jimi Hendrix cast, the towering inferno of the collection. "I'd like to do a casting of Geoff," said Cynthia defiantly. "Let's see what *he's* got!"

Cynthia was finally reunited with the replicas of her casts just before Mother's Day and they went straight to a bank vault, a very large bank vault at an undisclosed location in Chicago. "I miss every one of them that is missing," mused Cynthia. "Maybe for Thanksgiving this year I'll have my vegetarian turkey in the bank vault with the casts all around the table."

I hear from Cynthia annually, when a phallic holiday postcard arrives in my mailbox. Few icons of rock are as original as Cynthia Plaster Caster. Her casted penises have been exhibited at major venues, among them, in 2017, at the famous MoMA PS1 in Brooklyn. I count her among the most significant rock icons I have met.

Up Against the Yippies

Rock 'n' roll had been choogling hard over the years since 1965 and from a distance it looked as if it were about to eat straight society alive. A viable counterculture had formed too fast to get any real perspective on its ideals. A closer look showed the alternative society functioning on as irrational a split standard as the one it opposed, and within the youth uprising, there were ugly divisive crosscurrents, and an element that hung on the periphery of the rock scene with political motivations.

Basically the music did not relieve their anxiety, it inflamed it. The capitalistic aspect of it infuriated them, and though they associated themselves with performers and performances they felt their intentions went beyond rock itself. Continual accusations were hurled at rock stardom as being co-opted by business, corrupt, elitist, money-hungry, and a shuck. From the other side it was, if not innocent, certainly understandable. "We were the youngest generation of moneyed people," said Cass Elliot, "and we were just bigger kids about it."

Hippie neighborhoods were becoming ghettos once again and a scarcity of grass brought speed and hard narcotics on the scene. Concurrently, delusions of revolution rose to the surface.

Things were not running smoothly in communities of freaks. Somebody jumped bail on the free bail fund in the East Village; free clinics in San Francisco were robbed of hypodermic needles, presumably by junkies. Riots erupted and neighborhood thrift shop proprietors gathered merchandise from free stores to sell up the block for money.

Abbie Hoffman was an arrogant, flashy malcontent at the time, a leathery and witty ex-actor in search of a role. Paul Krassner had been living in a loft in the East Village and publishing *the Realist,* a flinty, iconoclastic magazine of political satire and societal sass. During the height of the action in the East Village he'd met Hoffman and the two became friends. Abbie was delighted by Paul's wit and eagerness to poke holes in lovingly upheld illusions and Paul was amused by Abbie's outrageous ambitions of disrupting society and his theatrical behavior.

Abbie had just gotten a contract and advance money to write *Revolution for the Hell of It* and Paul was interested in finishing a film script he'd been working on. Neither of them had had a vacation in quite some time, so they planned to take a winter vacation together—a month of writing, tripping, and heavy hanging out. Krassner had recently separated from his wife and didn't know any girls he wanted to take a vacation with, so he asked the editor of the underground newspaper *East Village Other* to run a note on the editorial page (as opposed to the personal ads, which were kind of seedy) saying that Paul wanted to meet a girl. "Any intelligent sensuous girl need apply," the ad read.

Friends, this author was always the kid in grade school who, on a rainy day, stepped in all the puddles on the way to school to prove her rubber boots worked: I answered the ad.

We were to meet outside an organic health food restaurant on the Lower East Side, have dinner, and preview an off-Broadway show. The play was *Conquest of the Universe*, the kind of theatrical disaster that sent Hoffman into the street for drama, rather than the theater. It was a painful thing to see. In one scene an extraterrestrial human's papier-mâché penis fell off during some complicatedly obscene piece of stage business, bouncing along the stage floor. The actor chased it down and stuck it into his waistband; in the next sequence an actress was supposed to wrench it from his pelvis. There were musical numbers such as "No More Nookie for You," during which time I told Krassner I thought the play was off-Broadway's bad parody of bad Broadway musicals. During the intermission Krassner said, to my suggestion of leaving, "On one hand it can only get better; on the other hand it's not likely to."

We left the theater, and later, over a cup of coffee Krassner invited me to come down to the Florida Keys with him, Abbie Hoffman, and Abbie's wife, Anita.

It wasn't a very cold December day as we made our way to the airport. It seems that when you leave New York for Florida it should be snowing and sleeting and two below zero just so it feels right. On the jetliner Abbie wondered how the East Village would get along without them for a month; Paul thought probably they'd do better. Abbie laughed sarcastically and nervously and cracked jokes throughout the flight. Paul unveiled the stash: a fistful of super pure acid.

At the Miami airport we rented a car and drove a few hours to the Keys. When we got far enough out along the road that bridges the water between the Keys we began looking for a house. There were very few vacancies for people who looked like us. Finally, on tiny Ramrod Key, there was a real estate agent. The sign indicated houses were available; the sign also said, very plainly, RESTRICTED.

We figured it couldn't mean Jews; it must mean blacks. Abbie and Paul exchanged questioning glances. Paul said, "Well, this is where we see how much we stick by our principles." Abbie laughed. We went in.

Our house was set atop a carport in back, supported by cement piles in front, far off the ground. Tropical hurricanes were not unknown in the area and houses built this way had a better chance of remaining intact during a storm. We moved in, happy to find a large dictionary among the cabin's features. A working phonograph was there and I was sorry I hadn't thought to bring any records. The dampness kept throwing the guitar out of tune. I tried to tune it for Abbie, asking what key he sang in. He grinned and replied "Ramrod Key." Paul imitated a drum roll.

The days were variably cloudy, long, and slow. We went sightseeing, made friends with local porpoises. Abbie and Paul rapped revolution. I was restless; I missed my rock 'n' roll. The only radio station we could get was one originating from Cuba, completely in Spanish, and the only rock 'n' roll I heard the entire time was "Lunes, Lunes" por Los Mamas y Papas. Abbie was impressed with the hold rock 'n' roll had on my consciousness; he considered that a pop festival would be a good arena for political activism.

I got very confused by discussions of revolution. First I couldn't decide whether they were kidding or not. They were talking guns and warfare and here I was a pacifist flower child with the flush of the Summer of Love still on my cheeks, a rock 'n' roll sibling trying to get my head straight.

There was an odd-looking bird that stalked up and down the road past our house at dusk and sometimes Paul would mimic it, clasping his hands behind his back, leaning forward, and following it down. A local grocer told us the bird was a fixture in the neighborhood and natives called it Alice. Every night we'd look out for Alice the bird, stoned out of our minds, laughing our heads off.

On our third day we broke into the acid. Paul had some writing to do so we waited until early afternoon when he had it organized. We swallowed and sat on the shore eating oranges while it came on.

The beach was on a coral reef that was very rough on bare feet. The water came to only a few feet deep at high tide, dropping sharply to way over our heads about a hundred feet out, where the reef ended. Close to shore there was a hole in the reef, a deep pool of water where all manner of sea life lived, unable to get out. Abbie slipped a mask over his face and jumped in, swimming underwater. His head splashed up and he hooted. "Woo! Nobody ever saw a fish like that one!" The acid was coming on.

Paul went back to the house for something and we all jumped into the hole. We swam around giggling, melting, merging with the water, touching each other all over, and finally slipping out of our bathing suits and throwing them up on the beach. Paul returned to find us all bare-assed in the water and frowned dramatically. He bent down, collected our bathing suits, and hung them out of reach, on a tree on the other side of the road. We were laughing so hard we could hardly swim, and we leaned against the edge of the reef to keep afloat. Paul came to the edge of the water and made gestures of antic mock disapproval. We looked at one another in feigned shame.

Swimming nude in these waters at this time with these people, playing out this naughty kid silent drama, I wondered bizarrely what meaning naughtiness had anymore.

Later we hightailed it across the road to our clothes and went back to the house.

We were so stoned all we could talk about was being stoned. "I never had a bad trip," Paul complained. "I've done everything, gone into the subway during rush hour stoned, I've done everything. I've never had a bad trip. I feel very left out."

Abbie looked out the window. The clouds were looking decidedly weird, moving, growing, grungy clumps of green and gray moving across the sky. Then it began to rain. Then it rained harder. Then it began to blow. A crack of thunder sent us scrambling. We watched lightning slither down the horizon toward us. "Sock it to us, God!" somebody yelled. "There's no such thing as God," retorted Krassner.

Things were blowing off the shelves and tumbling to the floor. The curtains were snapping around the windowsills, and papers were flying around the room. Anita and I attacked the windows, trying to close them down. "It's a hurricane!" We looked at the sky and it sure looked strange, all twisted and violent and beautiful. "What do we do at a time like this?" shouted Krassner. "Who do we ask, Tim Leary?" The house seemed to reel, swirling madly, spinning into the *Wizard of Oz*. Abbie ran outside on the sundeck howling, "This house is going to blow right on to Cuba! *We're coming, Fidel!*" Anita and I hung dearly to a couple of chairs, helpless with laughter. Paul Krassner sat in the midst of the utter chaos, chin in hand on a sofa saying over and over, very quietly, "Pretty powerful acid."

Later that night, as we were coming down, we tuned into President Johnson's State of the Union address. He was intoning as to how great this nation's citizens were doing with the exception of certain protesters, and he made some comment like, "We all know who we're talking about here," and that just about did it. We fell on the floor outdone. Our talks had already gotten down to what might be done to protest his re-nomination the following year. "What if he doesn't run again?" I asked Abbie. "What, are you kidding?" he replied, surprised at my naïveté. "He loves that job!"

Abbie and Paul were exchanging philosophies, gag lines, ideas. Paul told me privately that in his life only two people had ever really influenced him. Lenny Bruce, and now Abbie. This was the first time since they had met that the two had any real time to spend together. We all laughed together at the repercussions of the Manchester caper, the issue of *the Realist* that claimed to reveal the parts left out of the Manchester book on the death of President Kennedy. The article claimed that Jackie Kennedy caught Lyndon Johnson fucking the hole in JFK's neck on Air Force One as the body was being brought back to Washington, D.C.

One night Abbie grinned and confronted Paul. "There's something I always held back from you," he began. "Remember when we met I told you I talked about you with Dick Gregory?" Paul nodded. "There's something I never told you about that conversation," said Abbie. "Dick Gregory thinks you're a genius."

Paul's face lit up. Abbie chatted happily. Krassner was sold.

It was coming time to finish the issue of *the Realist* Krassner was working on and he began writing the paper's central essay during the tail end of that day's acid trip. It was titled, "Reason Let Us Come Together," and its essence was that this society is violent and we must fight it with violence. Next to *the Realist* logo it would read, "The Magazine of Cherry Pie and Violence." It would be the first time the word *Yippie* appeared in print. It would suggest some sort of coming together to protest the renomination of Lyndon Johnson at the Democratic National Convention during the summer of 1968. Abbie thought a lot of rock bands would attract millions of kids from all over and the Yippie Festival of Life at that point was an idea for just that—a giant rock festival. It was coming to an impasse, my being there. Our discussions were semantic acrobatics; I was becoming intrigued but a little leery of these people though I liked them very much. I was not in much of a mood to hassle out my own political ambivalences right there, so we discussed it and it was mutually agreed that I split.

As we drove back down the highway toward Miami we came across a chain gang, mostly black prisoners, carrying heavy tools. Abbie stopped the car next to one of the black prisoners, opened the door, and urged him to get in. The man smiled and shook his head, no. We screeched away as a guard, carrying a rifle, turned around.

They dropped me off in Coconut Grove, a picturesque, tropical, and hip community on the periphery of Miami where there were significant communities of hippies among the Mission-type architecture, banyan trees, and marinas.

I thought I might be able to find Fred Neil there; I was wondering how he was anyway and it seemed time to explore a new place for adventure. The Grove already had a reputation amongst the rock cognoscenti. Folk-rock songwriters played the area clubs and coffeehouses; John Sebastian had written a languid, musing, celebratory song about it:

> *It's really true how nothin' matters*
> *No mad, mad world and no mad hatters*
> *No one's pitchin' cause their ain't no batters*
> *In Coconut Grove*

and David Crosby kept a sailboat there.

In Coconut Grove, the Head Shop South was packed. Hippies sat on the stoop and the Rolling Stones' song "Why Don't We Sing This Song All Together" came churning out the front door.

Coconut Grove had long been a place for moneyed transients, students, resort hounds, dealers, vacation house celebrities, and now, its very own breed of Jet Set hippies. I met the owners of Head Shop South, Howard Zaitchick, twenty-four, and Michael Lang, twenty-three. "The climate is perfect, people are into a stimulating variety of artistic things and there was no place for them to get together. We first tried to open a head shop in Coral Gables, but we were closed down for violating some licensing regulation. So we found this store and fought City Hall to open," said Lang. "They can't cope with what a hippie is," said Barry Taron, attorney for the shop. "They felt a head shop and the kind of crowd it generates would be bad for other businesses and discourage tourism."

The shop was harassed continuously. Police pulled in the driveway and gave out summonses for everything from jaywalking to failure to have a rear reflector on a bicycle. The assistant police chief stated in a newspaper: "They have to put up with a certain amount of police supervision and the more unorthodox they get, the more they'll have to put up with. I just don't understand their whole attitude toward life."

A sign on Head Shop South's bulletin board read:

This is *your* store. We want to stay in business, so keep your dealings off our lawn and it will be better for all of us.

A psychedelic discotheque, the Experience, had recently opened in North Miami, where a local rock band, the Blues Image, provided the music.

The same day that Head Shop South was harassed by the police another head shop, the Mushroom in Ojus, Florida, north of Coconut Grove, was also visited by police. According to the owner, when the police entered the shop area, the owner read them an appropriate passage from the Bible. One officer nudged his partner. "You see what we have to put up with?"

After Christmas, before New Year's Day, I went back to New York City. Abbie, Anita, and Paul had already left Florida, cutting short their vacation. They got bored out there.

The leaders of the National Democratic Party are planning to meet in
Chicago in August; there to enact, for the television audience, all the drama and
excitement of an American Political Convention, culminating, it is understood, in the
nomination of L. Johnson for President of the United States, and Leader of the Free
World.

In the face of this act of sado-masochistic folly the free youth of America
will simultaneously hold an enormous International Youth Festival in Chicago; there
will be music playing and people swaying, dancing in the streets. Johnson and his
delegates, locked in their slaughterhouse conventionhall theatre, will make ugly
speeches and play ugly campaign music, while we, the living breathing youth of the
world, will make the city a theatre, and every restaurant Alice's. Already, throughout
parks and vacant lots in and around Chicago, agents of the Potheads' Benevolent
Association have planted hundreds of thousands of pot seeds. The long hot summer
of 1968 is expected to produce ideal weather for marijuana growing, and most of the
crop should be ready for smoking by the end of August. F r e e people, free pot,
free music, free theatre; a whole new culture will manifest itself to the world,
rising from the ashes of America. Rock groups will be performing in the parks;
newspapers will be printed in the streets; provos and police will play cops and
robbers in the department stores; Democrats and dope fiends will chase each other
through hotel corridors. Longboats filled with Vikings will land on the shores of
Lake Michigan, and discover A m e r i c a ! Chicago will become a river of wild
onions!

YOUTH   INTERNATIONAL   PARTY

CHICAGO, AUGUST 25-30, 1968

Yippee!

Shortly after New Year's the first Yippie meeting was announced, to be held at the Yippie headquarters on Union Square. A flyer, the first piece of Yippee propaganda, was distributed. [See previous page.]

A press conference was arranged at which Judy Collins spoke and Phil Ochs took time off from the McCarthy campaign to attend. The folksingers were still political—it was hard to figure what their politics were, but they were political. Some months before Phil Ochs had organized a "War Is Over" demonstration. Cynical observers assumed it was a promotion scheme for his latest record of the same name.

Jerry Rubin, Abbie Hoffman, and Richard Goldstein all spoke at the press conference; then the press asked questions. One reporter from a major paper asked why there were no blacks among the Yippies. Abbie Hoffman floundered, saying something about this being a white middle class youth revolution while journalist and activist Jim Fouratt stood in the back of the room shouting, "Bullshit!" It was never much of a conspiracy.

A spring Yip-In at Grand Central Station was being planned. Hard-core political crazies were beginning to attend Yippie meetings. During one meeting one of them attacked Abbie, grabbing his neck and screaming. He was pulled off but not evicted. What, after all, could they do about violence under the circumstances?

Spring came, as it does, to New York and to Yippies, and on one of those sweet green new days of spring, when the brave buds opened their faces to the city pollution, there was a meeting. Though Yippie, espousing anarchism, was supposed to be anarchistic, there was definitely a leadership clique. It consisted of Paul Krassner, Abbie Hoffman, Jerry Rubin, and Bob Fass, whose underground public radio show on WBAI had become a Yippie organ. Keith Lampe's wife, Judy, designed the Yippie button and Jerry Rubin's girlfriend, Nancy, and I took it downtown to the button maker, picked out the colors, and put in the first order. Bridgit Potter Fass crocheted pink berets for the girls to wear to the Yippie benefit at the Electric Circus.

The men had already been to Chicago to apply for a permit and managed to generate some press while they were there. They were reading the columns, laughing over the inaccuracies, pondering worriedly that one of the editorials came out in favor of the city issuing a permit to Yippie. All of a sudden out of the spring day and up the stairs a marching band was heard. The Pageant Players, a band of street-theater people, were invading the meeting. At that point the Yip-In at Grand Central Station was under discussion. The point of difference was the matter of a permit. It didn't look as if one could be obtained but most people felt that we shouldn't even apply, just take over the place and be done with it. There was general agreement to this sort of action; after all, it was what Yippie was all about, wasn't it?

The Pageant Players marched into the room tootling kazoos, banging tambourines, dressed in colors and funny hats, and shouting, "Enough of this. It's a beautiful day, let's all go outside and play." They circled the room and marched out again, singing, laughing, jingling bells. They marched up Fourteenth Street and entered the park, where they played leapfrog and one couple did a suggestive dance with a hula hoop and a long balloon. The meeting went on. Nobody dared challenge the idea of taking over Grand Central Station for a public gathering without a permit. It was, after all, revolution.

The spring Yip-In at Grand Central Station was cool for the first few hours. Thousands of kids showed up. Some climbed on top of the information booth and removed the hands from the giant clock. People started reciting, "The clock don't work 'cause the vandals took the handles." At that point the Tactical Police Force burst loose. The station became a blood circus. Demonstrators were shoved against a wall, with no escape, by a cordon of cops who rushed them. A boy got pushed through a plate glass door by a cop, ripping the flesh off his hands. Don MacNeil, a young reporter from the *Village Voice*, whose working press card was prominently worn on his jacket, got cracked across the head by a nightstick. He went to a hospital for stitches, then went to his typewriter to write a report. The piece appeared in the next issue of the *Voice*, deploring the police brutality and deploring even more the irresponsibility of the organizers of the Yip-In. He noted that the Yip-In was the fourth and largest demonstration held in Grand Central Station and the three previous ones had all ended in battle. "It was a pointless confrontation in a box canyon," he concluded, "and it somehow seemed to be a prophecy of Chicago."

The night the report appeared in the *Voice*, Paul Krassner, Abbie Hoffman, and Bob Fass dissected it over the air, finding fault with, of all things, MacNeil's grammar, as if that somehow undermined his credibility. I listened to the radio, unbelieving. I planned to be missing when they all got to Chicago.

In the wee hours of the morning Danny Fields walked into the Tin Angel, a hangout on Bleecker Street. He walked over to the table where I was sitting and bullshitting some boys and slapped a morning paper in front of us. The headline read, "Johnson Won't Run in '68." He smiled wryly.

"April fool."

Yippie continued anyway. They'd had that first rush of power and they weren't going to let it go.

Bobby Kennedy got shot. Chicago happened on television. It was a gut-wrenching riot. No rock bands agreed to perform there, except Country Joe. It was just about a year after the

Monterey Pop Festival and in that time we'd had our guts wrung out again.

I packed a pair of jeans into a typewriter case and flew to Los Angeles.

My friendship with Paul Krassner continues to this day. Anita Hoffman and I renewed our friendship, after her divorce from Abbie, when we both moved to L.A., and continued until she passed away—at a day and time of her choosing—from breast cancer. Abbie Hoffman and I came to serious differences after he tried to disrupt the Woodstock festival, screaming, "I think this is a pile of shit! While John Sinclair rots in prison!" and, thwarted at that, went on to disparage and accuse the festival of all kinds of deliberate negligence.

In August 1969, I lost my mud and wrote a long, fulminating, profanity-laced open letter to Abbie Hoffman, challenging the self-serving disinformation he was spewing—attacking Woodstock and the entire rock music culture, then a few weeks later, capitalizing on it, writing a book about it. My editor at the Los Angeles Free Press, *the late John Carpenter, told me there was practically a revolt over publishing it. It was published September 5, 1969. This is how it began.*

Abbie Hoffman plans to extort money from promoters of future pop festivals by threatening to burn down the stage. Any promoter who gets taken in deserves what he gets. The kids who go to pop festivals deserve better.

Abbie Hoffman, you're a liar. You told me that you confronted a festival official with a broken champagne bottle and said you'd kill a performer if helicopters brought champagne in while they neglected medical emergencies in the field. I bet you would have liked that to be true, but it turned out that it was a gross exaggeration of what actually went down. Same as the story you told me that you got $10,000 from them by threatening to burn the stage down. Seems they gave you money to run Movement City under less dramatic circumstances. Now you tell me you're going to try to extort money and privileges from future pop festivals.

To be perfectly fair, you never claimed to be anything but a liar, but you rationalized it out, rearranged the faces and gave it all another name: mythmaking or something like that. Now that you're a self-admitted "celebrity" (to use your own word) you've become a power freak, a structure freak and everything else you so charmingly and eloquently would have us believe you despise. You're so enraptured with the vision of yourself as a latter day Che that you'll make anything and anyone your enemy in order to continue this bullshit. You fucked with the highest authority you could think of and now you're being indicted by the federal government. You write that you consider it an academy award for your performance. But you're fucking with the music now, Abbie, and you're way out of line—your own line at that.

You tell me you're going to use lyrics and anecdotes from and about the Who, Janis Joplin and the Jefferson Airplane in your writings and in the same breath you say you're going to rip off future pop festivals and infiltrate them. You want to use them as mobilizing grounds to organize "revolutionary" activities. Fat chance, Abbie. What you fail to see is that they are already revolutionary crucibles, parapolitical and far beyond the lame kind of political activism you proselytize. You don't kill a legislator because you hate anti-marijuana laws, just smoke dope. You don't create riot situations to protest establishment repression, you share and dance and get high for three days. Or ninety days. Or forever.

Abbie, the age of politics is over. The revolution is finished. It served its purpose and it's irrelevant now. To hit out with violence is just plain stupid, you'll get your upraised fist shot off. The only way you get freedom is by deciding that you're free. If you fight authority, you acknowledge it, you give it power. If authority is ignored, it doesn't exist anymore. Dig yourself, Abbie, you create the evil you fear if you seek to conquer it by terrorizing. You can't carve a new society with old tools.

Fuck your rhetoric, man. Get it on, dance, dance to the music and stop trying to exploit it. You'll never get away with it, for one thing. For another thing, it's more fun to dance and sing than fight. Sure as "Give Peace a Chance" is playing on the radio as I write this, it's gonna change a lot more heads.

You can't rip off a pop festival then write a book (as you tell me you are now doing) claiming the whole phenomenon as your constituency. The culture is what it is, man, it's mine and yours and the groups' and the people's. If you don't like what's happening, don't bother coming around. Everybody else loved it at Woodstock. The only unhappy people there were the political crazies. What are you trying to do, man, ruin what is genuinely healthy about the new society, mess it up for everybody so everybody will be bum-kicked and violent? In a pig's eye, man, it's much bigger than all that crap.

Violence is a means to itself only, ain't nothing good gonna come of it never. Never has, never will. Use your head, Abbie. Join the festival. It sure as hell isn't going to join you.

—Ellen Sander

Concerts and Conversations

Some encounters I recall warmly.

Buddy Miles
September 5, 1947–February 26, 2008
Hit Parader/May 1969

The first time I saw him was at the Monterey Pop Festival with Mike Bloomfield's Electric Flag, but you could tell at once the enormous black percussionist who thundered out that frantic rhythm had been around. That he has, with Wilson Pickett, Otis Redding, and many other greats from which he's absorbed a great deal. He started playing professionally when he was nine years old, doing gigs in a local nightclub in Omaha. He gigged all the way through high school earning his living and is proud of the fact that his parents never had to buy him anything but that first drum set on which he began to play at age nine. He's just turned twenty-one, signed a fistful of contracts and assembled a big brassy band built around five members of the now disbanded Electric Flag. And if I thought about it at all at Monterey in '67, I now really know that he's about the best American drummer in rock 'n' roll today.

ELLEN: How did you like working with Wilson Pickett?

MILES: Very strange. He's crazy. I sometimes get the impression that he's tough because he likes to push people.

ELLEN: How come?

MILES: Just on g.p. (general principles) because he didn't like my actions. Because all the other guys could get his attention and I didn't pay much attention to him.

ELLEN: What happened between Wilson Pickett and the Flag?

MILES: I got it [heard it] once from Harvey Brooks that Wilson got mad at Michael Bloomfield and asked him why he took his drummer (meaning Miles).

ELLEN: When did you meet Michael Bloomfield?

MILES: About two and a half years ago after the last show I did with Pickett. It was like a flash. I was having too many hassles with Pickett. I was going to play with Mitch Ryder, too, but I went with Michael. The Flag started almost two years ago. I had been with Pickett about eight months. Took us about three months to get together. Then we had only about two months to get ready for Monterey.

ELLEN: Whatever happened to Nick the Greek (Nick Gravenites) who was with the Flag at first?

MILES: He was an outasite singer.

ELLEN: He didn't stay with the band too long, did he?

MILES: He came back.

ELLEN: Were there any difficulties when you signed with Albert Grossman?

MILES: Well, I wasn't even supposed to be in the band in the first place. I was told by Harvey Brooks—he told me as we were driving down Fifth Avenue one night before the final decision was made—that they didn't want any brothers in the band because of uh, conflicts. The next day I went over to the Albert Hotel and talked with Michael and Barry Goldberg and he called Albert (Grossman) and Albert had seen me play. I had sat in at a jam session a couple of nights before with Eric Clapton and Larry Coryell and Elvin Bishop, and others. Albert had seen me and told me he liked my playing and the next thing I knew I was with them. But I don't think it matters. Something happened. I don't look at situations like that because I don't want to—that's a racial crisis and I don't want to be considered like that. I want to be considered as a man that just wants work.

ELLEN: How about the question as to whether a white boy can sing the blues as well as a black boy?

MILES: You don't have to be black to sing the blues.

ELLEN: Or play the blues?

MILES: No.

ELLEN: The reason I asked is because a certain critic has been kicking that around for months and it's really giving me a pain.

MILES: Well, he has a good reason to think that.

ELLEN: What?

MILES: He's never had the blues. He doesn't know what the blues is about and he doesn't know what music is about. He seems to think that he does but if he did he wouldn't criticize people the way he does. If a person didn't think that he couldn't do any better he wouldn't be around. I think it's wrong to criticize a person like he does. There are better ways. I realize that he's trying to be correct to the best of his knowledge but as far as I'm concerned you just don't downrate a person like he does.

ELLEN: Are you talking specifically about his feud over the question of white bluesmen?

MILES: Yes and there's others. Me for one.

ELLEN: He was into you? What for?

MILES: He called me a King Kong or something. I realize I'm big and I'm proud of it. I'm sure my mother and father are proud, too, 'cause they done it. It just so happens that I dig food.

ELLEN: Your band is into a number of things including, but not exclusively, blues. Does there seem to be a general tendency away from strictly blues bands now that there are so many of them?

MILES: Everybody doesn't play blues correctly. There's a lot of groups that adds the name "blues band" but they don't really know what it's about, a lot of them.

ELLEN: Are your arrangements charted or do you improvise a lot?

MILES: I hum parts and Herbie Rich and I do the arrangements. Herbie writes.

ELLEN: What were some of the things you did before you put together your own band?

MILES: I was going to put a group together with Steve Stills. Me and Steve Stills and Eric Clapton. Stevie Winwood was going to put a group together with me, too. I did some demos with Steve Stills last summer but that was just for fun.

ELLEN: Are you happy with the band now?

MILES: We have a long way to go. We need more tightness and fullness, it has to be played. Time will take care of that. Right now I'm very uptight because one of my horn players is very ill and I'm going to have to let him go.

ELLEN: Was the album cut live?

MILES: No, I think that was bad. I wish we could have cut live. It had to do with the studio. This was our first album and we just sort of experimented and it didn't turn out really the way I wanted it.

There are some good points on the album and there are some bad. As a whole it's a fair first album, though it could have been a lot better. Time had something to do with it, to an extent we were rushed. We did the album in five days and all the music is there. But the mix was rushed.

ELLEN: I should think it would take less time to cut live than it would to overdub portions.

MILES: It does. But the studio we were in didn't have the facilities we needed to cut live.

Speaking of cutting it live, I can't remember who cuts it better live than the Buddy Miles Express. There's a full, rich funky sound and the big black bear himself, souling and howling through "I Got You, Babe," "Got the Love," "I Love Lucy," and some original tunes. Buddy does an interpretation of Otis Redding's "Don't Mess with Cupid" that is just inspiring.

That Buddy, he beats the drums black and blue while Jim McCarty goes through some incredible guitar work. Herbie Rich charges up the scene on organ and his brother Bill thunks out a solid bass line. Horn section is Marcus Doubleday on trumpet, Terence Clements and Robert McPherson on reeds, and Virgil Gonsalves, who plays sax. Ron Woods plays drums in back of Buddy because Buddy likes to get up and sing, moving to the edge of the stage, right up close to the audience, leaning forward and digging on the girls in the front rows. He's dressed in velvets and satins and colors and cool and he's just so outrageously alive. He'll swagger and smile, he'll close his eyes and croon the blues, and he'll open them and belt you out of your seat. He's mean, man, which means heavy and he's bad, real bad, which means he's great, and the same goes for that big brassy band he's put together.

◆

Paul Butterfield

December 17, 1942–May 4, 1987

Hit Parader/December 1968

I intended to interview both Jimmy Cotton and Paul Butterfield together, but Jimmy Cotton was exhausted when I arrived, because he'd just come back from doing a Ban Deodorant Commercial. Although Butter did all of the talking, Cotton was present and nodded in approval throughout.

It's a pretty tasty interview considering Butter was not known to be the most articulate of musicians.

ELLEN: Where did you first meet James Cotton?

BUTTER: We met on a reservation (*laughter*). He was with Muddy Waters's band then, that was about 1957.

ELLEN: What do you mean, a reservation, was that the name of a club?

BUTTER: No, I was thinking of—there was this Apache reservation out in Phoenix, Arizona, where we played this club called JB's and cowboys and Indians, real cowboys and Indians, used to come down and hear us. That has nothing to do with it, really, where we got together was in Chicago and we used to play a lot of the same gigs. I was working in a show band at the time.

ELLEN: What do you mean, a show band?

BUTTER: It's where you all wear the same uniforms and play lounges and stuff.

ELLEN: It's interesting that you met Jimmy Cotton while he was with the Muddy Waters band. Almost every musician I've spoken to mentions Muddy as one of their most important influences. It seems that he inspired a great deal of blues-oriented music that is today's pop.

BUTTER: I don't think so. I did listen to Muddy a lot; I really dug him. I don't think it's his playing that influenced me so much as his feeling did—there's so much feeling in his music.

When I couldn't play any music, when I really wasn't very good on the harmonica I used to go down and play and cats who didn't know me or what I played wouldn't let me sit in. Muddy always let me sit in. But nobody sings or plays like Muddy Waters. The closest I've ever heard was Robert Johnson, who was one of the greatest blues singers and guitarists Chicago has ever seen. He died when he was just about twenty-one.

The thing is, when I was going down to see Muddy in Chicago—Cotton was playing with him then and a lot of really good musicians used to come and play with them all the time. There was a lot of interest, a lot of things happening. The blues was really a scene.

A lot of people who are aware of people like Muddy or Howlin' Wolf didn't know about him until this last year or two because things are just opening up now, it's not just in Chicago anymore. As a matter of fact the Chicago scene is really dead. But a lot of people like Albert King or B.B. King are a big influence on the pop scene, because Michael Bloomfield and Eric Clapton and Jimi Hendrix and cats like that have taken licks and things from their style and used it in their thing. But even though Muddy himself influenced me a great deal, sitting in with his band and all that, it has nothing to do with my harmonica style or anything. Little Walter and James Cotton and all those cats have their own thing going. The feeling is what's important, though, that's got to be there. I haven't really heard any young groups that play like Muddy Waters. I mean Muddy really had a great band, then, Cotton and Otis Spann were in it and a lot of heavy stuff went down.

ELLEN: Elvin Bishop is really a distinctive guitarist. What do you think influenced his style the most?

BUTTER: Elvin is trying to do a number of things, trying to break through some of the barriers. There are a lot of guitarists in the Midwest doing a new thing, like a jazz thing. That's why Larry Coryell is breaking through— because he's using different things that are coming from different places and putting it into a jazz thing. Elvin is something else again; he's opening it up a lot. I've heard many guitar players who have more technique and more facility, but Elvin opens it up with feelings. He's only just developing a style.

I started out with Elvin. At that time he didn't play any guitar, he played harmonica. He started playing guitar in about 1960 and we used to hang out and play.

He's not with the group anymore, though. He quit. He's out in San Francisco to rest for a few weeks and see if he can get something together. I think he's going to start his own group.

ELLEN: Who's your new lead guitar, now?

BUTTER: A guy named Buzzy Feiten. He's from New York. He's nineteen years old and he's a monster on the guitar. Really together. There are so many really young cats around now who can really play blues.

ELLEN: It's kind of curious that so many younger musicians are into Chicago blues, which is essentially a form that emerged about thirty years ago and is, say, music of the last generation rather than music of this one. That is, what is loosely termed "rock," even though there is a lot of blues in it, is music of a contemporary generation and what you play is essentially an older form.

BUTTER: Blues is not an old or an older form. It has no label, it's not Chicago or anything, it's feeling. You play the music you feel. There's different ways of approaching it, naturally, some people spend years studying it but some people have a natural feel for the blues. For example, our piano player, he was born and raised in San Francisco and he's just got a natural feel for the blues. I've run into a couple of guitar players here in the Village that have just studied for the last two years, practicing the harp and things. I don't practice the harp anymore, to tell you the truth; I just play it.

ELLEN: I can see why you object to categorizing the music, but certainly you'd have to hear it somewhere. You play Chicago blues because essentially it was your environment.

BUTTER: Sure, you have to hear it and when you hear something you dig you play it, but it really doesn't matter where you are. Like the Chicago scene right now is really dead. But we were lucky; when I was there working and playing, everyone was playing blues. As a matter of fact at the time it was the only place anything was happening, except maybe at the Apollo Theatre in New York. They'd have, say, Lightnin' Hopkins or Sonny Terry and Brownie McGhee in the Village but they'd never have any blues bands.

Take Albert King. He's not from Chicago, he's hardly ever in Chicago, but he plays some of the heaviest blues you can hear. Just as heavy as Muddy or Wolf or anyone that's been playing from Chicago.

ELLEN: I would still say that there's a distinctive form to Chicago blues, it's a recognizable sound. And there really has been no innovation as with rock groups who will pick up different kinds of instruments, like the sitar, which makes a drastic change in the character of the music. Blues bands stay pretty much with the same rhythms and instrumentation.

BUTTER: Well, right, it's developing within its context; it's not really innovating. But it's going to develop into different things, naturally.

The thing about that kind of music for me is the feeling. I know cats in Chicago, especially young Negro cats right now, who don't want to play blues, they put down the blues, they want to do something different, a lot of them want to play jazz or top forty or R&B stuff. They put down guys like Muddy and Wolf because they want to get away from that scene, the ghetto scene, I guess. See, they think it's an old form, too. I disagree.

ELLEN: I'm curious about something else, too. Over the past few months several blues bands have added horns.

BUTTER: I started out playing in a band with horns and when I got my own band I talked about getting horns for a long time. I always wanted to work with them. Right after I added the horns, about a year ago, I guess it was, we cut that *Pigboy Crabshaw* album.

ELLEN: Do you like that album?

BUTTER: Not particularly, no.

ELLEN: Which is your favorite so far?

BUTTER: This next one coming up.

ELLEN: It's finished?

BUTTER: Yes. And things are changing for me, I'm really learning about how to arrange the horns. The thing just naturally develops. Like we're playing the blues, but I think it's really going someplace. I'm not really a purist, I like a lot of the things that Blood, Sweat and Tears did with their horns.

ELLEN: Well, they did all kinds of material on their album, a Nilsson song, for example, an entire orchestra in some parts, an R&B chorus and a string ensemble, to mention just a few things that don't fall into the category of blues.

BUTTER: Well, again, I wouldn't say that they were really a blues-oriented band. Kooper can play some blues but the rest of them are not blues musicians. Bobby Colomby was with a show band, that's why his playing is so tight and Steve Katz doesn't really play blues. But their horn section is really beautiful stuff. Not just on their album, I'm really talking about them live.

Some people put me down when I got horns, they'd say "man, why'd you do that," but there's so many things you can do with the horns. We're playing a few things now that aren't really blues—like some jazz-oriented stuff and spirituals. I really dig working with the horns, I don't dig leaving them just stand there and play along with us—that's why I don't like the *Pigboy Crabshaw* album too much. We went in and played the session without having the time to experiment with what we could really do with the horns. It was too new.

ELLEN: Do you write charts for your albums or just do head sessions?

BUTTER: We play the things we've been working with so we have them down pretty much. We don't write charts or make plans or anything.

But I don't feel I used the horns like I could have if I'd had them a little longer. Like we have a tenor sax, alto sax, and trumpet. The alto player plays baritone, tenor, and flute, the tenor player plays flute and soprano, and the trumpet player plays piano so we can really change around and get a lot of new things together. Like we could use two sopranos and a trumpet and the guitar player also plays a French horn.

ELLEN: French horn!

BUTTER: Yes, we're really going to use the French horn. We're writing almost all of our own material now; we do a few old things like "Pity the Fool" off the last album. Things are changing with James Cotton, too—he was in Chicago for twelve years with Muddy and now with his own band he's out of that scene. Next year different things are going to go down, he's gonna have new tunes and everything. That was the thing about Chicago: it got so dead, nobody rehearsed, nobody played anymore or tried anything new. People who really wanted to stay with the blues got out of Chicago and that's how it opened up.

I do like the *Pigboy Crabshaw* album for one reason only. We just got in there and played. No going through any of this junk of overdubbing again and again.

ELLEN: It was recorded completely live?

BUTTER: Right. That's the way I think all music should be recorded. Groups should cut live and play the thing, not overdub and use all kinds of tricks.

ELLEN: I'm surprised you feel that way. I can understand it with a blues band, which is basically a spontaneous kind of music, but with something like the Blood, Sweat and Tears album there were a lot of things on there that would have been a great strain to do live.

BUTTER: Sure it could have been done live. Have you ever heard Ray Charles's big band recorded? All of it is live. I'm not downing Blood, Sweat and Tears; I really dig the group and the horn section and everything. But this Ray Charles sound was better and they did stuff that was really more difficult to play together, more involved, and it was all live, no overdubbing at all. There's more feeling when you're playing with another musician than playing with a tape. Every time you overdub you lose some of that feeling. What I'm into is playing live music, playing with my friends. I'm not just into production and overdubbing and all that. I could do that all the time, and I did do it for a long time, overdubbing on the harp, but I didn't like it as much as just playing.

ELLEN: I think production techniques are one reason that records are so much better and more together than they used to be.

BUTTER: Sure. But look what's happened. You get a lot of groups that go into a studio for weeks, lay down a basic rhythm track, put in other instruments, put the voices in and add more stuff—but then they have a great record and they can't do the stuff live in performance.

ELLEN: I guess that's right to a large extent. I remember how great the original Byrds records were; they had all this charisma from their albums but when you went to see them live—it just lay there.

BUTTER: That wasn't their only trouble. Sure they did a lot of overdubbing and production tricks but they couldn't play live because they weren't competent musicians. I've heard bands that can play anything that they recorded and play it better live.

ELLEN: How then do you account for the fact that, just musically, the Byrds records were pretty together?

BUTTER: Well, you spend enough time in the studio—the first thing was, and really now, they brought in another bass player and another drummer to play on their records. A lot of groups do that—for instance the Monkees didn't play their instruments at all on their records.

ELLEN: That's not a fair comparison at all. The Monkees were never a real group; they were a package. You can't compare them with a group that's serious about making music, at least in their intentions, if not in their musicianship.

BUTTER: I played with the Byrds a couple of times and they just couldn't play live together. Partly because they just didn't dig each other and partly because they couldn't play. Jim McGuinn is a good guitarist but the rest of them couldn't play. I just didn't think they were any good. I like to play live and that's what I like to hear.

ELLEN: I have to agree with you up to a point. Like the Beach Boys—since they have decided they were "art," they don't have very much feeling to them, the sound is tight and slick and gimmicky but it gets to a point where it is all showmanship and no soul.

BUTTER: There is one cat in the Beach Boys, Brian Wilson, who does all the arranging and has all the ideas. But I talked to one of the other Beach Boys the other night and all he had to say about anything was "Will it sell, can it be marketed?" It all had to do with producing and selling and money.

The only thing I think about music is that it should be honest. Honesty in playing and feeling is the most important thing about it. That's what it is for me and that's why I dig it so much.

◆

Johnny Winter
February 23, 1944–July 16, 2014
Hit Parader/August 1969

On December 13, 1968, the second set of the evening program at the Fillmore East was Super Session and it was, or course, Al Kooper and Michael Bloomfield doing their things from the album of the same name. They eased into the razorback chordings of "Season of the Witch" and Kooper began to sing. "When I look over my shoulder/what do you think I see . . . Terry Reid looking over my shoulder/that's what I see."

The Super Session jam, to which a number of other musicians contributed, was a pleasant enough set, all things considered. Nobody expected very much of a jolt. But when Michael Bloomfield introduced a guitarist by the name of Johnny Winter with unprintable superlatives, the easy grooving audience at the Fillmore East woke up a little bit. Onto the stage shuffled a young man with silky white hair, a broad-brimmed black hat and an electric guitar. He played licks that sparkled, melody lines that shimmered, and harp that cut though the brainfog like a cerebral reveille. It took twenty minutes and Johnny Winter was the talk of the town.

The story actually begins with a December 7 issue of *Rolling Stone* in a major feature on the Texas music scene. A large picture of Winter and a paragraph or two described him as the hottest item outside of Janis Joplin (who also came from Texas).

The Scene impresario Steve Paul, on a hunch, flew down to Texas and brought Johnny Winter up to New York. Whatever it was that caught Steve Paul's eye, ear, or imagination served him well. Johnny Winter is one of the most remarkable musicians I've ever heard, and mind you I'm spoiled rotten—I've filled my life with the best music I could find.

Winter jammed around town for a few days at the Scene, a small, cramped club in the bowels of West Forty-Sixth Street, a neighborhood known as Hell's Kitchen, where the candles stay lit 'til the wee hours of the morning. It's the only hip place open that late and the most likely spot for jams to ignite as musicians playing other gigs in town finish their night's work and come out to play.

A couple of months later, Winter, with two sidemen, played a billing of his own at the Fillmore East. Rehearsed and prepared, sharp as a whip and twice as clean, Winter won them over, hands down.

He plays flashy straight-ahead twelve-bar blues with mercurial side trips up and down the scale. Each note he throws is tasty and right, always close to the melody in a tightly controlled pattern. His two musicians, drummer "Uncle" John Turner and Tommy Shannon on bass, complete a tight ensemble, filling in the spaces, keeping Winter up front. It's a tight, flexible knot, blues with flair; melodic, fresh and energetic.

It starts with Sonny Boy Williamson's "Help Me" followed by an adaptation of "Killin' Floor" by Howlin' Wolf. Winter tunes down for "Black Cat Bone" and the slinky ringing chordings make the blues your own. B.B. King headlines that evening's performance and Winter, with Bloomfield soloing, in tribute to the king of the blues, sings B.B.'s "It's My Own Fault."

His voice is solid, it loons and raunches, growling out the phrases, sliding up the scale from contralto to counter tenor falsetto, always secure and full of feeling. He's got the blues and he's got them down pat.

The last few months have elevated many blues virtuosos, but there's something so special about Winter. For one thing he cuts a sharp figure onstage with that white hair falling out of the gaucho hat. His visual impact is as cool and as clean as his name. His playing is always under control, flamboyant but not pretentious. It contains more substance than frill and the licks that pepper up the sound belong. He arranges rich clusters of notes, stringing them along long fluid melody lines like ornaments. The rocking blues fairly bubble, the slow ones moan with soul. The dust of the down-home little blues clubs of Texas is entrenched in his style and though he's a provocative sight on stage with his burgundy jeans, black shirt, shrimp pink scarf, and unforgettable hat, he never distracts from his music. He moves very little, his mind's on the music and so is yours. His heart's in the sound he makes and he's on top of it all. Slender, almost bony, ghostlike with that white hair, his style, both personal and musical, is not one anyone's likely to forget.

Major labels were fighting over Winter. He's made about as much commotion as any major happening on the music scene in New York, and the scene, if not exactly bleak, has been pale for a while as overripe supergroups fade or break up and little other than what seems to be an authentic blues revival fills the gap. He seems rather astonished about it all, but not unnerved.

Backstage he ran down the set to reporters, identified his musicians, chatted quietly and a bit uneasily to some members of B.B. King's band who came to tell him, "You're bad, man" (which is blues talk for great). "The next superstar," Steve Paul beams.

Superstar is an unfortunate choice of words when speaking of pop music at this juncture. Superstars are personalities first and foremost, confident mythmakers, scenestarters and style setters. They're the stuff good copy is made of and, in turn, publicity surrounds them like a coat of many colors. A superstar bluesman is an incongruity to my way of thinking, a contradiction of terms. Blues, however inventive, is traditional music drawing from a rich, inviolate black heritage. Superstardom somehow rearranges convention drastically, and Winter doesn't exactly live up to a case built on extremes. Hopefully he won't have to live it down, either.

He's a musician first and foremost, a really heavy guitar man who plays competent harp as well. His voice is confident and he's got enough soul to move an audience twice the size of the Fillmore East. Still, it looks a little strange to see him walk offstage in a flutter of strobe light; it's just not his scene.

With a little luck and a lot of efficiency, Winter will be touring and recording very soon, and I'd say he's a performer you wouldn't want to miss if you dig blues. If you don't let the inevitable but well-meant hype affect you, it will be a performance that will reach inside and move you through the joys and desperation of the blues that claim us all. Johnny Winter is a main man rather than a prime mover, but then again, how many bands have you ever seen that can upstage a lightshow?

A short time after the previous piece was published, I had an interview with Johnny Winter, which was published in a subsequent issue of Hit Parader. *It was a remarkably unguarded conversation and I found him to be humble and personable, a very respectful and mannered man with endearing honesty and focus.*

ELLEN: You must be going through some incredible changes.

WINTER: Yeah, well, really. I'd thought about it so long and planned it and waited for it so it really didn't catch me that much by surprise. I had things pretty well figured out but still, it's shocking, really groovy that I'm not wandering around again, wondering what to do next. It's everything that I've been working for for ten years. When I got up every morning, I'd hope that would be the day when it would happen. It's been a long time coming. I've been putting out records, playing, traveling.

ELLEN: I was under the impression that you were strictly a Texan area performer.

WINTER: Everybody is. That's what's so strange. I was never in the Texas area much. Most of the time was spent out of Texas. For two years we had an agent in Atlanta, Georgia, and we played lounges and things, the go-go circuit. We played R&B, ballads and things. You know, a drinking type crowd. The response was kind of good; it was what they wanted to hear. But that scene just isn't—well, it was just a way for us to stay alive. We got well known on the circuit. I was making $400 a week just for myself, which is okay for just a club musician. But we had to do "Misty" and "Moonlight in Vermont" and those kind of things. We'd do "Funky Broadway," just all around stuff.

ELLEN: Have you made records?

WINTER: Yes, just too many to count, it's just unbelievable. I was on major labels, got a lot of local labels, too, regional hits. A couple looked like they were gonna break out, but y'know just never did. Every day I'd say, well maybe tomorrow, y'know things were looking good but it never happened. I was never allowed to play blues because it wasn't something that people could dig. I'd sneak one in once in a while but . . .

Steve Paul, Winter's manager, came in the room: "We'll go to Nashville tomorrow and bring the guys out on Thursday. All right? Then as soon as we know it's cool, I'll call Marshall Chess in Chicago and get Willie Dixon. Is there anyone else you want?"

WINTER: Maybe a harp player. Any cigarettes?

STEVE PAUL: We'll get some for you in a few minutes. (*leaves*)

ELLEN: You were saying that you didn't play too many blues numbers [on the go-go circuit]?

WINTER: Blues was always a personal thing for me. I never really considered making a living as a blues singer at that time. Nobody was liking it. I started listening to blues when I was about eleven. I would listen to WLAC in Nashville, a 50,000-watt station that played those post-war blues things. I'd buy the records and take them home and listen to them and everybody hated it. I didn't have one friend that I could groove on it with. If I'd play it in a club, I'd maybe do a B.B. King thing and jive it up, make it real commercial, but still it was a lull for them. I didn't want to force the situation. I'm not the type that would say, okay, you gotta dig this, this is good. I can't play my best if I think people aren't enjoying it and I know people wanted to hear that other stuff. It was just a personal thing that I did when I could because I loved it. I'd go to colored clubs and play with colored musicians and for colored people.

ELLEN: That must've freaked them out.

WINTER: Oh, they loved it. When I was fifteen and sixteen, they loved it and I felt really close to them.

But all of a sudden, things changed with blues. British groups started doing it and white people started accepting it. It started really ticking me off. Here, for years, I was really loving it and nobody ever listened. And then these people were recording it and I thought they weren't even as good as me. Some of 'em were excellent, but a lot of groups that are making it aren't any good at all. People that copy Eric Clapton and Jimi Hendrix instead of Muddy Waters—I've talked to some of them and they don't even know who the old guys were. They really believe they're copying some form of British music! It's unbelievable!

I bugged the record company in Texas to do a blues record, please to let me do it. I never got anywhere with them.

ELLEN: What was your childhood like?

WINTER: It's really strange. I had a band when I was fifteen and my whole life changed.

I guess I'll start from, well, Daddy had a cotton business in Leland, Miss., right in the delta. His family has always been into cotton things. Most of the blues people you picture as coming out of cotton plantations and my Daddy owned one. I often wonder if the delta had any influence on me when I was younger. Daddy went out of business because he had a small concern and bigger companies were moving in with big machines and stuff and we moved back to Beaumont, Texas. I was about five when we moved, just before I started school. I guess you'd call my folks middle class or upper middle class. We got a nice house and my mother's parents had some bread.

I've never needed anything; everything was always cool. I had great parents. Musical people. Daddy played banjo and sax and Mama played piano and they sang so I sang soon as I could talk. Daddy dug barbershop quartet stuff. We'd all sing harmony, me and my little brother.

ELLEN: Is your brother (Edgar Winter) albino, too?

WINTER: Yes, that's unbelievable. The chances against that happening in one family are unbelievable. There's never been an albino in the family before; both my parents have dark hair.

First part of my life was probably the lousiest because I was an albino and the kids in school were really cruel. You can't rationalize with kids. People were rotten to me for no reason except that I had white hair. It really bothered me. Like one of the big things when you're young is to get your first car and like I couldn't drive because I had bad eyesight and I couldn't get a driver's license. And you know the most popular guy in school is usually the star football player or a big baseball player and a lack of vision kept me from doing all those things. My eyesight is 20/200. I can't really see except real close up. But when I got into music, it didn't matter. I've never felt impaired at all.

ELLEN: Do you think that because you were an albino you were treated like a Negro?

WINTER: Certainly. I think one of the reasons that I got into feeling so close to colored people is I saw people discriminating against them and I felt a common bond. People were rotten to them and I, for the same reasons, cos I was different. I was even a smaller minority than the colored people! We're not even organized! I felt more accepted in the Negro clubs than I did around white people.

But when I was around fifteen there was a station in Beaumont, KJET, which played black music. I used to listen to it all the time. I got to be friends with a disc jockey on KJET that was also a guitar player; he played clubs and everything. I did gigs and played with him. I loved blues from the minute I first heard it. I didn't care who hated it or what. It wasn't just because it was black people's music or anything; I just loved it. Blues makes you feel groovy. You hear other people sing and you know they've got the same problems as you. When you sing it yourself you're letting it all out, telling people how you feel.

ELLEN: When did you pick up the harp?

WINTER: I did that because I loved harmonica and there wasn't anyone else in the band that played. I didn't really consider myself to be a harp man, but I like to mess around with them. Guitar is really my instrument.

ELLEN: You were still in school, weren't you, when music took first place in your life?

WINTER: Yes, I went to school but I didn't study or anything, didn't give a darn. I played guitar.

ELLEN: What was your social life like? Did you finally get into kids your own age? Did you have girlfriends at all?

WINTER: No, I was completely different. I was hanging out with Negroes and nightclub broads. Everyone else had hot girlfriends and went to proms and I'd go out to the clubs and get drunk. All the girls' mothers were terrified of me. Even if one of those girls would want to go out with me, their mothers probably wouldn't have let them. I only stayed in school because I loved my folks so much. They never did anything wrong to me and I didn't ever want to hurt them. I went to college for a little while, too. After one semester, I knew I had to do something; school just didn't cut it. I quit college and went to Chicago. I had some kind of strange idea in my mind of maybe going to Chicago and playing with Muddy Waters and Little Walter or something. I was about eighteen then.

I had one friend who played bass up there and I stayed with him. He didn't have a place for me in his group and I didn't know what I was going to do. So I went to a music store and pretended like I was going to buy an electric guitar. I'd dig the people coming in; if they looked like they were going to be a musician then I'd turn the guitar up real loud and play every note I could play. Then I'd go talk with them. After I'd been there two or three hours, I had several gigs lined up.

ELLEN: Did you ever play with any of the blues bands you imagined playing with?

WINTER: No, I never even got near them. I lived on the North Side and I couldn't find anyone who would take me into the colored club section. They were all terrified to go there. When I went by myself it was just so bad. I wanted to go back, but not alone. I played State Street lounges, but it was the same thing I'd always been doing, not blues. Regular businessmen's lounges. I read somewhere that Michael Bloomfield had a blues club on State Street called the Fickle Pickle and he was bringing in people like Big Joe Williams and Little Brother Montgomery and lots of blues people that nobody had heard of. He was finding them and paying them like $25 a night out of his own pocket. I wasn't even sure who Mike was. I walked in one time and he was sitting there over the counter. I took my harp out and started playing. I started jamming with him and other people of the Fickle Pickle on my night off. I had his name and address and I went back to Texas without really telling him I was going or anything. I wanted to get in touch with him, but I never did. I didn't see him again 'til I played the Filmore East in New York. He was so nice. Mike is such a great person. I never kept in touch and I guess I should have, you know, maybe get a band together with him some years back. But I guess it all works out for the best.

ELLEN: It always works out for the best. You look back on the worst crisis of your life. Everything works out for the best, always.

WINTER: I believe that. I think I'm a lot more ready now than I was before.

I went with several different bands for a while. I was unhappy. I didn't have a good group or anything. I met Red, the drummer. I met him in Houston. He'd just quit a band in Dallas. We started talking and we sat in. He had a friend, Tom, and that was how the group got started. The whole idea of this group was we weren't going to play for anyone but ourselves. We had a good combination. They both gave up everything to do it. Right away we found out no club dates. We started working head joints in the area. You gotta travel, but there are head places, where teenagers and groovy people go. For months we really just starved through. I didn't have to work, I had my parents. But they didn't have anything. They really slept on the floor and didn't have enough to eat.

ELLEN: There's been criticism that your band isn't up to your playing.

WINTER: I understand why it is, but we don't have a Cream-type group. It would never work in the first place. I want guys that are primarily following me. I think they're excellent for that. One of the main reasons I wanted to do blues so bad is, before there wasn't anybody to play for. As soon as I realized that John Mayall was making albums, I started thinking "How can I get there?"

ELLEN: What does it do to your head when people tell you you're going to be a superstar?

WINTER: I love it. I don't really mean about being a superstar, because I don't care that much. I know I play good blues and I want people to hear me and I wanted people to like me. The greatest part of it all to me is that people really do enjoy it. When somebody comes up to me and says, "Man, you really did a great show," I just love that. That's the greatest part of it all. I've been waiting for it so long and wanting it and I thought about it and I really think that nothing's going to happen to me that I really haven't thought of. I feel like now, everything is cool; it's the way it should be. I've got a chance to do everything I want to do.

◆

Cass Elliot
September 19, 1941–July 29, 1974
Crawdaddy!/April 1972

It is said of some that they are born stars and if that is indeed true, one of those must surely be Cass Elliot, Earth Mother of the Mamas and the Papas, and in her time, Grand Dame of Rock 'n' Roll. She has always exerted a presence on the scene, always the articulate highlight of any one of the many television shows on which she's appeared (save her own special, but more about that later).

She defends it hotly. The TV show was the last time she ever resisted asserting herself with whomever she worked. Not doing so was perhaps a bad habit left over from being excluded from the business end of her life for what turned out to be too long.

"When I was touring with the Mamas and Papas, I felt I was kept from a lot of things I should have known. There are a lot of decisions you have to make out there, that no one can make for you, things like money and coordinating interviews. The Mamas and Papas were a tremendously symbiotic relationship. John was the father figure. He handled everything: the business, the contracts, where we would work, where we wouldn't work and there was a sort of tacit agreement, because the three of them had been singing together before I joined them, that I would not become involved with the business. It was never explained to me."

Though she resented that arrangement at the time, she regretfully accepted it. It turned out to be a symptom of what was generally amiss within the group. "I don't know whether it was because John felt threatened by me or that it was just easier for one person to handle it, but the end result was that I didn't really know much about what was happening."

Later on she found the same attitude recurrent, even when she tried to handle, or at least inform herself about, the business end of her career. "You always find that record executives tend to treat a woman in a slightly conciliatory way. Pat you on the head. I know how to do my job, I had been doing it for ten years, let me do it! I learned a lot about the business since, and I have an instinctive thing, I know what's right for me. Being alone, I had to learn to exert more control over it.

"When I did my TV special, the people who produced and wrote it had no idea who I was. No idea! And they had written all this stuff and it was just a nightmare. I wanted the audience up close, everybody to be a part of what was happening, television *verité*. So I sat out on the front of the stage and rapped with the audience. The first thing they did was cut all that out."

After she left the Mamas and the Papas, she opened in Las Vegas, which was a colossal bomb, the inappropriateness of which was made much of in critical circles. "I had this tremendous vision of going to Las Vegas and blowing the top off of it. Just doing a very honest, unprepared set where I'd talk to the people, a type of show that had never been done there. I didn't want a prepared act, but my advisors said, have an act. Mason Williams wrote me an act. I looked at it and I said, 'I can't say these things, I just can't go on and say that it's me and Julie Andrews fighting it out for those parts.' It may be funny, but it's just not me."

The unhappy reminiscences concluded, she says, "Now I've reached a position in my career where I can say no!"

There had been many other lessons learned along the way, things you'd never expect to come up but there they are and you have to—in the middle of the dizzy circus that was rock 'n' roll stardom—deal with them. "There was a certain amount of jealousy between myself and Michelle [Phillips], not because she was pretty but because she was with John. It made it a little easier for her. I was mostly alone. If you've got a string of one-nighters, it's not very easy to run around a lot. If you're successful in the business and you want to be somebody's old lady and he's not as successful as you are, ultimately, it gets to him. It has interfered. The tighter you are with the people you're working with, the easier it is. The reason I left the group the first time is because I couldn't take the loneliness of the road.

"I worked up until the eighth month of my pregnancy. It got pretty difficult. On our last dates I had to do the second set sitting down because I went into false labor. I was really overweight.

I weighed three hundred pounds and I couldn't jump around and dance. After that we recorded an album called '*Deliver.*'"

Among other indignities she recalls with resolve and distaste, she said, out of nowhere: "I didn't like the constant inference that I was on drugs and screwing everybody."

Whether stardom is a born or acquired attribute can be argued. With Cass it doesn't really matter. She is one of those rare stars that can speak openly, honestly, blowing myths with every sentence without dissolving the excitement or the strength of a stellar personality. It comes with experience, it comes with the ups and downs of an erratic career, it comes with the incredible confidence she has, and much of it, she enjoyed telling me, came with motherhood.

"You lie less to yourself when you're a mother. You cannot bullshit a child. I told Owen (her daughter) when she was very little that I couldn't be super patient with her. I'm not a super patient person. I had to explain that to her because when I had a screaming temper fit she would wonder who the stranger was." Surprised, I asked if a child understands that. "You're damn right she understood. Kids understand. I became more concerned about ecology because of Owen. Motherhood is the first time in your life you think of somebody else first. Even when you're in love, you don't always think of somebody else first. When you have children, you're concerned about them and I'm concerned about the fact that she may not have air to breathe.

"I think to myself some nights when I come home, maybe I've been working sixteen or seventeen hours and I'm tired, 'Wouldn't it be nice to have a man who really loves you, a couple of kids, stay home, cook dinner rather than get up at six in the morning and be "Miss Show Business."' Sometimes I just say 'Screw it! Stay around the house!' But I know I just can't do that. I may get incredibly bored in six months, go batty from it but I just don't know because I've never had it.

"I'm not your basic type of girl. I dropped out of high school; it was the only way I could get out of going to college because my parents had me enrolled already. I was of age and I just quit, hung around for a while and decided to go into show business because my girlfriend was in it. When I got married, I didn't know what I thought was going to happen, but it didn't happen."

I mentioned that the general impression when she had the baby was that she wasn't married. "I was married when I had the baby," she grinned broadly, "conveniently enough." She looked at the ceiling and laughed to herself. "And that's all I'm going to say about that." [It's complicated. She was married, but not to the father of her child.]

"I'm much older now, I'm thirty and basically I want to tell you that I don't think a woman can be a father to a child. I've been going with a guy for eight years now, before and after I got married, and now we're thinking about getting married. I guess I have kind of old-fashioned ideas. Or maybe it's just me. When you've been fat all your life and insecure about it, I find I need the security of being chosen and loved and being married."

Cass Elliot was and remains a unique and irreplaceable voice.

◆

John Lennon
October 9, 1940–December 8, 1980
Yoko Ono
February 18, 1933–
Saturday Review/June 28, 1969

This is an account of time spent with John and Yoko Ono Lennon in June of 1969. Following this article is the full transcript of the interview, published in the L.A. Free Press *on July 11.*

William D. "Pat" Patterson, publisher of Saturday Review, *forwarded it to quite a few politicians he knew to try to advance Lennon's cause, or at least his admission into the U.S., which drew praise—but no intervention—from, among others, then New York City mayor John Lindsay and U.S. senators Jacob Javits and Ed Muskie. John Lennon did eventually take up residence in New York. And there he died, a victim of incomprehensible violence.*

When I read the tag line of this piece, I could weep to understand how wrong, how wrong, it was.

John and Yoko Ono Lennon: Give Peace a Chance
Toronto, Canada/May 1969

There is more to rock than music. There's a lifestyle, and an ethic, even a politic to it, and it all adds up to a very healthy if somewhat desperate mirror of the visions and intentions of the turned-on, tuned-in generation that is through with dropping out, a generation that has ceased to be an age bracket.

Rock is music come of age in a time of continual global crisis that pours from every media outlet. Rock is the sensibility of the young, the unsheltered generation; rock is music that asserts and reflects the visions and rebelliousness of its audience. The music protests loudly and celebrates itself widely. It is considered not only an art or society's sideshow, but a social force with which millions identify. Every beat of the new music creates and reflects unrestrained cries for change, for liberation, and, most of all, for peace. Rock is, for those whose lives are intimately involved and even dominated by it, a creed, a religion without dogma.

Synonymous with decadence to its critics (few in number but loud in censorious comment), rock is actually the healthiest mass art form a generation ever had to speak for it. Rock may be beautiful to watch and hear, but its surface beauty is mere glitter, if one considers the stuff its substance is made of.

Beatle John Lennon and his wife, Yoko Ono, have recently returned to London after several days in Canada, where they were finally denied a visa. They held open house in Montreal, then had to go to Toronto for a hearing at the Canadian Department of Immigration to establish whether or not they could stay. The answer was a "No," but officers of the Immigration Department still wanted their autographs, and they obliged.

In March, the couple had honeymooned in Amsterdam, opening their doors to reporters while they stayed in bed as a demonstration for peace and against all violence. The press was skeptical. They wanted to know if the reports that the couple would not hesitate to make love in front of friends were true.

Perhaps a genuine demonstration for peace was incomprehensible to the cynical-sharp Establishment press, which by now is inured to reporting the constant barrage of violence and injustice marking this epoch. The impact of evil is special to this generation—the young who literally see, hear, and experience all of it at once—and particularly to the Beatles, who have committed to an art form admired so widely it cannot be ignored—the experience of being young and all that goes with it. "How can evil be rampant in the world (as it clearly is) when I do not know one single evil person?" a Berkeley youth writes, and I understand exactly what he means. There is an innocence in rock's plea for a new world, an innocence born of the painful reality of idealists living in a sea of bigotry, assassination, greed, and dehumanizing bureaucracies. It can no longer be passed off as naïveté; today's young and today's music live in the "global village" Marshall McLuhan has defined.

There is a knowing innocence about Beatles music particularly, an innocence that often gives way to savage social satire and criticism when its spirituality is threatened. Lennon, long known as the cynical, iconoclastic Beatle, at this point— with full knowledge of the implications of his public behavior— turns his life to a major (and personally expensive) crusade for peace, and he's deadly serious about it. He's willing to subject himself to the press for ten hours each day for extended periods of time, and he's determined to fight for his right to demonstrate throughout the world. Because of a marijuana conviction, Lennon is not eligible for a visa to enter the United States (to demonstrate for peace). The ruling is being appealed. Horrified by the hypocrisy of such a restriction, Lennon parked himself, his lady, her child, an entourage of press aides, and a film crew north of the border to give radio interviews for the States, and to reapply for a visa. The application had to be withdrawn because of legal technicalities.

Drugs are the excuse here, not the issue. Marijuana laws have made potential felons out of a significant share of the population under thirty, and have created most of the hostility between the youth and the law in this country. Inextricably entwined with rock music, the drug controversy rages as the single most irritating source of conflict between generations. It's a simple way in which the Establishment can hit out with real force against its children who embarrass it by refusing to accept the errors of their elders as a way of life. If John Lennon's drug conviction is used to prevent him from fulfilling his mission for peace, we may be missing a brilliantly appropriate opportunity to see the kind of change rock music proselytizes. It makes no sense at all.

Lennon, however, is implacably optimistic. "I'm sure we'll get there," he said confidently. "It's just a matter of under what conditions. We won't play games with the guv'ments." He is particularly distressed about student violence. "The students are being conned! It's like the school bully: he aggravates you and aggravates you until you hit him. And then they kill you, like in Berkeley. Establishment, it's just a name for [he paused to consider the next word] evil. The monster doesn't care, the Blue Meanie [fictional, malevolent, music-hating monster in the Beatles film *Yellow Submarine*] is insane. We really care about life. Destruction is good enough for the Establishment. The only thing they can't control is the mind, and we have to fight for sanity and peace on that level. But the students have gotten conned into thinking you can change it with violence and they can't, you know, they can only make it uglier and worse."

Nothing has ever been made better by violence, and nothing ever will. Violence on the part of the young is the product of a frustration they won't outgrow. At the basis of that frustration is the certain knowledge that this planet and this society could provide a much better environment than they do. They experience the joy of being among kindred minds at a rock concert. Their music is their communication medium and their catechism, their treasured product and their hopes, turned up so loud that nothing can be heard above it. It's a vital force generating hope positively and constructively in this, the last half of the century that could sentence the globe to destruction. The Beatles were the leading edge of the rebirth—who better than a Beatle, now, could stand up and provide a figure around whom youth can mobilize and end all this madness?

Lennon's Canadian stay was characterized by the mayhem and adventure that attend all Beatles doings. He was visited by hundreds of reporters and guests that included Allen Ginsberg, Timothy Leary, and Dick Gregory. A TV special was made and shown in the States. The telephones were busy with calls from American and Canadian disc jockeys. The Hare Krishna people showed up. Fans followed him from Montreal to Toronto, bearing poems and gifts.

Al Capp was so hostile to the Lennons that he had to be asked to leave. He was thereafter referred to as "Al Crap," and Lennon said, "How much time do you spend with the Al Craps? I think it's better to get at his children. They haven't had fifty years of building up their wall." If John Lennon is prevented from coming to this country and pleading his case to "give peace a chance," it will be America's great loss. If the mother culture loses its children, the future is lost and the present will continue to be unbearable. There is great beauty fighting to flower here, but if the repression of the young continues, they will surely regurgitate all the ugliness forced upon them. Lennon wants to stop youth's violence. And he may be just the one able to do it.

Interview transcript published in the *L.A. Free Press*

ELLEN: I understand there was a very uncomfortable scene when Al Capp showed up.

JOHN: Al Crap, if you don't mind.

(*Yoko laughs.*)

ELLEN: Perhaps some people are so far beyond reason that there's no touching them, no reaching them.

JOHN: Dunno! Somebody asked him afterwards if it was interesting, two points of view meeting, and he just refused to recognize that we had a point of view! Yoko thinks we need him for ten days in a room to brainwash him.

YOKO: He'll come around if John and I work on him, don't you think so, John?

JOHN: Naw, we need him for two years.

ELLEN: I can't believe how people become so cynical. It's so precious what the two of you are doing here; I can't comprehend anyone not being able to relate to it all and being hostile like that.

JOHN: They just can't see themselves in the mirror.

YOKO: Sometimes in the middle of all of this we wonder, we ask ourselves, are we naïve? But I think you need that.

ELLEN: Naïveté in numbers is power.

JOHN: Sure, naïveté isn't stupidity.

ELLEN: I guess it could be, but when you're in your middle twenties and have come through that much hassle it's not naïveté; it's just coming around again where you belong.

JOHN (*Singing, imitating Paul McCartney*): Git back! *(laughter)*

ELLEN: I sure hope you do get to the States because there's a lot of beauty there as well as a lot of very distressing things going on.

JOHN: I think we'll get there all right; it's just under what conditions.

ELLEN: I read you were asked to come out with a statement against drugs as a condition to your entry.

JOHN: That was the original offer. It's gotten more subtle.

YOKO: Yes, it's so easy to sell out. That's another thing that's disturbing us.

ELLEN: John, for better or for worse you have a reputation as the cynical, intellectual Beatle. What's brought you around, seriously?

JOHN: Ah, I figgered for meself that I needed more protection as a Beatle so I built up a protection racket around me. And now I'm out of it. I guess I always had a chip on me shoulder for a long time, oh, from my teen years on and I kept it going through Beatle, ah, mania as they call it. 'Cause it came in handy—I thought. And now I don't need it. I just find I've no use for it. Oh, I retain a certain amount of cynicism so I have something in common somewhere along the line with Al Crap. I think he's pretty well trapped in it. I mean how much time do you spend on the Al Craps. I think it's better to get at his children. They haven't had fifty years of building up their wall.

ELLEN: Don't you think a certain amount of disillusionment is necessary to commit yourself to something positive? It was that way for me, I think.

JOHN: You go through the disillusionment and you drop out mentally. And then you find you're still here. Then, what to do about it? You either go through your whole life disillusioned and complaining about it or you go and do something about it. I'm on the try and do something kick because what else is there to do?

ELLEN: Don't you think you'll find a position of leadership in a peace movement an overwhelming prospect?

JOHN: I don't intend to be tricked into leadership.

ELLEN: I don't see how you could help but be.

JOHN: Well, people laid leadership on the Beatles but it never existed.

ELLEN: You don't think so? Whew!

JOHN: No, identification isn't leadership. A lot of people are aware that the Beatles weren't leading anything, they were just part of it. The Beatles were aware that they weren't leading anything. The people that thought that the Beatles were leading something are the ones that say "Oh, there are only nine kids waiting outside the door this time." *(laughs)* They think we've been outvoted or whatever. We never took that responsibility. Because leadership is what's wrong here. Johnson did it, the guv'ment did it. I guess we all did it.

ELLEN: We were talking—Derek [Taylor] and I—about that before. An organized movement with a leader and a hierarchy is the old way of getting something done. It's probably impossible to accomplish something new in an old way.

JOHN: We can lead in as much as—the same way as the way the Beatles led or were supposed to have led. Here's something, for example: instead of sitting on that example, sitting on the bed, we move off again. Anyone that's following up to that point will have to find the rest of the way themselves. We can't do it for 'em. We don't mind being Abbot & Costello, King & Queen *(laughs)*, but . . .

ELLEN: Laughter conquers all. The Beatles are all about that.

JOHN: Yeah, heh, that's what we hope to do.

ELLEN: What about the other Beatles? Are they with you, where are they? Are they behind you in this mission?

JOHN: Well, they're not against me. I mean Paul's more of an intellectual ostrich and George is the most positive, active member and Ringo—is. I couldn't expect, I . . . I have no idea what they'll do. I'll still be myself about it and myself seems to want peace, so I'll inspire peace. I hope.

ELLEN: What's next after sending acorns to world leaders?

JOHN: We'll play it by ear, I guess. We don't know.

YOKO: It's very strange, you know. It's becoming a big issue now. If the prime minister decides not to receive acorns that means that they're afraid of it and what's wrong with the acorns? *(giggle)* I guess [Pierre] Trudeau decided it was a dangerous affair or something: it's very interesting to see them do that. I'm sure they wouldn't do that if it's just somebody sending flowers. There's not much difference between flowers and acorns, no?

JOHN: Insecurity. And then you build up a wall around it. You're a cynic.

ELLEN: Maybe cynicism on that level is, well, you just treasure your visions so much that any threat to them makes you deny them. Hopes, fears, they're so close.

JOHN: How do you mean "deny"?

ELLEN: I see it happen with my friends who have turned into radical "politicians" in America—home, you know. Everywhere they turn they come up against a wall so they get violent, angry, frightened, really. They call it self-preservation, but, well, I was on that trip for a while I guess; it's so easy to get caught up. But it felt so wrong. I mean all those people walking around bum kicked and throwing off negativity when there's so much to gain on the positive side, I just can't follow that anymore.

JOHN: We think they're being establishment. The establishment is like the bully. It aggravates you and aggravates you until you hit it. And then they'll kill you. That's how they're playing it now. They're testing people!

ELLEN: You think they have full knowledge of what they're doing then?

JOHN: Sure! They know exactly what they're doing!

YOKO: You know, well, instinctively. Like violent animals.

JOHN: Yes, exactly, that's, well, Al Crap is a perfect representative. First of all he comes in and tries to undermine you, y'know, he says, he smiles, I'm a fascist. He presumes then you're relaxed. We're relaxed anyway, but that's his game. Then he irritates you 'til he hits you. Then he uses full force. That's exactly what's happening to the students. They relax them a bit and say, "Yes you can make 'make love not war' banners." Soon as they relax the students go "Aw nothing's happenin'" and they play them around in circles. Then they gotta do something physical about it. Once they do that then the establishment declares a state of war.

You gotta remember, establishment, it's just a name for— evil. The monster doesn't care whether it kills all the students or whether there's a revolution. It's not thinking logically, it's out of control, it's suffering from, it's a careless killer and it doesn't care whether the students all get killed or black power—it'll enjoy that. Whatever the rabbit or the sheep does, it doesn't matter, the cat is playing with it. And whether the rabbit gets away a few hundred yards, it doesn't matter; they'll get it. We've got to realize that it doesn't care which way we go. But the only thing it can't fight is the mind. But the students have got conned into thinking that they can change it with violence.

YOKO: It's a very dangerous thing and everybody's playing that game. Because people are so insecure they need to try to put somebody in the position of a leader. The hippies will do that with John. But they have to trust in themselves, understand that there's no such thing as a leader. Nobody can stand that responsibility. All the presidents of the United States. You criticize them, but just put yourself in their place, you'd be the same hysterical shouting bastard. After they make someone a leader then they make him the scapegoat. Now America is the scapegoat for the world, now America's to blame—everybody has their own way of escaping responsibility.

ELLEN: I believe that, that America's a villain. We're caught in an angry negative cycle.

YOKO: No, don't do that. You're falling into the same trap. Try to rely on yourself.

ELLEN: I understand. Instead of leading, you're an energy center around which a movement will mobilize itself. On the other hand I think if America keeps going the way it's been going, the extension of that is the end of the planet. And people don't relate to their environment as a planet, they relate to it as a room.

JOHN: You really think so? The end of the planet? Nuclear war?

ELLEN: Sure, America will crumble politically if there's enough of an uprising to declare martial law. We'll be politically vulnerable and outside forces will just move in. It'll be global havoc.

JOHN: I don't think the planet will be destroyed; I think America and the West will collapse money-wise. That's not so bad, it's the death-poverty-disease bit that'll be the worst. Technology will survive. A lot of the Buckminster Fullers and whoever they are will instinctively know when it's coming and they'll leave.

ELLEN: One alternative is to get out and hide. But for myself I see too much growth, too much beauty—it's being disheartened but it's there.

YOKO: Well, it was probably the same before the Second World War. I'm sure there were many beautiful Jewish people that had beautiful artistic ideas and they couldn't believe that that beautiful culture could be destroyed. All of a sudden everyone got shot. There's the same kind of vulnerability in American culture now. And they don't realize how vulnerable they are. The beautiful ideas can go like that when they're shot. People have to be aware of that.

ELLEN: We are, we're afraid. You know I've come this far in life and I really know for sure that I'm not an evil person. And I can't believe that anybody else is really, basically evil.

JOHN: There's hope for them all in degrees. But you have to think about—well, get out and live to fight another day. Their minds can live anywhere. What we're saying is don't die for the cause, the cause lives on outside America and it's better to leave than die. Stay till the last minute but don't die. If and when America collapses there's gonna be more need of them outside America.

ELLEN: There's such a thin line.

YOKO: If every peacenik in the U.S. would immigrate to somewhere else—anywhere—and build their own empire. Then to whom would they put their violence?

JOHN: The guv'ment is using the students and the peaceniks as a diversion. If there were nothing for the guv'ment to point their finger at, they'd be shown. People don't believe it, that it could be so bad. If there was nobody the people would have to realize that . . .

YOKO: That there's something dumb going on around here.

ELLEN: In a way. But I think that it would just give them an opportunity to perpetuate this horrible inhuman bureaucracy.

YOKO: The rest of the world wouldn't let them do it. All right, it's a beautiful country and you don't want to leave it. It's like a property; forget it! Leave it to them if they want it; the rest of the world is beautiful too. I understand, you know. I was in New York for a while and I got attached to it. I didn't want to leave there—and I'm a foreigner. If you think what you say about the end of the planet is true, you're responsible to the rest of the world to leave, not fight, not have a civil war. Leave it all to the establishment. The greedy ones. The Pigs. Then the rest of the world will be beautiful, all the peaceniks will be in the rest of the world and the rest of the world will be more powerful.

ELLEN: The hippies tried that—dropping out without physically removing themselves, that is. Then the mother culture comes in and gobbled them up. It was a threat in a strange sort of way, all of these people refusing to make money, refusing to make enemies, refusing to compete and sitting there, enjoying each other, the establishment moved right in on them. Dope is the excuse, it's not the issue, but that's what they use.

Yoko: So then you have to leave.

Ellen: Well, I'll stay 'til I know there's no more hope. It's my job to do that, I think.

John: Oh, yes, do that. But see, if you die then there's less of us. Don't wait 'til the boat's nearly under. Once you get the smell of it . . . like you might have a year. That's the minimum.

Ellen: But there's a chance for some kind of flowering of hope in this year. I feel that, too, even stronger than I fear total . . .

John: We feel that, too; that's why we're trying to get into the States.

Yoko: I think that would be the biggest threat to the establishment if they find out that the whole of the peacenik generation is ready to leave, that they're not ready to fight. Everything that they're proud of in the culture is ready to leave for Europe! Okay, that's a laugh for the establishment to think that you're ready to fight. It's like a rat fighting a cat. That's fun; they say come on, come on. If they think you're going to leave, that's not funny to them, that's a threat.

Ellen: I wonder, I really do. How many of us there are. A couple of million. Sure, more than that. But they might be just as glad to get rid of us. I'm not so eager to take the thorn out of their side.

John: Well, what we're really talking about is a last resort. Get out. But until then—that's why we want to go there. We're in the same kind of confusion as you. One half of us thinks, well, that's it, the other half is hoping for a miracle.

Yoko: You have access to communications media. If you could present in some way that if the establishment pushes too hard they're going to lose the whole bunch, not that they're going to fight, if they understand that, that people are just going to leave. You have to infiltrate ideas like that.

Ellen: I think it goes a little deeper than that. Once people know how good you can feel when all that fear is gone, once a person has a taste of that, nothing is settled until they arrange their lives that way.

JOHN: We have to make people aware of that.

ELLEN: I rather believe that most of America is so stuck in that that they just can't comprehend that there's any other way to be. Oh yeah, the Beatles, they're cute and dandy and all that but the establishment in America, they can't understand all that—JOY! SING! DANCE! They don't know what it's like to feel that way, walk down the street and just hear music; it's there!

JOHN: YES, we've got to try and help them become aware of that. Because if they don't become aware of THAT then that IS it. But like you say they have to see it themselves. It's no good the Beatles and us dancing amongst ourselves.

ELLEN: It sure is. It's a lotta good. Sure is good *(laughs)*.

JOHN: Aw, but we got to make them sing and dance, too; otherwise they just won't know what it is.

ELLEN: You really think you can do that?

JOHN: We wouldn't try unless we thought there was a chance.

ELLEN: I know, it was a rhetorical question. I mean I wouldn't be here either if I . . . I . . . well, I think you can do it, too.

JOHN: But they can't just let us do it and pretend to follow it thinking, well, John and Yoko will do it or the Beatles will do it. They have to work as hard as we do or there's no hope.

YOKO: What surprises me is the differences between the peaceniks. It makes them weaker. Black power is different, it's stronger. Dick Gregory was here and we were talking about it. Like say there's John and I and Kyoko, three of us, we are fighting and that's three powers. But say a man has five children like Derek and he has to take care of the wife and six children so he can't fight. So the powerhouse, which is the man, cannot fight because he has the family to protect. In black power the whole family is the power, the woman and the children, too. We have to be like that.

ELLEN: Yes it's true, we all have to realize that we're one family. The divisions in the revolutionary community is a ridiculous thing, it's self-defeating. We're really all a family and that's a strength. In this revolution it's the children who are fighting.

YOKO: I tried to tell that to Al Crap. I said, listen, we're in the same world together. And this world is a small village as Marshall McLuhan says, but it's not a small village anymore, it's a hysterical ghetto. And we're stuck with each other. I said, you're married to me. So he said, huh, ah, no, well, I'll leave that up to John *(laughter)*. So I said we have to do something about it. People don't realize that.

JOHN: They're just retarded children.

YOKO: But you have to take care of them.

ELLEN: There's the jealousy, too. They're taught that if they don't fight it somebody will take everything away from them. They don't understand that if they stop fighting everything is theirs.

JOHN & YOKO: Yeah.

ELLEN: It's easier maybe for you two to get through. You've been through adult problems; they can't say that you, or I, are too young to know.

YOKO: Al Crap and me fighting is like a man and a wife fighting. It just weakens the tie and the family power. The whole earth is like a family, right? And it will destroy our globe and no other planet is going to care.

ELLEN: I think of that every time I see the pictures of the earth as seen from the moon on the color TV. It's just sitting there like the rest of them. And here we've got a population that civilized, tamed the planet and then proceeded to make it unlivable. It doesn't make any sense and it's all so simple. So why is it so difficult to ram that home?

JOHN: It doesn't make sense because the monster's insane. The Blue Meanie is insane. We're the only ones that really care about life. To them it doesn't matter. Destruction is good enough for them. It's not just the guv'ment, it's power or the devil or whatever we call it. It doesn't matter to him. Either way he gets his kicks. And his kicks are control or destruction. If he can't control, he destroys. We're the only ones interested in life, the peaceniks or whatever. We've got to make the others aware of it—the ones, the borderline ones who don't know.

YOKO: There are people who really think, well, sometimes you do have to kill people. Anybody who is saying that—we have to convince them that there is no time to kill people.

JOHN: There will be some members of the square brigade that we can get through to. You don't go to Africa and speak English to them; you have to learn the language. If we can infiltrate on those levels to the part of the establishment that isn't completely insane they'll help us. They're unaware of what they're doing.

ELLEN: I know it's a horrible question to put to you but what, really WHAT, causes that. How can they be so completely oblivious?

JOHN: Evil, the same thing that's caused it for millions of years. Evil is a way of life. We've got to get through, we've got to get past that. We want to live.

At Large

Laurel Canyon was very mellow. During 1967–68, groups had broken up. Everyone was wondering what was next, a little worried, but grooving nonetheless on the time between. Days were permeated with a gentle sense of waiting, summer blew up the hills, past the painted mailboxes and decorated VW buses, and musicians were floating about. Cass Elliot's dune buggy (with a racing stripe) was parked outside David Crosby's house in Beverly Glen and she was inside visiting, sitting on a huge unmade bed with David and her old man, Jim Hendricks. They all looked forlorn. The Mamas and the Papas had broken up and Cass wasn't working. Since leaving the Byrds, Crosby had produced Joni Mitchell's first album and the Jefferson Airplane were recording his song "Triad," the one McGuinn refused to let the Byrds record, an innocently daring invitation to a *ménage à trois*. He would survive on what those two projects would bring in, but he wasn't playing and he wasn't happy about it. He had been trying to put a solo album together but just couldn't find the right producer. "Cass," he implored, "somewhere on one of the tracks on the tape in your head you must be thinking of a producer for me." Cass took another hit and continued talking about something else.

Litter spread outward from the bed onto the floor. Clothing, blankets, boots, laundry, luggage, and some guitars filled the small room.

Crosby was living in the downstairs apartment of his own house, having rented the upstairs to deejay and radio personality B. Mitchel Reed for a few months to save money. He picked up one of the guitars and sang some new songs, "Guinnevere" and "Long Time Coming" among them. He sang with his eyes closed, mustache drooping, red hair folding around his face.

The days were long and lazy, ivy-tangled hills and houses sat quietly as summer went by. The sun glittered on swimming pools pulling one day into the next with shameless ease. It was a time of endings and beginnings.

Joni Mitchell, newly come to Laurel Canyon, was decorating her cottage with antiques, colored glass, and small carved creatures. Her opening at the Troubadour had been triumphant, her career just about to crest, her music unleashing all the changes of every girl who ever hurt from having loved too much. "She's a love gangster," said Stephen Stills. "Every man within fifty feet falls in love with her."

Stephen Stills was playing some tapes for producer Barry Friedman down the canyon, some sessions done just for fun with Buddy Miles. Eric Clapton was running around the canyon with an advance pressing of the Band's *Music from Big Pink*, playing it for everyone, helping establish it as a musician's music.

Judy Collins was rehearsing her band at Cass Elliot's house, out by the pool. Everything else was going on at Peter Tork's pool.

Peter Tork had quit the Monkees and was growing a beard. When they were first casting for the television series, the production company had auditioned someone recommended to them as a highly promising youngster, Stephen Stills. They liked his music but his teeth were wrong, and they didn't feel he had the wholesome, American boy-teen appeal they wanted, so they asked him if he had a friend. Stills recommended Peter Thorkelson, who got the part and shortened his name to Tork. The series was successful. Stills went on to join the Buffalo Springfield, one of the most infectious and beloved bands to come out of Los Angeles in the mid-Sixties.

Tork became quite rich and bought an estate in Laurel Canyon behind a sentry gate that was always open and where crowds of the pop elite and the obligatory hangers-on would come all summer long and swim nude in the huge pool. All day long Tork was host to music people and supported a houseful of resident freeloaders. It was almost as if he were apologetic of his bogus group's huge success and afraid of being alone. It must have been hard being a Monkee at a time when rock 'n' roll was just beginning to be taken seriously.

In time, with the money running out, Tork assembled his own group with his girlfriend, a singer, and a bass player. On the day people were coming to audition the group at his home, a few friends showed up to swim. Peter cautioned them that the company men were coming and please don't freak them out by screwing on the jungle gym or anything. The guests laughed, talked about the fuck flicks made there the summer before at the pool, threw off their clothes, and jumped into the water. They took a quick dip, then ran upstairs into the sauna, afterward bathing together in a huge bathtub. Tork was earnestly trying to impress the agents downstairs, whose attention was diverted to the naked nubiles who scampered about the house with the boys. Finally the band started to make music and the musicians there sympathized with Tork. "Okay, everyone, let's put our clothes on, go downstairs, and show the agent people which parts to boogie to."

Somehow it didn't work. The company men went away unimpressed and the band fell through sometime later. Peter Tork began to collect $75 a week unemployment, his only income. His accountant called him frantically a few days before the telephone was shut off. "You can't support eleven people in your financial shape!" he insisted. Peter listened until the accountant was through and told him to pay the bills and let him worry about it. Some months later the money was all gone. Peter told the accountant to tell the creditors to do what they usually did when people had no more money and he moved from his estate to the downstairs apartment in David Crosby's house (Crosby having moved back upstairs by then) with his pregnant girlfriend. It was over, that was all; it was a great ride and it had ended for the time being. He accepted it completely. Stephen Stills, with a new group forming, bought the Laurel Canyon estate, shut the sentry gate, scrupulously screened visitors, and later entertained the Rolling Stones there.

Sunset Strip was a mess in the summer of 1968. Cops had moved in on it and rousted packs of kids each night. A big billboard of Lenny Bruce looked somberly over the scene.

The Mamas and the Papas had once recorded a song called "Twelve Thirty," about having once lived in New York, coming to California, and living openly and freely. Neil Young had moved to Topanga Canyon, far away from the center of L.A. "It's beautiful," he enthused. It was secluded; his house was on a hill overlooking a pasture with horses. "There are about eight girls who go around, keeping house, cooking food, and making love to everyone." Groupies and groups in pop mecca, all living out their fantasies.

◆

Janis Joplin, unveiling her new band, played Forest Hills Stadium in New York, the stage where years before Joan Baez and Bob Dylan had reigned supreme. It was a mannered but enthusiastic crowd, the night was balmy and clear. Her agent took his seat in the best section and settled comfortably. Richie Havens opened the evening in rare form, singing in a powerful staccato style, alternating songs with long languorous stony pauses, making his familiar warm jokes about tuning up and breaking guitar strings.

The agent chattered all through his set, discussing business with his guests ("This is the only business where you can be a hero on paper") and fidgeting, anticipating Joplin's appearance. He showed small signs of worry. "I bet she's going crazy backstage," he chortled; "she's probably putting her fist through the wall. 'Get him off there!'" he mimicked.

Joplin came on to a thunderous ovation. She performed, all blues and dues and spitfire bitch, crooned and wailed and gave herself inside out. She danced into every number, the band cooked hard behind her. The set swelled as she continued and the agent was overjoyed. "She's not even in great voice tonight and they love her! Boy, does she know how to shake ass!"

Janis wooed the audience. She was at once a little tease and an ancient siren, full of earthy lust. She had caressed and inflamed them, beaten and loved them with that sound she sang and then she prepared to ease them down. She announced her last song and a unanimous protest went up at the words *last song*. "Noooooooooo," sang the audience, in unison.

At the sound of the rising voices the rent-a-cops marched out in dignified single file from both sides of the stage and stood in front of it in a solid line. Janis's eyes popped at the sight of them. She held the microphone away from her face and let out a stream of curses that stopped them dead.

"Go!" she demanded. "Get the hell out of here!" she screamed, this time right into the microphone. Her command echoed around the stadium and the audience cheered. The cops went back the way they came and a great cheer went up. "They got to understand, these pigs, that what's going on here is for us, it's not for them!"

There had ceased to be any general direction to the music scene. In every way it had grown too big for any one phenomenon to symbolize. Some music was at an in-between stage; some was buckling under the weight of its own influence.

The Doors and the Who had been booked as a double bill in the Singer Bowl at the World's Fair site in New York. It was coming toward the end of a long hot summer in New York, an irritable scene that sharply contrasted the mellow Los Angeles climate from which the Doors had flown in to New York to play. They were at a slick motel getting ready to leave for the gig. A film crew was traveling with the Doors, another of the countless attempts at rock *verité*. Cameraman Babe Hill was anticipating a good night for shooting.

There had already been some trouble. "The Who don't want the Doors' equipment onstage," Hill muttered as he prepared his gear. "They're sore because they didn't get top billing and they're threatening to wreck the Doors' setup if it's on the stage."

It was a sticky, hot night and the Singer Bowl was large. There would be kids in from all the boroughs that evening and the concert had long been sold out. It looked like a good possibility for some kind of trouble. "That's what we want," said Hill, "film of unruly kids."

The film crew loaded themselves and their gear into one limousine and waited for Jim Morrison to appear. The rest of the Doors got into a second limousine and promptly drove off toward Queens.

Morrison walked through the lobby doors of the motel to the delighted murmur of about twenty-five kids waiting on the sidewalk. Wordlessly, with his head down, he got in and closed the door beside him.

Morrison was the one cool renegade to reign over the pop scene for a length of time whose style and personality differed vastly from his fellow superstars. He was an arrogant loner, the *enfant terrible* a mystery poet of mystical liberation. He was a pro, a performer who could manipulate an audience with invisible reins, steering them through the deep complexities of his songs and movements. He could silence them with a stroke of his hand, he could arouse them with a primal scream, he could unleash them into his own vision of theater, set them free of even his own control and out into one another. The band behind him was a threesome of impeccable timing and musicianship. Together they were synergistic, they rose to the top, arched their heads with stroke after masterful stroke, then began to topple wildly.

Morrison and "the boys" had grown apart. He was too crazy, too unreliable, too intellectual, and too conceited for them, but mostly he was too insecure. They shunned him socially and he retaliated by terrorizing them with the threat that he would quit. He was lonely, as all writers must be, and he was outrageous in public, often drinking himself blind and creating a scene. He considered himself a poet, rock 'n' roll his vehicle. He was also an actor, a cinematographer, a screenwriter, and a rather pleasant guy when he wasn't acting out.

In contrast to the arrogance and depravity he projected on the rock 'n' roll stage, he was endearingly bashful, particularly at the height of his fame. He affected indifference, aped bravado, and generally gave the appearance of deep thought, glib observation, or helpless stupor, all covers under which he could size up a scene (a scene often was galvanized by his very presence there). He sat that night in the back right-hand seat of his limousine, flipping pages of the *Village Voice* back and forth and mumbling about nothing happening in New York.

He tossed the paper to the floor and began to sing "Eleanor Rigby," scattering the lyrics into gibberish. "You're weird, man," came a comment; delighted, Morrison grinned. "I tries," he drawled, settling back into the back of the seat.

The driver lost his way close to the Singer Bowl. Someone made a nervous joke about time. "This is anarchy," Morrison accused the driver. The limousine became tangled in the traffic jam around the Singer Bowl. As it finally rounded the bend toward the stage entrance, a crowd of fans charged it. They ran up to the car, which stopped halfway to the building to avoid running them over. They ganged it, pressing hands and faces to the windows. Before someone could reach across Morrison's chest to snap the door lock closed, he opened it. Hands reached in and bodies followed. The car was full of kids playfully grabbing at Morrison, who winced and hung limp. "Will some of you girls escort me backstage?" he asked huskily. "I might get mobbed or something."

The backstage area was a locker room in a cement cubicle, rather large but very hot and steamy. Jim decided he wanted to walk around outside. Checking to see that the cameramen were following, he stepped out into the arena, at once both matador and bull. He got about twenty feet before he was noticed; then hundreds of people mobbed him, running up to him, wanting to get near him, afraid to get too close.

It was an evening destined to go ascrew. It was just in the air. During the Who's set a revolving stage malfunctioned and got stuck. A portion of the audience couldn't see and they were getting mad. The Who played badly and the drama of their breakup finale was taken down a peg by an equipment man in full sight (as the stage was in the round) lighting smoke bombs behind the amplifiers. But the crowd was roaring. There were fifteen thousand of them and they were in the mood for some action.

The Who left the stage in a foul mood. the Doors took their time going on. A half-hour passed, then an hour. The audience was frothing. They pounded loudly and rhythmically, demanding the Doors. The band—Krieger, Densmore, and Manzarek— appeared onstage and vamped, waiting for Morrison, who was very deliberately taking his sweet time. He stepped out of the doorway and a cry went out through the audience. He smiled, posed, drew himself up intensely. I thought I saw him shiver. The sound of the crowd changed—it was voracious, vicious, predatory. Girls hung over the tiers, sobbing. He was escorted by a cordon of security police to the stage through people who leaped at him. He lifted the microphone and began to sing.

A good portion of the audience still couldn't see and they were furious. Crowds stormed the front of the stage and were turned back by police. The set proceeded sporadically, further infuriating the crowd. Some were trying to scale the stage and others cheered them on. Morrison spun around and ground the songs out half-heartedly, ad-libbing, improvising, doing an ominous dance. Hysteria was building.

"Cool down," he urged seductively, "we're going to be here for a long time."

"'Light My Fire,'" the audience demanded. "'Light My Fire!'"

Morrison shrieked, moaned, gyrated, and minced to the edge of the stage, hovering. Hands reached out and grabbed him and the cops had to pry them away. The camera crew ducked a piece of broken chair, which came flying onto the stage. Morrison caught it and heaved it back into the crowd. Moments later it was thrown again, by someone in the audience, and came sailing through the air again, hitting a girl on the head and cutting her. the Doors were hardly visible from any angle because there were about twenty cops onstage.

The set ended under great protest and the Doors had to be dragged by police through a tunnel of fighting kids. Everyone not with the Doors' party was removed, some forcibly, from the backstage area, which was then locked up tight. The audience banged on the doors and the walls. It was like being under siege.

A few cans of beer were passed around to fill the time it took to clear the area. Jim Morrison was in the hall talking to the injured girl. Densmore was batting an empty beer can against the wall with a stick of wood he'd found. He then threw the slab of wood angrily against the wall, picked up a mop propped up in the corner of the room, took it out into the empty arena, mounted the stage, and began swabbing it down. He called for the cameramen to shoot it, cursed when they remained with Morrison. Morrison came back into the dressing room. "Do you think it looked phony, me talking to her?" he asked nobody in particular. Nobody answered. The area was cleared and the Doors headed back toward the limousines for the return trip. This time John Densmore and Jim Morrison rode together.

"That was a weird gig," said John Densmore. "If those kids really got together and figured 'We're fifteen thousand and there are only a couple of hundred cops,' they'd really do something. I can't decide if I dig it or I don't. Do you dig it, Jim?"

"They'd really do a revolt thing if I jumped off the stage, wouldn't they?" asked Morrison.

"You'd get pretty messed up, man."

"Aw, we should do something. They were throwing things and stuff."

"I threw them about twenty drumsticks."

"We ought to throw money. Yes, let's get a few hundred ones and throw them into the crowd. It'll be great for the movie."

One of the cameramen laughed. "Movie, hell. I'm not going to be shooting, I'm going to be picking up the bread."

John's head was back at the concert, trying to piece it together from his point of view. "All that unrest," he mused.

Back at the hotel the group ran into Pete Johnson, rock critic for the *L.A. Times*. He was a shy man, with long lanky hair. Banana hair, people called it, all tight and wavy. When he used to show up at the *Times'* office, they kidded him about it, asked him to take off his hat. He was in town on some freelance business and had not even known the Doors were playing locally, a fact he quickly told them to explain his absence at the concert. Morrison whooped, slapping Johnson on the back. "Man, when you wrote that we were the ugliest group in captivity, that was your finest hour."

Upstairs they sipped cold drinks together, coming down. The riot had depressed everyone. John wished they'd planned something to do. It was Saturday night, not even very late, and there was nothing to do. "There's got to be more to it than this," he said. "Play a concert, cause a riot, then sit up in a hotel room by ourselves the rest of the night."

Johnson asked him what happened at the Hollywood Bowl some weeks previously. Kids had thrown things at the stage, laughed at and booed the Doors. In their hometown, yet. It was taken as a dramatic loss of prestige in the scene, a real challenge to their supremacy. "Every time we get together we ask ourselves what went wrong that night," said John. He referred to the Doors as "the dupes" and acted embarrassed. "Hey, I know 'Hello I Love You' [a huge hit at the time] is bullshit, but we've never been played by those kinds of radio stations before."

In the months that followed, the riots at concerts continued. Each story was more outrageous than the next, culminating with Morrison's arrest for exposing himself at a concert in Miami. It took about a year to come to trial and Morrison had criminal lawyer Max Fink defend him. At the trial the witnesses were discredited; he was convicted on some charges and appealed. The whole ordeal had inspired a "decency movement" of Florida youth under the auspices of Jackie Gleason. Had he done it? Had he really exposed himself? The popvine was speculative. Most people thought he had; the whole thing was a farce anyway. Still, there was no real answer to the question. For weeks Morrison's live-in girlfriend, Pamela, a young, charming, and glib strawberry blonde, tried to pry it out of him. She couldn't believe he'd done it; she couldn't believe he hadn't. Finally, one night when he was drunk, she asked him again. He gave her a mischievous little grin, the kind she loved him most for. "Aw," he giggled, "I just wanted to see what it looked like in the spotlight, that's all."

Hungry, insatiable crowds were devouring concerts. The riots at the Democratic National Convention in Chicago had set everyone running scared and pieces of the scene were falling around our heads. We were ducking, dodging, running fast and furiously. The leaders of this country never confronted how badly we were being torn apart until too late. The nation's children were seceding from the union and forming their own, something new and unafraid, not without its own flaws. The leaders of the new culture refused to face its insufficiencies just as carelessly as the leaders of the old. The difference between the two faded; it became a matter of which one was more fun.

It was not as if there were a certain portion of revolutionary youth that had violent intentions and another portion that was pacifist; it was that each and every one of us teetered on that edge, releasing all our anxiety and energy into one another. Songs got braver. Groups got bolder. Enthusiasm was inflamed by response. We got higher and more finely sensed. The tide seemed unstemmable and rising. We could only push so far, they could only push so far back. It was clear that whatever it was that was happening would come to a head again and again in different and more outrageous ways until something, somewhere changed.

In the wake of the riots at the 1968 Democratic Convention in Chicago, David Crosby and Stephen Stills were moping around in Crosby's Los Angeles home one morning as summer was drawing to an inconclusive end, reflecting on the urgency, and at the same time the idiocy, of revolution.

"I don't think a violent revolution is what we're going to have here," said David. "I think it's going to go down in a way it's never gone down before. There's going to be some of that, the spades are going to give it and they're going to get it. That's probably what will happen to the cities."

"If you don't believe it," said Stephen, "go hang out with some of those little old ladies with blue hair that elected Lyndon Johnson. The right wing is a lot stronger than the left wing and that's where the trouble is going to come from. It's a fact. And when it starts to come down, boy, I'm going fishing!"

"I'm just trying to stay alive," retorted Crosby. "Nobody's come along and sold me a political bill of goods. I'm not playing parlor revolution; that is not a game. Those idiots are endangering us all, the best they can do is to take some of the heat off me."

"It's not a game!" glowered Stephen, jumping to his feet, grabbing Crosby's rifle which was sitting in the corner of the room. "It's not a game but that's how they're playing it and it's dangerous, just as dangerous as having this gun in your room!"

"Of course," agreed Crosby, "if we get into that we're beat; they've got us totally covered. They've been doing it for years and they know how to slaughter."

And later, one stony night in his Beverly Glen house, Crosby sat hanging out with Carl Gottlieb, of the Committee, discussing a medal Joni Mitchell had given Crosby "for conspicuous nudity in the face of the enemy." They were improvising on the possible history of the porcelain medal for the benefit of the household and everyone was giggling at his own clever repartee.

"In this house, even bullshit is an art," I yocked.

Crosby grinned on me and squinted his eyes. "Everything is an art," he rumbled, scrunching his mustache, "and it's all bullshit."

David still had no gig together. Stephen had been sitting around since the Buffalo Springfield broke up, staring at the side of a mountain. They had been hanging in and hanging out with one another, jamming, singing, trying out new songs. Graham Nash, having left the Hollies, came to Los Angeles from England. It was simply the place to be in that quivering of time when everyone was in between groups and trying not to think about it while the days got imperceptibly shorter and shadows of insecurity crept up the canyon wall.

One afternoon Crosby and Stills were at Cass Elliot's house, sitting on the floor and singing. John Sebastian was there, too, and some other friends and Nash dropped by. Crosby and Stills were wailing, into their songs so heavily they were unaware of where they were. They harmonized, trading off lead parts by instinct, their voices twining like longtime lovers together, sure and rhythmically. Nash followed the song in his head for a few moments and then opened up his throat and laid a high harmony over the top of them, skimming the sound, peaking the energy, completing the soul of the song. Something in the room changed the moment he did that; it was like a split second of destiny come to pass, after which none of them, or their music, would ever be the same. In the months that followed they did little more than sing together; there was nothing more gratifying for any of them to do.

In every other respect those boys were a mess. Crosby had never really gotten over Joni Mitchell, who had jilted him for

Leonard Cohen, who had jilted her. Stills was sensing that his desperately involved affair with Judy Collins was coming to a real end. He spent half his time agonizing over it, the rest of it trying to convince her to marry him. To keep his sanity, he sang his hungry heart out. Graham Nash was falling in love with Joni Mitchell; she was falling in love with him. And quite perceptibly Crosby, Stills, and Nash were falling in love with one another. Their sound sent everyone within earshot into rapture.

As winter bore down they went east to Sag Harbor, a small whaling town near the tip of Long Island, New York, and lived there with John Sebastian, polishing their music. Sessions bassist Harvey Brooks was called in briefly to play bass with them but, according to Crosby, he was too good. He put Stephen Stills uptight and was dropped. Brooks didn't even know he was dropped until the day he went to pick up some tickets to join the boys in London and was informed that there were no tickets left for him.

Egos were high and flying. The sound got tighter and tighter. Recording together was going to be a problem contractually because they were all signed to different companies. David Geffin, agent, industry *wunderkind*, worked it out so that Atlantic traded a then new group, Poco, to Columbia for Graham Nash's release so they could all record for Atlantic, and it was set. They would make a record soon but for the time being they went to London to rehearse and hang out some more. A friend of long standing, Dallas Taylor, would be the drummer.

Contracts took all winter to work out; huge amounts of money changed hands. Came the first glimmerings of spring, it was time to make an album.

By the time Crosby, Stills, and Nash were halfway through making their first album, it had been raining for forty days and forty nights in Los Angeles. The town was uptight, people were cabin-bound, and nothing was happening in the clubs. News of the new association of the three musicians was around but nobody saw hide nor hair of them during that time. They were locked up in closed recording sessions almost every night. On a rare night off they hung out together with a very few friends, piecing their voices together, conspiring on the technicalities and metaphysics of making a beautiful album.

Crosby's house in Beverly Glen was glowing. Inside it was all redwood, candles, and incense and they were watching TV. It was a rerun of an old Pete Seeger program featuring the then-deceased Mississippi John Hurt and the three were watching intently, rocking softly to the late old man's music. The program ended and they each tried to pick out Hurt's peculiar style of double-thumbing the guitar. Stills got close and started to sing "You Got to Walk That Lonesome Valley," culminating in a self-parody so perfect it might have been intentional.

At twenty-four, Stills already qualified as a veteran of the American music scene. He'd been on the road since he was fifteen. His first job was as a stable boy at a racetrack down south. He craved success, money, and stardom so hard you could feel it in his voice, but he came on like a stone hick whenever he lightened up. His presence was a studied forbiddingness; he said little, smiled less, dropped perfectly uproarious one-liners when they were least expected.

Star Trek was interrupted by a visit from Jim Dickson, who came to play the original Byrds demonstration tapes for David, to get his permission to issue them as a record (the album that eventually became *Preflyte*). They sounded like a bunch of guys who used to be the Everly Brothers and wanted to be the Beatles. "Mr. Tambourine Man" swarmed out of the speakers, its euphoria filling the room, plunging everyone into nostalgia, a remembrance of innocence, a promise of experience, a paean of joy. David

Crosby looked at the listings on the tape box and alerted Graham Nash. "Wait'll you hear the next one!" And the next one was a song that reeked of phrasings embarrassingly derivative of the Hollies, but nowhere near as good. "Wot, did you listen to oos?" exploded Nash, slapping his forehead and laughing. "Sure," said Crosby with an overly casual flap of his hand, "the folk process." Crosby winced as he listened closer and heard himself hit a particularly sour note. He giggled. "Sure," he said to Dickson, "go put it out, I'll be a sport if the others will."

Dickson stayed and inquired about the new group endeavor. By that time Van Dyke Parks and the writer and *Crawdaddy!* publisher Paul Williams had joined the household for the evening. "Let's play the album," suggested Nash, grabbing for a guitar. Stills picked up another and began to play the opening riff of "Suite Judy Blue Eyes." They ran through the entire album, singing and playing without a pause or a spoken word between them. When it was over the room was silent and stunned, overcome with amazement at how beautiful they sounded. They sang "Blackbird" as an encore and dickered about putting it on the album. Paul Williams had written a poem called "The Word Has New Meaning." David Crosby thought it might make a song and wanted to compose music to it. Paul wrote the words down and Graham Nash looked over his shoulder. "I know that word," said Nash, "it's the same word as, you know, 'all you need is word.'" He grinned at his own cleverness. David Crosby raised his eyes and shook his head softly. "Graham," he said quietly, "you are so stone beautiful I can hardly believe it."

The following evening they were at Wally Heider's studio on Cahuenga Boulevard, piecing together tracks for the album. The engineer, Bill Halverson, a beefy blond man, hunkered over the control board, locating instruments on each track of the tapes, isolating and labeling them, playing them one at a time to get a reading on each. The boys were in the studio, through a glass wall. The connecting microphones were shut off and they played and jabbered silently. They were joking around with songs, feeling out parts, and goofing on each other's riffs. A light on the panel indicated someone was at the door, a massive, soundproof door that took great strength to open. Outside stood Donovan like a scrawny scarecrow, coming to visit after taping a Smothers Brothers show. He came in and they played the tapes of material already finished. Donovan danced around the room in delight. They all went into the studio afterward to let Halverson finish reading the levels. Donovan and Graham Nash played Beatles songs together.

It was time to record again. Graham Nash sat alone in the studio and played "Lady of the Island." It was perfect, that one take. Everyone was amazed. All the other songs took about thirty takes each to get right. David Crosby went into the studio to sing a second part over it. Bill Halverson played the take Nash had just completed, opened up another track on the tape for Crosby to sing into, and rolled it. Crosby freewheeled it, creating harmonic circles around Nash's voice. He came back in the studio and they all listened to the three parts together, one guitar and two voices. It was perfect. Halverson moved the volume controls around on the board, adjusting each part to the other and fading it gracefully at the end. Everyone watched the oscilloscope as he did it, to make sure the parts were in phase, not combating one another. The green signals formed ellipses that spun around and around, creating circular designs, winding, spreading, quivering, finally shrinking as the sound faded, compressing into a tiny agitated dot that skipped around the very center of the instrument, then disappeared. The lights were dim. Pungent smoke was heavy in the air. There was silence—heavy, meaningful silence.

The doorbell light flickered again, intruding on the almost darkness. The lights were faded up and the door answered. It was Jerry Wexler and Ahmet Ertegun. Stills, from the studio, saw Ertegun through the glass, ran through the door, and gave him an enormous bear hug. They were made welcome, and in walked their faithful Indian companion, Phil Spector. They played the finished material for everyone again. "Yessir, we're working hard," said Crosby, trying to sound credible. "At two bucks a minute we can't afford to socialize. We may even bring this one in on time, Ahmet. That'll improve our reputation in the business a lot, right? 'Specially Stills."

Stills yocked and guffawed, the laughter hissing out in throaty spasms between his crooked front teeth. Ertegun ruffed his hair affectionately.

They hadn't yet chosen a title for the album and Jerry Wexler suggested *Music from Big Ego*. It was flatly rejected. "Guess they don't have the distance to appreciate it," mumbled Wexler, amused.

Spector, Ertegun, and Wexler left, smiling. A few moments later, with a clatter of hooves and a hearty heigh-ho guru, Donovan left and they got back to work because a more difficult task was at hand: the frightened, outraged, prophetic "Long Time Coming."

In the summer of 1969, Crosby told me he'd written the song the morning after Bobby Kennedy was assassinated. "I couldn't sleep," he said, "and I sat up and wrote the song." The song just wouldn't hang together the way they had been playing it; it sounded overweight, clumsy, preachy, and preposterous. Crosby sang it and he sounded like Stills. It was getting to the point where they were wondering whether it should even be on the first album after all. Crosby was frustrated. Stills was impatient. Nash was concerned. The arrangement between them had been for an equal distribution of each other's songs and whose song it was, in a difference of opinion, got the last word. "Long Time Coming" was coming to a short dead end.

It was very late, they had been in the studio for nine straight hours, and had accomplished a great deal. They prepared to go home and get some sleep for the next night's sessions. Stills grumbled something about putting away the guitars and stayed late. When the others left, he worked all night long and into daylight, going home on the verge of collapse.

The following night the group assembled in the studio again. Stills sat at the control board and ran the tape. Out came an entirely new arrangement for "Long Time Coming" which he had single-handedly put together the night before. It was gorgeous. It churned out rhythmically, the lines meeting with the incredible force the song contained. An organ part undulated along the top of it, insinuating a siren. David was agog. He swigged a lug of wine, went into the studio, and sang in an entirely original way. As if possessed with the immensity of the music, he broke through. He was tearful at the end. "I finally found my voice," he said afterward. "Five years I've been singing and I finally found a voice of my own. Every time I had a lead vocal part with the Byrds I choked up because I was so scared. But these two loved me enough to let me find my own voice."

He thanked and complimented Stills on the arrangement for the song. "You make me ashamed of myself," he said, with no small measure of admiration, and even more affection. Stills, who always had trouble accepting open praise from anyone, had his eyes down, and when he raised them the expression on his face said plainly and silently: *I arranged your song better than you could have in a thousand years. And don't you forget it.*

Crosby didn't respond in kind but it wasn't lost on him. The time for real ego clashes was yet to come. They loved and fought like a family. They made up to make music and money together. None of them singly had the same kind of weight that they had together.

Joni Mitchell, who was working on her own album at the time, dropped in later that night with a big box of homemade cookies. She played some of her new songs for the group. One of them was a song for Nash, whom she'd nicknamed "Willie." She sat at the piano and sang, "I will be his lady all my life. . . ." Nash leaned over the piano, enchanted, and went misty. Crosby watched from across the room, the utter heartbreak on his face unnoticed by either one of them, they were so wrapped up in each other.

Shortly the group started recording again, doing the last vocal overdubbings on another song. It worked out so beautifully it even surprised them. Everyone was excited, happy, enthusiastic, tired, and hungry.

A break was called. The road manager, Chris, had brought some wine, cheese, fresh fruit, and deli. Everyone dug in. Joni and Graham were off getting kissy with one another. Stills muttered something about getting back to work. Crosby slumped on the couch, cuddling a bottle of wine. He closed his eyes and his mouth curled into a smile behind his mustache. "I've never had so much fun making an album in my entire life!"

In the interim between the time the album was released and their first tour, they had to find a bassist and a keyboard player. Stills got hold of Bruce Palmer from the old Buffalo Springfield. Palmer tried, but couldn't cut it. "It got low," reported Crosby. "We were trying to tell him he wasn't making it and he was insisting 'Yes, I am.' It was really hard to do." A bassist appeared, a very young black man from Motown who played with them on the first tour only.

Stills politicked very hard to get Neil Young into the group over Crosby's and Nash's angry protest. Neil Young was still intent on making it as a single artist but he hadn't broken out yet. By that time Stills was the power in the group and he wielded it with a heavy hand. They broke up, re-formed again. Young was in.

The original group was Crosby, Stills, and Nash. The deal was that they were financial partners in the group. They wanted a bass player and keyboard man to tour with them for salary, earning good money but considerably less than the group members, who would get percentages of whatever they brought in, which by that time, they knew, would be in the area of seven figures. Bill Halverson got a small percentage of album receipts, but one that amounted to a great deal of cash. They finally, under protest, gave Dallas Taylor some kind of minute percentage also. Greed was setting in. But when Neil Young joined the group, he joined not only as a keyboard man but as a writer and an additional superstar, giving the group more weight. He was cut in for a considerable percent. Their concert price skyrocketed, promoters revolted but gave it to them, having to raise their ticket prices.

Dallas Taylor so resented Neil Young's getting a bigger piece that he would mess him up onstage. Young hit the roof when it happened once too often to be accidental and insisted he'd never play on the same stage with Taylor again. Taylor had to leave the group.

They never got a better drummer. They broke up and re-formed again and again. Finally Graham Nash, who by that time had parted company with Joni Mitchell, became involved with Stephen Stills's new girlfriend. Stills, whose heart was much too vulnerable, said he was splitting for good.

That time Ahmet Ertegun believed him and was quite upset about it. "That group is gone." He shook his head mournfully. "The only way they'll get back together again is for the others to go to Stills and ask him to come back and they'd never do it; they're too proud and they're too hurt."

"Why don't you just get another bass player," suggested a well-connected friend. "I know of one just as famous, talented, even as crazy as Stills and I bet he's looking for a new band himself."

Ertegun, without a trace of suspicion, brightened and bit. "Who?" The friend grinned triumphantly. "Paul McCartney."

Ertegun, without missing a beat, replied, "That's a tremendous idea, tremendous! I wonder how much Apple would give me for the other three?"

I was on assignment in Los Angeles. Chuck Berry, who was called Charles in his private life, was dating a friend of mine—the petite, button-pretty, sharp-as-a-tack ebullient blonde publicist, Diane Gardiner. Diane and I had plans for the evening. She called in the afternoon to ask if I wouldn't like to go out with her and Charles for the evening and after making sure I wouldn't be intruding, I happily accepted the change of plans.

I went to her apartment in Hollywood at 7600 Fountain Avenue. She lived downstairs from Jim Morrison, who was peeling the fender of his girlfriend's car off the side of the too-narrow driveway as I arrived. Shortly after I got there, Charles showed up at the door. After introductions, we walked out the driveway to Charles's brand-spanking-new RV, a huge, luxuriously appointed land yacht. Charles was a little stiff, and I was afraid he either hadn't been consulted or hadn't been happy about my joining them for the evening.

I'd never seen the inside of an RV before and Charles graciously showed me around. Everything you could want was in there. "Even a commode," said Charles, pointing to a narrow little door toward the back of the cavernous vehicle. Since the RV was so new, he had to put some miles on it before the first local service, so we drove quite a ways up the freeway. Diane, I could tell, wanted to show off at a fancy restaurant, but Charles had other ideas. We drove for more than an hour. Charles was in the right lane with his left turn signal on, and cars kept passing us. He seemed a bit hesitant to change lanes. I said, "Go ahead, Charles, you could put that Chevy in your commode!" He flashed me a huge grin (that's how I knew I was finally okay with him), sped up handily, and changed lanes smooth as a silk.

We stopped near Oxnard. When we pulled off the freeway and headed toward a family-style restaurant, Diane voiced her disappointment at such a modest eatery. "I thought you said you wanted chicken . . . dear," said Charles. The restaurant's marked parking places were too small to accommodate the RV, so Charles parked it alongside of an adjacent gas station and we crossed the parking lot to get to the restaurant.

We entered the restaurant and seated ourselves in a booth, studying the menu. And studying the menu. And studying the menu. I noticed that people who'd arrived and been seated after us were getting served. More time went by. We were being conspicuously ignored. I was astonished. Diane was indignant. Charles was sardonic. We'd been there over forty-five minutes and no waitress approached our booth. The moment Diane made a remark about horrible service Charles gave a hand signal for us to get up and leave. They weren't going to serve a table with a black man and two young white women.

We walked silently across the parking lot. A cluster of late teenage boys coming the other way passed us on the way to the restaurant. Behind us we could hear one of them turn around and exclaim: "Did you see that? *Did you see who that was?* That was Chuck Berry! Fuckin' Chuck Berry!" The other boys turned around in wonder, exchanging epithets as they recognized the tall brown-eyed handsome man leaving the scene, shaking his head and smirking at the obscene incongruity of it all.

We did not acknowledge the boys. We walked silently back to the luxury RV and got in.

It had been raining most of the previous two weeks in New York but that day in 1969, the day before the Woodstock Music and Art Fair, the sun was shining and it was comfortable and warm. The people were already there, a capacity crowd and more still coming in. The neighboring households were out in their front yards watching in amazement as all those cars paraded by. The local kids flashed peace signs experimentally, nudged and poked each other as the people in the cars returned them. It was something they hadn't seen before. Although during the weekend to come most of them wouldn't be allowed on Max Yasgur's farm because their parents were afraid, they were getting excited.

On the grounds, there was anything but excitement. There was sheer panic among the staff. Construction had been held up by the rain and the performance area was only half completed. The stage, twenty feet high, was a bare platform surrounded by metal scaffolding. They were furiously working on a hydraulic elevator for heavy musical equipment, certain it wouldn't be operative by showtime, only twenty-one hours away. No elevator, no show; there's no way to hoist a half a ton of amplifiers twenty feet without it. They were tearing their hair out. If there could have been a way to cancel out at that point, they would have gratefully done so. But there wasn't, and they worked through the night to get the area finished.

A starry night promised a clear day ahead. The promise was broken. It was a compound fracture.

The first day was mostly folksingers and acoustic music. There was still time to set up complicated electrical systems. By that time the New York State Thruway exit for the festival had been closed off. A cheer went up as this was announced. People somehow arrived in droves anyway. The few skinny country roads leading to the farmyard were choked with cars parked on both sides of them. Shoulders were muddy and too many cars were stuck. People outside were desperate to get in. Inside, nobody cared about anything but what was going on there. Most of the action was in the field. Campsites were buzzing with activity, free food concessions were doling out incredible amounts of macrobiotic fare. A procession of popstars arrived at the Holiday Inn in a nearby town that afternoon. By evening a caravan of cars from the Holiday Inn decided to visit and see what was going on.

We arrived on the periphery of the crowd while Joan Baez was singing, and wandered among the campers, not able to see, barely able to hear. A group was playing on a makeshift platform in one of them. Periodically, we could hear the crowd roar. It began to rain and we ducked into a tent. The driver of our car, one of Jefferson Airplane's road crew, decided we'd better get out while the getting was good and seek a more privileged and easier entrance in the morning. We found our car miraculously, started it, and headed out onto the road. At one point the drivewheel got caught in the mud. Seven teenage boys ran toward us and grabbed the rear bumper. "Heave, heave, heave," they laughed as they rocked the automobile, and in a few moments the car was free, heading down the road back to the Holiday Inn.

We'd been touched by the unexplainable rapture of the crowd. We partied all night long. The Airplane and the Who had just played Tanglewood a few days before so they were already there. The next day the rest of the festival arrived.

It was raining bucketfuls and if you had to run ten feet from the car to the motel, you got soaked through to the skin. Several miles away the culmination of pop history was unfolding but a couple of dozens of its superstars and their touring staff were stranded at the Holiday Inn.

Somebody had changed a $5 bill at the bar and put all the quarters into the jukebox, playing "Hey Jude" sixty times end to end. The whole bar sang along with the chorus, linking arms, swaying from side to side and laughing, among them Country Joe, Jack Casady, Marty Balin, Richie Havens, Janis Joplin, Tim and Susan Hardin, and Jerry Garcia. A high-stakes poker game was going on in the corner of the bar. Later, Rosalie Sorrels and Jerry Garcia sat on the floor with guitars and sang folksongs together. Judy Collins headed a long luncheon table in the dining room with both Clive Davis and Jac Holzman in company.

A little guy called Arturo ran around like a chicken with his head cut off, assigning helicopter space, hysterically asserting that helicopters were for performers only and he would personally deck anyone else who tried to enter one.

The eight-person copter was the only way in that afternoon but nobody was particularly uptight about it. The Holiday Inn was rocking along on its own steam. It was probably the first time so many San Francisco musicians had had a chance to get together in two years. Great hugs and lots of music were exchanged.

By afternoon there was a break in the weather. It was Jefferson Airplane's turn to go to the festival. They were due to play late at night, to close the show, but they wanted to see the festival, as did all the performers present. Stories of the size of the crowd and amazing mess in the fairgrounds came in hourly. It sounded like their kind of gig.

The Airplane were called to the lobby for departure. It was getting to sound like a wartime operation. They were told that they and they alone could go, in some escorted cars, to the festival area. They refused, saying that they wouldn't play unless their old ladies could come, too. Arturo, up against a wall, had to agree. The Airplane's old ladies turned out to include everyone in the Holiday Inn who wanted to go to the festival that afternoon and a caravan of at least a dozen cars assembled.

Among those gathered was a man called Bear, who was in fact Augustus Stanley Owsley III, previously known as the acid king of San Francisco, a renowned soundman and keeper of the stash that could levitate the entire festival. And escorting the Airplane, their old ladies, and this mammoth stash were four state troopers who headed the caravan and brought up the rear, escorting a good dozen cars right onto the festival area.

The stars and their guests unloaded and walked to a pavilion where fruit, wine, sandwiches, and punch were plentiful and flowing. Somebody immediately began putting acid into a huge vat of punch. A few moments later they were caught in the act and ten gallons of punch was poured out on the ground, but not before some of it had gone into the bloodstreams of people unsuspectingly drinking what had been poured into paper cups. Al Aronowitz, alerted as to the contents of his glass as he was drinking, spat and sprayed a mouthful out, cursing angrily.

Santana was playing onstage in the late day, their jungle rhythms boogalooing out on the crowd. We walked a monkey bridge from the performers' area to the stage, a suspended path of slats that went twenty feet up from the ground, over the wall separating the stars from the main mulch and affording them a star's-eye view of those hundreds of thousands of people, meadows full of them, stretched out over a field that dipped slightly like a shallow bowl and rose slightly at the edge about a half-mile away. And all of them were on their feet, dancing to Santana's Latin-based rock; they were like a great writhing mass of T-shirts and bottles of pop and smiles, with clouds and clouds of sweet pungent smoke rising from within their midst.

The Dead played after Santana. They played for a long time and left the crowd howling for more. They had worked them up to receiving Janis Joplin and her new band with a rousing cheer, one that echoed into the setting sun. She danced with them as if they were one; they shouted back at her, they wouldn't let her off until they'd drained off every drop of her energy. The energy seemed at a peak but there was no letting up 'til morning. In the dark, Sly and the Family Stone came on and socked it to them. Sly looked so fine with his fringe and his sass, his band in colors, and his funky minstrel show. He got the crowd up on its feet again and whipped it around with sweet rhythm and blues, simple compact phrases that make you shake yo' body down. His last number was a frenzied dance, one that caught both the audience and the crowd on stage. Grace Slick and Janis Joplin were dancing together, with their eyes tight shut and their fists clenched and their bodies whipping around. "Higher!" Sly shouted into the crowd. "Higher!" they boomed back with the force of half a million voices at their loudest. He threw up his arms in a peace sign, a billow of fringe unfurled around them, and the audience responded, shouting "Higher" in unison and raising their arms and fingers to the air, joyously, desperately, far as a huge searchlight could pick out, arms and hands and fingers raised in peace signs, heads and voices crying out into the night, crying the anguished plea of the Sixties, "Higher, higher!"

And the act was over, and they cheered as even they had never cheered before, these of the biggest crowd in the history of American entertainment, that audience, the biggest star of the biggest festival to date, they were cheering Sly and they were cheering themselves and that moment became another metaphor for the movement, the most spectacular moment of its time. And I looked out and could hardly believe it. "Have you ever seen anything like it?" I demanded of Grace. Wide-eyed, she looked out over the crowd and growled, "Nah!" Hours later, the Airplane would have to follow that act.

But the Who were on next. It was way past midnight and Peter Townshend was not in what could be called a good mood. All day he'd been leaning disgustedly against an abandoned pile of lumber by the stage, surveying what he quite plainly felt was the biggest mess of a gig he'd ever seen. The group had refused to go on unless they were paid right then and there. They'd come all the way from England and they quite rightly surmised that the finances of this scene were in as much of a turmoil as the rest of it. Their agent got a certified check out of one of the promoters and they agreed to go on. The group walked onto the stage and began to plug their instruments into the amplifiers. The spotlights were down and the stage was almost dark, except for the tiny pinpoints of red that indicated that their amplifiers' power was on.

Abbie Hoffman sat dejectedly on a pile of twisted electrical cable on one front corner of the stage, complaining he was on a bad acid trip. He crabbed about the medical facilities, claiming the performers were being given preference. Champagne for Janis Joplin's band had been flown in by helicopter instead of medical supplies for the hospital tent, where a bunch of kids were in bad shape. "Who are the biggest stars here?" he demanded. "Is this a big thing? Is Dylan going to show up? The Beatles aren't here!" He looked out over the crowd. "This is what we wanted at Chicago," he grumped. "No musicians showed." Some friends were trying to talk him down.

"Abbie, wake up," I urged. "This is the revolution, can't you see, it's all the same thing."

"Naw," he retorted. "I'm the conscience of this movement."

The lights went up. Peter Townshend was about to hit that first chord to begin "Tommy." Abbie leaped in front of him, grabbed the microphone, and bellowed something about everybody leaving this scene and going down to free John Sinclair from prison. The mikes were killed in the middle of his outburst. Peter Townshend knocked him down with his guitar. The kids who noticed him shouted, "Sit down, we can't see, shut up, we can't hear!" Abbie was crushed and furious. He jumped off the stage, made his way through the crowd, split the festival grounds, and hitchhiked back to New York City.

Monterey, Chicago, Woodstock. The three events had occurred almost exactly a year apart, each distinguishing its year as a turn in American youth consciousness. Innocence, anguish, and an orgy of souls. They were culminations of movements that will never quite be duplicated, as each changed the symbols and substance of the culture recursively. The future sat on the edge of apocalypse as supreme joy alternated with supreme tragedy, stirring up challenge and desperation among apocalypse's young constituency, abandon's young collective, hope's young front line.

The Airplane went on after a long set by the Who during which the sun rose majestically over their encore. They were exhausted and played to an exhausted audience, many of whom slept right there in the mud. There was another day and night of music during which the Band made a rare personal appearance; Crosby, Stills, Nash, and Young made their major national debut as a performing band; Johnny Winter, Blood, Sweat and Tears, and Jimi Hendrix played, closing the festival with a ringing, twisted "Star-Spangled Banner," to a rapidly thinning crowd. The Airplane piled into several rented cars and headed toward New York to do the *Dick Cavett Show*, a show at which David Crosby, Stephen Stills (who showed off the Woodstock mud on his boots), Graham Nash, and Joni Mitchell all showed up and participated. The Airplane sang "We Can Be Together" as the show was taped, and the following day the pop press all gathered together at Ungano's, a rock club uptown, to see if in the airing the offending word in the "Up against the wall, motherfucker" sequence was censored. It wasn't. The Woodstock had landed. The euphoria was fertile, widespread and historic, but it wouldn't last long.

They sauntered in, single file, across the back of the room, miming some kind of formality by default, down the center aisle of set up chairs, and arranged themselves behind teacups on a long white table at the front of the room. About fifty reporters, photographers, newsmen, cameramen, and assorted hangers-on had assembled in a banquet room of the Beverly Wilshire in Los Angeles to receive the Rolling Stones after several years' absence from the United States. Legal, domestic, and other problems had beset them in the meantime, and they had been sorely missed.

The Stones had been in town only a day or two, but their presence had made itself felt. "The world's best rock 'n' roll band," proclaimed the *L.A. Free Press.* If nothing else, this proved that Los Angeles is practically their second home. It is the only city on the planet insane enough to absorb, engulf, and contain the Rolling Stones, or take them in stride. Here the Stones have always been patron demons, madcap musicians on the loose in twentieth-century Sodom. The assembled reporters— some natty envoys of long-esteemed Hollywood papers, some shaggier members of the underground contingent, some cool, compromised company freaks, and practically every house hippie in town—were prepared for a traditional Rolling Stones assault on the questionable dignity of the communications profession.

The brutalization began. In rare form, the group fielded questions, parlayed answers, evaded definitions, put on a riotous show. In Los Angeles, the press either doesn't know enough or

Mick Jagger, 1969   Photo by Ellen Sander

knows far better than to be insulted and they just laughed. In the laughter was more recognition than amusement, more a welcome than a reaction. The Rolling Stones had arrived.

Famed for reducing members of the press to "stuttering, embarrassed heaps," as one English paper once described it, the Stones lived it up and lived it down. Mick Jagger—vocalist, lyricist, and head Stone (or stone head, depending on where you were sitting)—delegated questions, growled halfway intelligible answers, mocked disdain, flashed his eyes and his leer, then, finally, put his head in his arms on the table and groaned, "That's enough." The pack, looking as if they'd been shaken out of a restless sleep, without time or inclination to change, shave, or rouse their dispositions, marched out of the room in single file, leaving a cheerful ruin of reporters behind. "A classic," muttered John Carpenter of the *L.A. Free Press*.

"It was all right," Jagger told me later. "Some of them are really great." He grinned heartily and turned his attention to one local paper's report of the debacle. "Stones put on press," he intoned condescendingly and giggled as he read on. "You'll see. We've got to have one when we get to New York."

At a press conference in London more than a year ago the group hurled a dozen cream pies into a flock of reporters. It was a direct and loving affront to the ever distant, very proper English press establishment. By now at last, Her Majesty's finest are at least inured to this band of musical ruffians, the amplified street gang the Rolling Stones have personified all along.

Unleashed on the idle pop market in 1963, the Stones have had a hectic history. Always the vagabond group in their appearance, their music, and the development of their artistic *gestalt*, the Stones have somehow, and much to their own amazement, pulled through. Responsible for such evanescent beauties as "Ruby Tuesday" and "As Tears Go By," and, more typically, such rock classics as "(I Can't Get No) Satisfaction," "Get Off My Cloud," "19th Nervous Breakdown," and "Have You Seen Your Mother?" typified by the raw, unadulterated insolence of their collective performing personality, they've capped their creative contributions with "Honky Tonk Women," a single that is undoubtedly song of the year 1969, their current release. They were in Los Angeles to finish an album and prepare for a twenty-two-day, fourteen-city performing tour of the States, their first American appearance since 1966.

Much has transpired in their absence, as this country's youth has trembled from the brink of flower power to the abyss of fist power and back in an agonized convulsion. Meanwhile, dissent has polarized much of the populace. The Stones have always had a genius for relating to the American social situation in a way no other group in the world has been able to sustain.

The nightmarish Convention riots last year were likened to a Rolling Stones concert, and their release then was "Street Fighting Man" coupled with "Jumpin' Jack Flash." Many radio stations refused airplay of the first side because of suppressed revolutionary undercurrents and violent implications.

Violence? The Stones typify it; they don't imply it. A Stones concert is a raging assault, a fiery menace of music and freneticism choreographed by the devil's disciples. The Stones confront their audiences; they don't mess around. Jagger on vocals, and various rhythm instruments, dances like a dervish, moves like a matador, teases, threatens, and taunts his crowd into submission; half the show is in the fight they give him. Performers and audience are one in a desperate, cathartic drama, and everyone loves each moment of the fray. The energy is siphoned off, the crowd breathless, elated, spent. The group stalks dramatically offstage.

They have carved an identity with their special brand of machismo and stoned soul sorcery; they've paid their dues and the result is the world's best performing rock band. Also, they've always been the underdogs of pop, and most of the time they've not been together enough even to try harder. They've had their problems, internal and external, and they've borne the brunt of abuse from the press.

Misunderstood, misused, and, in many ways, classic misfits even in their own milieu, the Stones are the original outlaw bluesmen. It's easy to understand why they are so well-loved by their fans, so passionately resented by their detractors. In the establishment "pop" has become, the Stones are the only real rebels left. Their recordings, their performances, their antics, their anti-style make no concession to order or predictability. Uneven, often sloppy, sometimes even lame, their product has never been uneventful. Their music is pure essence, basic hot-tempered rhythm rock and blues tapped from rich black roots, honestly assimilated, and delivered with confident finality. Their act, onstage and off, is an art built on sexuality and anger. The effect is chaotic release.

The day after the press conference Mick Jagger and Keith Richard, the writing team and creative nucleus of the group, sit behind the mixing board in a studio listening intently to a playback of an album cut. The track was completely recorded and the mixing (the process by which the sixteen tracks of vocals and instrumentals are adjusted and refined proportionate to one another) was in process. "I want those drums out," says Jagger; "I want them like 'Hey, Bo Diddley.'" He throws out a pair of hands and approximates drum sounds to demonstrate.

"Midnight Rambler" thunders from the enormous studio speakers at top volume—mean, quick, blackhearted. It is mixed to satisfaction and the next cut is played back for inspection.

It is "Monkey Man," a tortuously disorganized rock 'n' roll extravaganza piled high with innuendo and a deafening, heavy beat. The album, which would become *Let It Bleed*, is scheduled for release immediately on completion, for maximum impact during the tour. (At the time this was published, about a month later, "Honky Tonk Women" had been high on the charts for weeks.)

The success of a rock band depends a great deal on the coordination of airplay, booking, publicity, and performance dates. Now the Stones must tackle the problem of a follow-up single.

Allen Klein has arrived at the session. He is business manager for both the Beatles and the Stones, a music business heavy with a mean reputation and a tough track record. He stands medium tall, a stocky, considered man, his arms bulging from a short-sleeved knit shirt, his hands knotted in each other.

Jagger, Klein, assorted acolytes, and I retire to a smaller room to listen to a few tracks of the album, trying to extract a single. One contender is played; it seems to be the best bet. Jagger closes his eyes, clenches his fists, and dances about, swaying, jerking, writhing, punching out the beat.

At the end Klein says, "I still like it."

"So do I," replies Jagger, "but is it a hit?"

"I don't know; I can't pick records."

Jagger is a picture of perplexity, his cool blue-gray eyes fixed elsewhere. He pouts silently.

"I didn't like 'Honky Tonk Women' at first either."

"Neither did I, right?"

"Look, we don't have to release a single for the tour; it would be good, but we don't have to; the album's still selling."

"We still have a problem getting it played, except for the FM stations. We can release a single or not. What do you want to do?"

"I don't want to; I don't know."

"Okay, we won't release a single. I'll put together a promo album, three or four cuts from the album, and we can tie in with local stations on the tour. If they want to cover the tour they guarantee us so many hours of airplay on the promo. That's not payola, right?"

"Let's not release a single, then."

"I'm with you."

"Okay, so what are we doing?"

Jagger leaves the room for a moment to check out the studio. Klein flashes an affectionate paternal glance in the direction of his exit. For a moment he glows.

"Honky Tonk Women" was the single of the year and they didn't like it at first? They're nervous about the tour, nervous enough to have a test concert somewhere in Colorado before the official opening in Los Angeles.

The unpublicized Colorado concert is already sold out. In this, the year of Woodstock, *Tommy*, Abbey Road, the Isle of Wight, and the Chicago conspiracy trials. The Rolling Stones' tour could blow the whole pop scene wide open with an explosion of energy and a tidal wave of rejuvenation.

Jagger returns to the room, and they quibble about airtime, singles, and payola. Jagger chews thoughtfully on a knuckle. The heel of his hand is scarred from a recent mishap: a gun on the set of the movie *Ned Kelly* went off accidentally while they were shooting in Australia. Once his arm was broken in the crush of a post-concert melee. The slight scar on his head is a battle wound inflicted by an overzealous fan and a piece of broken chair during a performance. These are hazards of the trade to a rock 'n' roll star.

People come in with photographs. Klein grabs them and squints through the transparencies in the light. "We gotta get this stuff out right away or those idiots will use pictures from the Year One. I'll bring them back to New York tonight."

Klein and Jagger hunch over a table. Klein is scrawling figures on a sheet of paper. "Don't you worry about the bread. If you need 30,000 pounds to live on, we've got to earn you 300,000, right?" Jagger brightens. Klein draws boxes around the figures. The conversation gets disjointed. Jagger goes back to the studio to help with the mixing.

In the studio, producer Jimmy Miller and engineer Glyn Johns are sitting in front of the controls. They are tops in their trade, viable alchemists to the finest rock product from England. Richards is reaching for the toggles and dials. Johns asks him to leave the board alone—too many hands, no control.

The room is heavy with concentration. The music is on the tape, the profile of the songs is taking form. Jagger crumples over the board. Annoyance, delight, a wince, a grudging smile, then a grin of satisfaction flicker in rapid succession over his face.

The mobility of his expressions tells more about the man and his art than anything he'll give to an interviewer. His smile is at once mischievously evil and warmly endearing. His careful eyes show both outrage and concern. Behind them is rare instinctual genius. His presence is electric; his movements are quick, spontaneous, with a kind of animal grace only children and born stars possess.

Faces behind the board are mesmerized. A charge of excitement flashes around the room. It's a wonderful album, bursting with excesses, characterized by impassioned finesse and doltish humor.

"Here, see where it changes, goes from fourths to eighths? There's a lot of time changes and every one is accompanied by a change in the sound; that's what we're trying to bring out on this one."

Staunch professionalism. The days of headlong record ramblings have passed for this group. In rock 'n' roll, they've got it covered. From the chaos on the tape the order of the excitement begins to take shape.

Somebody comes in with paper sacks full of soda and chips. They will be working far into the night.

In the next few months the Stones toured America, their first tour in years. They took the pop scene by storm, bringing crowds to their feet with fists uplifted with "Street Fighting Man," plunging them into urgency with "Satisfaction," and at each concert showering roses all over the audiences as their last song faded. They were the theater of the times, strutting the angst, machismo, and hope across each stage they descended upon and whipping up a crossfire hurricane in their wake. Then they got the brilliant idea, the ultimate ego trip: Woodstock West. With the exception of Newport '65, every momentous pop event before Woodstock had taken place on the West Coast, and the surprise about

Woodstock was not that it happened at all, for it was predestined and even predictable, but that it happened when and where it did. But East Coast kids are a tougher lot; they hassle that miserable winter every year, and their lives are far more regimented than their cohorts' lives in California. East Coast kids could sit in the mud and rain for three days without freaking out. Californians are used to much more room.

With the same kind of problems that could have turned summer's Woodstock into a disaster at any moment, the Stones' crew prepared for the free concert at Altamont in December.

With my friends Earl McGrath and Diane Gardiner I took a flight to an airport in Livermore, where we hailed a cab. The cabbie wanted to go to the festival, so we stopped at his home so he could change his clothing and at a liquor store so he could lay in a supply. He drove us to the festival, parked his car. We all got out and the driver disappeared into the crowd camped out at the gate. It was a cold, clammy night, but kids slept on the ground on the hillside. The moment daylight revealed the speedway, they charged down the hill en masse and stormed the gates, tearing them down to get in.

That was the first indication that this event—which, like Woodstock, teetered on the edge of crisis—would fall on the other side of the line.

Bad wine spiked with bad acid got loose in great quantities in the crowd. Bad vibes multiplied. We found the Jefferson Airplane retinue, who put us up on the stage. We didn't stay long. We decided to get out of Dodge immediately after Paul Kantner stopped their set because one of the Hell's Angels working as security punched out Marty Balin.

On my way out I paused to try to comfort a boy of seventeen who was sobbing uncontrollably through a bad trip. I embraced him and stroked him as he screamed and wept. He eventually quieted down but couldn't tell me what was the matter. My friends and I hitchhiked to the airport courtesy of a Mexican couple who picked us, and a couple of other festival escapees, up. Five of us jammed into the back seat. The Mexican couple asked us if Altamont was what all festivals were like. We were too miserable to answer either way. We looked at each other, muttering "Livermore, oh Livermore, quoth the raven, 'Livermore,'" again and again until the whole car was singing it.

Just as the Sixties had begun several weeks late, they ended a few weeks early, and we were riding the downhill fall. The Technicolor whirlwind had picked up a generation and spun them into a surreal collage of fantasy and reality that flared across the imagination of our most daring dreams and deepest feared nightmares. It gave us wings to fly and landed us ceremoniously on our asses with the unassailable truth that it was us, all us, the good and the bad of it, ours and ours alone. In a pragmatic sense little had been changed. The war was still on, bigotry still existed. Very little had been altered but our minds. In the light of stark reality the revolution was only a prelude and the movement had not yet even been defined. For where the real revolution occurred was in our consciousness, in the way we found we could choose to live no matter what, if in fact we could make it matter at all. There was still an open question, and we were "it" in a game of media-tag.

Altamont was not the ending; it was only the symptom. We had learned everything in the previous decade but what a self-made tragedy, a youth culture assassination as evil and senseless as a presidential assassination, could teach us. And the dream had come full cycle once more. How ironic.

The myth of power to change the world by magic dies hard. The revolution was no longer in the hands of revolutionaries, but neither was it in the hands of politicians, gurus, or poets. What came to be known was that the revolution was a process of changing minds in changing times, a process evidenced in a symbolic lifestyle that served to unite and signal individuals into a recognizable mass that is just as easily described as a market. It exists in the souls of the people it touches, where it cannot be seen, where it cannot be charted, where it cannot be organized, and, most importantly, where, come what may, it cannot be stopped. And as a history and byproduct of those uproarious, mysterious years, its music emerged as its banner and its art.

At the height of anything, it begins to topple. That is what has propelled the human endeavor through the march of time. The Sixties—their phenomenal strides and vibrant culture—live as an intermittently evident subliminal radiance in the core of those who've experienced it. No other American musical era has been more culturally significant, more durable, or more lasting. Rock music of that luminous epoch was—and remains—emblematic of the freedom, foolhardiness, pathos, and courage of the times.

Appendix:
For the Record (Albums)

fikken

finger tipping icons bloom
33.3 RPMs
drained spider skull style
transistor sic Gloria

A few Sixties records I still love and reviews of them—some discs and some dish.

The Rolling Stones
***Beggars Banquet* (London)**
Saturday Review/January 25, 1969
"Beggars Triumph"

It begins with a crazed wildcat yelp and the primordial rhythms of hand drums on a rampage. It builds maniacally in intensity and complexity, the vocal brawling, the drums double gunning, the bass pumping, and the piano twisting the melody and rhythms together like so much heavy two-ply twine. The guitar whines, the voices hoot, and the lyrics blast the consciousness with a pageant of chaos. It's a bit pretentious in spots, has a couplet or two of unadorned truth and some specious nose-thumbing at history, but it gets you moving, jiving, and throttles you with its raunchy nastiness, the furious ranting that ranges far beyond the lyrics. "Sympathy for the Devil," the opening cut from *Beggars Banquet*, is a song full of what rock 'n' roll is all about, and for all who lament the bastardization of rock, the Rolling Stones have finally come through. They show all too clearly that what had generously passed for 1968 rock was just a scene of loudmouthed mediocrity and studio claptrap.

The Stones have created a primer in rock 'n' roll, blues and country rock, assimilating honestly and energetically. It's a definitive 1960s rock album, the best the Stones have ever done, perhaps one of the best rock albums ever assembled. It has a staunch, secure style, a crude artistic vigor, and it dishes the dirt with turbulent glee, raving wildly, restrained only to the point of coherence.

The blues songs on *Beggars Banquet* have sinewy melodies, careful harp work, and slinky bottleneck acoustic guitar figurations. "Dear Doctor," one of them, is a rectilinear country blues, a perfect vehicle for the drawling vocals, the loony falsetto, and cornball harmonies. Their country and blues songs are truly inspired, their assimilations of these older song styles are pervasive and unaffected, unlike the nostalgic tomfoolery on the Beatles or the campy re-creations on the Mothers of Invention's latest album, *Cruising with Ruben & the Jets* (the former is superficial, the latter a visionary resurrection of an old form intact). The Stones' derivative product is the result of four seasoned rock 'n' roll men affectionately goofing on Johnny Cash, Buck Owens, Son House, Elmore James, the Byrds' *Sweetheart of the Rodeo*, and Dylan's

John Wesley Harding. Like the latter, the Stones "drink to the hard working people/ . . . drink to the lowly of birth 'raise your glass to the good and the evil . . . drink to the salt of the earth'" (from "Salt of the Earth").

One of the finest songs on the album, "Jigsaw Puzzle," is openly reminiscent of Dylan. It's a narrative, flowing with characters and instant vignettes, a preoccupation with outlaws and outcasts in their latter-day incarnations: tramps, grandmas, soldiers, and a rock 'n' roll band:

> . . . *the singer looks so angry at being thrown to the lions*
> *and the bass player looks so nervous about the girls outside*
> *and the drummer he was shattered*
> *trying to keep on time and the guitar player looks damaged*
> *they've been outcasts all their lives.*

"Me, I'm waiting so patiently," goes the refrain, "with my woman on the floor, just trying to do my jigsaw puzzle/before it rains anymore."

The Stones have always enjoyed and excelled at lusty music and joyfully lecherous lyrics. They're the evil loners, the Marlon Brandos of pop, Hell's Angels on a rock 'n' roll stage. Mick Jagger, a prancing, lascivious satyr, is the prototypical sex symbol of rock. The bluesy backbeat of "Parachute" is couched in the heavy concupiscent symbolism of the lyrics, a tradition of the folk-blues heritage from which it draws. On the other hand, "Stray Cat Blues," one of the outstanding rock songs on the album, is explicitly lewd and sadistic.

It's a raw, leering song about a fifteen-year-old girl climbing the stairs to find the Stones. It begins with a salty snicker and driving beat. It builds and twists with brutal rhythms, an explosive balance of tensions and a shattering release. "You say you got a friend, she's wilder than you," Jagger gloats. "Why don't you bring her upstairs/If she's so wild she can join in too/ . . . don't scratch like that/Oh, yeah, you're a strange stray cat/bet your mama don't know you bite like that/I bet she never saw you scratch my back."

A classic Stones song, brilliantly done. *Beggars Banquet* is not an album that will be cooed over by condescending classical music critics or patronizing college professors trying to be chic. There is nothing for either here, no intellectual profundity or melodic innovation, no avant-garde experimentalism or mixing board contortions. It's a raw and raunchy rock album, delightfully vicious and deliciously bestial. Its depth is in its dark, tangled textures, and its weight is in its kinetic density. With their new producer, Jimmy Miller, the Stones have outdone everyone trying to recapture the slavish intensity of rock (including the Beatles), and, most amazingly, they've outdone themselves. The heights of fury they reach on *Beggars Banquet* are awesome, almost terrifying.

◆

Joan Baez
One Day at a Time (**Vanguard**)
Saturday Review/March 28, 1970
"One Day at a Time"

The poet Richard Fariña died in the spring of 1966 at a tender age, leaving this world his earthly remains: songs, poems, a book, and a widow, Mimi, Joan Baez's younger sister. While he was alive, Joan was fond of referring to Fariña, affectionately, as "my sister's crazy man." Crazy (in the way it has come to mean human) he might have been; Fariña was a rover and a lover, ever the rambler and gambler a long way from home, and who is there to say that, wherever he may be, that is not still what he is? He was an observer with an eye for the absurd, a writer so possessed with the quixotic that each time he touched his world to his pen it emerged more uproarious and more ironically real. Fariña's sphere of influence might have been select and esoteric for the times, but his persona was such that he moved every soul he touched. In those inevitable "if-only" reminiscences of the folk movement that was in bloom during the early Sixties, eyes go misty at the mention of his name. The poet Richard Fariña died in the hell-bent-for-leather manner of his writings, in a motorcycle accident, on his way to a party celebrating the publication of his first novel, *Been Down So Long It Looks Like Up to Me.* Nobody thought it was to have ended quite that way.

Mimi Fariña remarried some few years later, to producer Melvin Milan, the subject of the first song on Joan Baez's new album *One Day at a Time.* "Sweet Sir Galahad" is the song, a rare and beautiful Baez original with a melody so supple, lyrics so feeling, and a vocal treatment so silken it heralds the most beautiful Baez album since *Farewell, Angelina.*

"Sweet Sir Galahad" must have been hard to sing with Baez's own sweet Galahad, her husband David Harris, now imprisoned in the federal penal camp at Safford, Arizona. His crime against society was draft resistance, and his sentence three years. This album was recorded just before Baez's first visit to her husband in prison. That was in September; their child, Gabriel, was yet to be born. A month earlier, at Woodstock, one of the most moving moments was Joan Baez standing in front of the hundreds of thousands gathered there, her guitar balanced on a belly full of child, singing "Joe Hill," a song done with touching brilliance on this album.

With the patience and persistence, the courage and love that are present in various forms throughout, this album was recorded in only two days, Baez on guitar and a slew of Nashville's finest supporting her. Of all the albums she has recorded lately, this one stands out as the finest marriage of singer, songs, and accompanists; of a woman, her music, her convictions, and her man.

If the new music has a singular heroine, it is Joan Baez, although she, in characteristic modesty, would decline any such label. She was the voice that set the folk movement ablaze, a leading lady who more than anyone brought Bob Dylan to the forefront of contemporary music by singing his songs, praising his talent, and introducing him in person to share many stages on which she was the star, before Dylan had a personal following outside the folk clique.

The folk movement in those days was inseparably involved with the civil rights movement. For some reason, I've been thinking back lately to that lifetime ago when we all thought peaceful demonstrations were the real answer to social injustice. Baez then, and still, personified the spirit of Gandhi with a strong commitment to nonviolence. Dylan bawled "The Times They Are A-Changin'," and by now they sure have a-changed. Most of the people I still know from that time have a-changed in terms of their reactions to what's happening now politically. Demonstration is not quite the word for what goes on when idealism and brutality clash with a force so disillusioning you cannot tell one from another. Baez led, participated in, and performed at so many of those early peaceful marches and demonstrations, always encouraging nonviolence as the order of the day. Times were a-changing, but Baez remained firm in that respect, although at a later mobilization in Washington, D.C., she was reported to have quipped: "Behave nonviolently or I'll kill you!"

Although she let the mantle of superstardom fall from her slight shoulders, her devotion to the belief in the better side of humanity was evident in all phases of her life. She met and married David Harris, practically on his way to jail at the time.

There is a strange, sad rendition of the Rolling Stones' "No Expectations," complemented by a traditional treatment of Bonnie and Delaney's "Ghetto," both interpretations of contemporary compositions in a folk style. She sings "Carry It On," the song for all movements, reworks a standard of hers, "Long Black Veil," and jives along with a happy-go-lucky arrangement of the homesick blues of "Take Me Back to the Sweet Sunny South."

"Jolie Blonde" is listed as being traditional, but I've never heard anything quite like it before, a country fiddle slithering into a bayou snake dance, while the incandescent Baez vocal instrument whoops and wails wordlessly at intervals behind it. The high point of the record is "A Song for David," where she sings:

> *In my heart I will wait by the stony gate.*
> *And the little one in my arms will sleep. . . .*
> *The stars in your sky are the same stars in mine,*
> *And both prisoners of this life are we.*
> *Through the same troubled waters we carry our time—*
> *You and the convicts and me*

It is an album that stands unique among many released this month, an album of a wife, a mother, a lover who sings of liberties and lies, of ghettos and prisons, of bodies and souls. There is the voice of the sorrows of her sisters and herself, each in its place, one at a time, carrying on.

And that is the heroism of this small woman and her music, a strength that is comprehending and still soft, a vision prey to the violence poured forth daily, the militance that has come to define this spasm of America's labor pains, a vision still strong, firmly rooted in the insistence of inner and outer peace as a way of life. The album is a voice in her virtual absence from the performing scene, closing with the title song, a final statement that is a lovely voice amidst the incredulity of her situation, sharing her philosophy and offering it to the spiritually needy:

I live one day at a time
I dream one dream at a time
Yesterday's dead and tomorrow is blind
I live one day at a time

◆

Paul McCartney
McCartney (Apple)
Saturday Review/May 30, 1970
"McCartney on His Own"

Several weeks ago, to almost nobody's surprise, Paul McCartney announced that he had left the Beatles and was releasing a solo album. He added that his family was giving him more pleasure than his group. John Lennon retorted: "It's a simple fact that he can't have his own way so he's causing chaos. I put out four albums [without the rest of the Beatles] last year, and I didn't say a word about quitting."

It was a bitter way to blow a myth. When I spoke to John last year he described Paul as an "intellectual ostrich." It seems there had been problems with the Beatles for quite some time. There was internal dissent about managerial affairs. You can hear Paul's feelings on it in "You Never Give Me Your Money" on *Abbey Road*, and the erratic nature of the material on the previous (plain white) album indicated a rift among the Beatles.

John Lennon's marriage to Yoko Ono and Paul's later marriage to Linda Eastman were moves in opposite directions for the writing Beatles. Beatle press aide Derek Taylor mentioned that John's absorption in Yoko was coming between him and Paul and they weren't writing songs together as they used to. McCartney's announcement was merely a conclusion of what any Beatle fan could hear in the music itself, and the "split" was not so much a breakup but a calculated play for publicity centered around McCartney's eponymously titled solo album.

A conditioned entertainer rarely changes his image; it confuses a faithful public. With groups the problem is more complex. The Beatles, who defied almost every show business tradition, are a collective image of four individualistic personalities, each growing in a different direction. A group's personality is based on the most obvious aspect of the conglomerate, but with the Beatles it was simply John, Paul, George, and Ringo—together. Beatle music may have changed from album to album or from song to song, but one thing was vital and inviolate: They were the Beatles— forever. It's a difficult posture to sustain when a man is as serious about his private life as he is about his career, and Paul McCartney cast an old showbiz rule and the public image of his group to the wind and chucked it. It was a most unsympathetically timed move: The next, and most likely final, Beatle album, *Let It Be*, was just about to be released, having been rescued from a state of utter disorganization by Phil Spector, one of pop's first and most widely celebrated producers.

McCartney's solo album—inspired, he says, by the installation of four-track recording equipment and a single microphone in his home—may not so much punctuate the demise of the Beatles as signal the beginning of a very promising something else.

McCartney is one of the few entirely successful "home" albums released. It's encouraging, after several failures by other artists, groups, and producers, to see that music of this kind can be recorded intact without a bevy of borrowed superstars and the Ikettes behind them. Linda McCartney is the only other artist involved in *McCartney*; her intimately beautiful photographs decorate the sleeve, and her uncertain harmonies waft through some of the songs (she can't carry a tune in a bucket, but her *oooh-ahhh*s are heavy and her presence is charming).

There is a great deal of padding on the record, and at that the album seems very short (neither the label copy nor the jacket gives timings). But the feel of the album is whole in the few songs that work, in the mystifying fragments that just sit there and sound pretty, in the roundhouse spirit of the entire package. One could spend hours listening to such simple, sparse, often unfinished music, and, having heard it all, never hear enough of it.

"La, la, la, the lovely Linda" may not be one of the most original or stimulating lyrics Paul McCartney ever wrote, but it certainly is one of the most engaging. "That Would Be Something" is another careful fragment, the rhythm irresistible, the dynamics complete. "Valentine Day" is a short instrumental, a little bit McCartney, a little bit Beatles, and a lot of something else, indeed. Like many of its companions on the record, it is unresolved, spontaneous, a shred of a few musical ideas strung together and left there. "Every Night" is the first complete song, but it somehow can't compete with the variety of enticing ideas set down before it. "Hot as Sun/Glasses" is a track of beautifully phrased melodic structures, broken by an uncut bit of shenanigans and ended right there. "Junk" is a lazy, laconic song, so simple and undemanding that the track is repeated on Side 2 without voices as "Singalong Junk."

"Man, We Was Lonely" is the exception on the album. A hearty, homebound tune, full of fireside jive and family fun, it comes off as a robust, full song. The spontaneous quality of the items (one can hardly call the majority of them songs) on the album was preserved by careful studio discipline in producing the homemade tapes. Since Paul plays all the instruments, they are all overdubbed, and the vocals are as they were, hardly touched or changed. The clinkers were all left in, and they only heighten the implicit friendliness of the music.

Beatle music has become a document of the individual Beatles, and Beatle albums a chronicle of themselves. An unknown could never get away with producing the kind of album that *McCartney* is; there would be no frame of reference to cradle it. *McCartney* is musically a primitive album, but its fascination lies in the unraveling of the life and times, at this particular juncture, of an individual whose participation in the Beatles has influenced the life and times of the millions in his audience. It is that audience which will appreciate *McCartney*. Whereas other Beatle albums have had a much wider range in appeal, being the product of the aspects of the group and producer/arranger George Martin, or an advance in the formalization of pop so critical as to merit attention from those outside that intense but select area of interest, *McCartney* is by and for the family. With the single exception of the Band's recorded music, no home pop album ever recorded has emerged as anything but egotistical and incestuous.

"Teddy Boy" was a song idea originally intended for the Beatles' *Let It Be* album, and the original (pre-Spector) tapes I heard have Paul riffing through it, teaching it to John, George, and Ringo, with each of them putting a piece of himself into it. It went on and on with nothing emerging but a glimpse of how the Beatles try to make a song together and don't. "Teddy Boy" appears on the McCartney album as a ditty, one where Linda's frail harmony fills in the open space where the rest of the Beatles might have participated.

There is some beautiful pop in the album. "Maybe I'm Amazed" is a song that would benefit any album and "Kreen-

Akrore" a track that extends as graceful and final a parting gesture as could be expressed. If McCartney was embarrassingly ungainly about the manner in which he released his divisive statement, *McCartney* speaks well for his decision on much more sensitive grounds.

◆

Jerry Jeff Walker, Joni Mitchell, Tim Hardin
Mr. Bojangles (Atco)
Song to a Seagull (Reprise)
Tim Hardin 3 (Verve Forecast)
New York Times/December 29, 1968
"Three Who Sing Their Own Songs"

Jerry Jeff Walker, one of the solo singers surviving the explosion of rock groups, can now be heard on his first album. "Mr. Bojangles," the song that gives the album its title, is a masterpiece of a pop song, one of the finest contemporary folk poems ever set to melody.

Its first public airing came about a year and a half ago during an underground radio show over WBAI-FM, on a midnight to whenever-they-feel-like-going-off-the-air affair called *Radio Unnameable*, hosted by Bob Fass. On that night, Walker and his long-time accompanist, David Bromberg, came up to the studio with their guitars and stayed to play and sing for hours. At 4 a.m., they did "Mr. Bojangles."

Bojangles is a weathered, tattered, itinerant street dancer with a liking for the bottle. Walker transfigures him and dances him through dreams and tales of streets immemorial, the way a puppeteer dances a marionette through its paces. Meanwhile,

Bromberg plays a nimble guitar countermelody which patters and highsteps like the wizened old man's shoes.

Though they must suffer a bit by comparison, Walker's other songs measure well against "Mr. Bojangles." "Gypsy Songman," a portrait of the artist as a Greenwich Village minnesinger, is as cunning a song sketch and as colorful a folk myth as "Mr. Bojangles." "Little Bird" is a soft, evanescent love song with an elegance born of simplicity and immediacy. "I Makes Money. Money Don't Make Me" is a down home, nitty-gritty statement of integrity. "The Ballad of the Hulk" is a long, scathing, free-form monologue done in talking-blues style, pleasantly reminiscent of Dylan's "Subterranean Homesick Blues." "My Old Man," a song about the artist's father, closes the album tenderly.

Walker's voice is supple and luxurious and his songs are handcrafted, skillfully constructed and buffed to a rich luster. His subject matter is homespun, rustic and as curiously inglorious as the old gent described in "Mr. Bojangles."

The programing on the album is significantly well-effected. There is a comfortable balance of material, which results in a genuine unity. The arrangements—which are particularly tasteful, and sensitive to the artist's nuances—explore different textures of the single tonal quality Walker and his guitar supply. As an album of a solo artist's work, this one is outstanding.

Joni Mitchell's songs are the product of her fascination with changes of heart, changes of mind, changes of season, and changes of self. She's written, in "Both Sides Now" and "Circle Game," two stunningly simple parables of life that have been recorded by dozens of other artists: Judy Collins, Buffy Sainte-Marie, Dave Van Rank, and Tom Rush, to name but a few, and that is why this very independent artist did not include them in her initial album. On *Song to a Seagull* Joni Mitchell writes and sings of the people and places she's been, from the windy Saskatchewan prairies where she was raised to the seaside which entrances her and to the big cities. Her lyrics are poetic portraits, artistically detailed and honest. Her melodies are exotic, taking unusual turns in time and tone. She takes the listener on a wistful journey in her quest for honesty, in her search for human values.

The songs about herself are songs for today's independent young woman and the peculiar problems she faces. "I Had a King" is a sad, backward glance at the artist's broken marriage, without bitterness or self-reproach. "Cactus Tree" speaks of today's young divorcee on the rebound, "so busy being free." "Nathan La Franeer" is her definitive comment on New York City cab drivers.

It would be good to be able to say that *Song to a Seagull* is as successful an album as Joni Mitchell is a performer and composer. But, the engineering is uneven, her voice sometimes sounds shaky. The songs, accompanied only by Miss Mitchell's guitar, beg for adornment and their sequence works to decided disadvantage of the material. The effect is monotony, albeit a gentle monotony. Any one of these frailties would ruin an album of a lesser talent, but *Song to a Seagull* offers rewards in spite of itself.

After several disappointing tries, someone has finally recorded Tim Hardin the way those of us who have seen him live know him. *Tim Hardin 3* is an immensely satisfying album, containing rare performances of the artist's best-known material: "The Lady Came From Baltimore," "If I Were a Carpenter," "Misty Roses," "Red Balloon," and "You Upset the Grace of Living When You Lie." The jazzy backup ensemble complements and embellishes Hardin's trembly, aching voice, which floats in the unlikely middle ground between folk and jazz, far removed from the gusto of pop. Hardin is a truly individual phenomenon, a man and a voice and songs that reveal his pain and hopes and fears. He strikes a crippling blow at human indifference.

He stands vulnerable in the midst of his music, articulating despair and loneliness, questioning the things that are lacking between people and, finally, questioning himself. There is deep comfort in Hardin's songs, as well as a document of feelings which run almost too deep to be controlled. In the communication of these feelings, the sharing of human pain and hope, lies the very highest sort of art.

◆

Crosby, Stills and Nash
Crosby, Stills & Nash (**Atlantic**)
Saturday Review/May 31, 1969
"Renaissance Fair"

Now and then, and not very often at that, there's a pop album that stands head and shoulders above the rest, one so characteristic and distinctive that it defies competition or comparison. It doesn't appear from out of nowhere; actually it may be rather predictable. When it is finally released, it is a source of the affirmation and joy which is the lifeblood of rock 'n' roll.

Rock has muddled around for several months, and while there has been enough jamming around and back-to-the-roots exploration, there has been no real breakthrough for quite some time. The field has not been fallow, but the music was out of breath, marking time. A fistful of refugees from prominent groups has been larking around and something had to come of it. There are now several second-generation groups at work, and if the first Crosby, Stills and Nash album is any indication of the best of what's to come, I, for one, can't wait for more.

David Crosby left the Byrds some time ago. Stephen Stills was a vital member of the now disbanded Buffalo Springfield, a very special group which, though it was hardly recognized until its dying hour, was one of the freshest, most distinctive bands of its era. Graham Nash has recently left the Hollies, the most fetching vocal group England has produced (other than the Beatles). All of them are gifted, experienced vocalists, musicians, and writers; each has several brilliant contributions to his credit. Together they have produced the most outrageously lovely album to freshen the pop scene in many months.

Their first album, *Crosby, Stills & Nash*, is nothing short of a treasure. They have created music that is both meaningful and new, yet natural and free. It is packed with songs of the changes that have made searchers of all of us.

Their music combines pure elements of rock 'n' roll, and still it is bashful and innocent, about the happiest sound since laughter. They've mixed the charged heights of the Byrds, the country coquettishness of the Buffalo Springfield, and the sheer tensile strength of the Hollies. With this album the rock revolution is over (in that it has irrevocably begun) and the renaissance begins.

The album is noteworthy, among many features, for its generous use of acoustic guitars applied in totally refreshing ways. They use harmonies, counterpoint, rhythms, and instrumental combinations deftly and sparingly. A combination of four songs by Stephen Stills, "Suite Judy Blue Eyes," is a bruised but undismayed series of love songs to the same lady on three different days, and the final verse, sung in Spanish against a Latin tempo, is a love song to Cuba.

Graham Nash's "Marrakesh Express" follows, an energetic, deliriously happy trip song that pulls out all the stops until Morocco. David Crosby wrote and sings "Guinnevere," a fantasy portrait of a golden lady. It shimmers with honeyed warmth and tender imagery, at times a shade too lush. Crosby's voice has mellowed considerably since the Byrds; he now sings lead as effectively as he's been known to sing harmony and has beautiful vocal control. The balmy resonance of "Guinnevere" is juxtaposed by another Stills song, "You Don't Have to Cry," accompanied by a single acoustic guitar and fancy-free finger-picking.

Side 1 closes with "Pre-Road Downs" by Graham Nash. His songs are charming and unaffected, yet always somehow humorously odd. Here he sets a musician's life to song, a song of leaving, traveling, the back-breaking schedule and heartbreaking restlessness a latter-day Pied Piper must cope with. Nash, though, is a sly bloke and manages to turn the tune into an impish tunelet, riding out the ups as well as the downs. It's extremely well done.

Crosby, Stills, and Paul Kantner of the Jefferson Airplane wrote "Wooden Ships" on Side 2. It's a dystopic science fiction creation beginning with two disembodied voices meeting after a disaster, sharing food, wondering why, and asking "Who won?" The song flashes back on the present, agonizes over civilization's shortcomings, then, almost resentfully, sails away on a radiant cloud of vocalized *ahhhhhh*s. "We are leaving, you don't need us," it reproaches, while an extended instrumental break vividly creates a scene of wooden ships at sea filled with bewildered but happy expatriates.

Both Crosby's and Stills's songs throughout their careers have reflected political concern. "Wooden Ships" has the added dimension of creative fictionalization, engagingly elusive imagery, a distinct and refreshing musical identity. Nash's vocal on his "Lady of the Island" was recorded on the first take; it fit just as it fell from his lips. David Crosby, in some of his most moving vocal work ever, sings a circular countermelody behind him.

Stills's "Helplessly Hoping" has a genuinely infectious melody. His lyrics mix alliteration and metonymy throughout, and the feelings fall through the playful tonal games like so much shyness. It is accompanied by an acoustic guitar and very economical use of wily vocal shenanigans.

Crosby's "Long Time Coming," with an insinuating organ line running through the outrage like a distant siren, was composed on the morning after Senator Robert F. Kennedy's assassination, and it contains the elements of pain and numbness that gripped those hours. Two songs by Stills, "49 Reasons" and "Bye Bye Baby," were combined to form the last song on the album, another "suite" to complement the first. It reels and rocks until the last sinewy guitar line quivers and fades, capping a magnificent song and a magnificent album.

Stills, it might be noted, plays most of the instrumental music on the album. In addition to his facile lead guitar, he composed and arranged many of the instrumental tracks as well as playing electric bass and organ on many of them. The "violin sound" on Nash's "Pre-Road Downs" is Stills on a doubled guitar played backward by reversing the tape and mixed into the arrangement through a sixteen-track board. Similarly, he is responsible for almost every piece of the arrangements on his own songs and the entire conception of the "Long Time Coming" instrumental track. All things considered, with this album Stills can be counted among the pantheon songwriter-musician-vocalists of pop, in the same league as Dylan and Lennon-McCartney.

Crosby and Nash are professionals—experienced, refined musicians with an enormous amount of recording triumphs behind them. They surpass themselves on this album, and when the three of them harmonize it's like a formation flight. Assisted by percussionist Dallas Taylor, the three have created a soft, happy morning of sound. For forty-three minutes, it's like not being alone anymore.

◆

The Beatles
Abbey Road (Apple/Capitol)
Saturday Review/October 25, 1969
"Abbey Road"

Whenever a new Beatles album is released it's generally a critical and social as well as a musical event. Rock fans spend an entire week listening to the blessed product, radio stations play it incessantly, teachers bring it to class for discussion, and retailers scramble for stock. Musicians listen and compare; opinions, analyses, hypotheses, and suspicions fly; much is written; much is discussed; and whatever else happens, millions of Beatles lovers on all cultural levels are intensely involved with the new album for a week or so. The world is more fun for a little while; then things sort of settle down to the usual general chaos.

This Beatles album, *Abbey Road*, is pure beauty, a wonderful album. Some folk poet once said that in ugly times beauty is the only true protest, and, if nothing else, *Abbey Road* bears him out. There are no nagging inconsistencies in *Abbey Road*, no finger-pointing or exasperating enigmas, just a whole mess of sublimely executed, elegantly composed Beatles music. Yea, team.

Shimmering brilliance and unbounded creative energy grace every moment of *Abbey Road*. It is alternately bright, silly, warm, funny, childlike, funky, and glib, seamlessly bound into a perfectly molded entity born fresh into the day. All the insecure raggedness of the plain white album is gone and *Abbey Road* emerges a glowing, cohesive tour de force.

It opens with a fresh, salty, rock 'n' roll stompalong, "Come Together," peppered with spicy Lennon one-liners, underpinned with a jolly boogie beat. It's a midnight mover, good old rock 'n' roll. "Something," a love song suffused with tenderness, follows; it is certainly one of, if not the most beautiful songs George Harrison has ever written. He feels his way through the song, instinctively cutting through its body and into the core, emoting so clearly and so gracefully that at the moment he peals "I don't know, I don't know," it is shown that even what is not known can be understood.

"Maxwell's Silver Hammer," in the best McCartney music-hall, rinky-tink tradition follows, a jolly ditty of mischief and manslaughter, full of musical imagination and lyrical buffoonery. You can hear his losing battle to keep a straight face while singing. "Oh! Darling" is a blistering rock 'n' roll wailing wall, a grand old John Lennon screamer. It's constructed simply around a conventional rock 'n' roll chord pattern, reaches its height with steamroller guitar assaults, the vocal roaring, gasping, and gagging until its relieved last, dying breath. Ringo wrote a children's song for this album, "Octopus's Garden." It's full of sweet silliness, cartoon images, and pretty guitar figures. The melody has the charm of a puppet show; the harmonies are sweet, lush, and innocently sincere behind Ringo's lead vocal. It's pure enchantment, very simple and colorful, and during the short upbeat instrumental break, bubbly noises rise behind the music. It's all carried off with straight-faced, childish delight, and on pure musical terms it stands up to any other song on Side 1.

The final cut on the first side is "I Want You (She's So Heavy)." It's another broad-beamed hard rock number that builds into an ear-splitting maximum-volume chord crescendo, then fades instantly, so dramatically that you don't know what hit you. The first side is spectacular, programmed for abrupt contrast and crisp definition of the material. Songs of completely different character are placed next to one another with a conscious sense of pace. The result is that each song is set off to the ultimate advantage of its contents and is surrounded by material that complements it, leaving its identity intact. Programing is what makes an album an album and not just a string of songs, and the programing on *Abbey Road* is as good as any and all of the material arranged on it.

If Side 1 is the study in contrasts, Side 2 is the ultimate in tonal blending and rhythmic balance. It is the sun side, suffused with mellowed warmth, woven together with motifs, bridging, reprises, surprises, with all the songs set within one another. It opens with "Here Comes the Sun," an awakening, an exaltation of the dawn, "sun, sun, here we come." "You Never Give Me Your Money," a song of estrangement, business, and art, follows, leading through with the same sonic quality. "Sun King," picking up the tonality and theme of the first cut, is next; then come five mini-songs interwoven in a casual suite, exerting the identity of each section gently but firmly in a careful but easy structure.

The racing upbeat is broken by "Golden Slumbers," an overflowing lullaby, leading easily into "Carry That Weight" and a reprise ("The End") of "You Never Give Me Your Money," back into "Carry That Weight," and, be it ever so humble, Ringo takes a ten-second drum solo in a rhythm break. The chords flood up again into a two-liner conclusion: "And in the end the love you take/is equal to the love you make," a moment of silence after a beautiful fade, then another chord burst, and a bit of McCartney sass about Her Majesty ends the album with an afterthought.

The album is completely cycled, ready to be played from the start again and again. The balance and feeling for the material on this album is a brilliant example of the Beatles' perspective on their own work, the variety and ultimately the synthesis of the sounds they make. The range of musical sounds in this album goes from tiny cricket noises to a Moog synthesizer and everything in between. Each cut is clear and full but never overloaded. The album changes shape each time I listen to it, each listening unravels new discoveries in every song. This is one Beatles album of which I will never tire.

◆

Delaney and Bonnie; John B. Sebastian; Crosby, Stills, Nash, and Young
Eric Clapton (Atco)
John B. Sebastian (Reprise)
Déjà Vu (Atlantic)
Saturday Review/April 25, 1970
"Friends and Neighbors: Alive, Alive-O"

Live albums are deceptively hard to record. Sound systems in concert halls and clubs are generally inferior and the ambience, the interplay between performers and audience, nearly impossible to capture without the visual and emotive stimulus present at a live rock concert. There are many groups that can rip it up in a live show and, minus an audience, seem pale on disc. On the other side of the coin there are those groups so reliant on the gadgetry of a recording studio that their live shows rarely approach their records.

Delaney and Bonnie can do it all. A little less than a year ago they released a studio album (Elektra) full of ballads, spirituals, rock, and soul. While it was far from a monster hit, the attention it received was so intensely favorable that it became a cause célèbre among the rock cognoscenti. Anywhere the duo and their band would play, there would be more stars in the audience than on the stage. At one point Eric Clapton, a bizarrely talented guitarist (refugee from, in chronological order, John Mayall's Blues Band, the Yardbirds, Cream, and the superhype disaster Blind Faith), began jamming with Delaney and Bonnie and Friends and wanted to join the group. There were contractual difficulties, since Clapton was signed to Atlantic, Delaney and Bonnie and Friends to Elektra, and Clapton's English managers would not allow a release for Clapton to record with the group. Elektra stepped out of the way and released Delaney and Bonnie and Friends to Atlantic, where, even though Clapton has split from the group, Delaney and Bonnie must remain.

They toured England with Eric Clapton and Friends, which also includes Dave Mason, formerly of the sorely missed Traffic. But an entourage of superstars included in the backup group of musicians ("Friends") is not the substance of the success of Delaney and Bonnie. They have an intrinsic vibrancy, an irresistible driving musical conception, unique and utterly refreshing. With the temporary addition of Clapton to the group they drew a large audience quickly. It wouldn't be risking much to say that it is theirs to keep.

One of the best live albums I've heard is *Delaney and Bonnie and Friends on Tour with Eric Clapton*, recorded by Jimmy Miller and Glyn Johns, the producer-engineer team responsible for the incandescent quality of more recent Rolling Stones albums. They have captured brilliantly the crackling excitement of a live rock 'n' roll show. "Come on, everybody!" urges Delaney, opening the concert. The music maintains a fast and frenzied pace throughout. The hoot and howl of the vocals, the shouting solos and piercing harmonies are an integral part, rather than a steering mechanism, of the show. The musicians throw in sparkling little licks, the rhythm section is particularly deft and pulsating. Delaney and Bonnie have everything—blues, soul, gospel, and rock—executed with the finesse only talent and good times together can bring out. I wouldn't be without either of their albums: the Elektra release for its variety and down-home soulfulness; the new Atco album for its living, laughing showmanship and Eric Clapton, too. *On Tour* is one live album that really makes it.

It must have been difficult deciding how to record John Sebastian's first "solo" album. Son of the classical harmonica virtuoso of the same name, the superlative singer, writer, guitarist was formerly the guiding genius of the Lovin' Spoonful. As a solo performer Sebastian is gently magnificent. His voice is supple, his songs ingenuously personal, and his presence magnetic in a very quiet, intense way. Alone, with his guitar and his wisecracks and maybe a friend who drops by to hear him and stays to play, Sebastian can pull tie-dyed colors out of a dark room and make music you'd never want to leave. He is also a musician's musician; Sebastian's fans are stars. This, his first solo album, was more than a year in the making.

The album, *John B. Sebastian*, contains eleven beautiful Sebastian songs accompanied by himself and friends, some prominent pop musicians with whom he often hangs out. They make an impressive collection of musical personalities, but tend to overshadow the special presence of John Sebastian alone. It may have been that the album is an attempt to project music made under the friendliest and most casual circumstances, but it doesn't live up to its promise. There are moments when the song itself will rise above the curious, often disorganized mixture of sounds behind it, but rarely does the peculiar brand of Sebastian magic come through. *John B. Sebastian* is easygoing music with side orders of Dallas Taylor, Harvey Brooks, Paul Harris, David Crosby, Danny Weiss, Stephen

Stills, Graham Nash, the Ikettes, Buzzy Linhart, and more; but nothing I can hear tells me why. Sebastian and friends are not as adept at combining talents (though those talents are individually spectacular) as Delaney and Bonnie and Friends, and what results is an album that, while hardly disappointing, leaves one with the feeling that letting well enough alone might have done the trick.

Neil Young, another ex-member of the disbanded Buffalo Springfield, joined Crosby, Stills and Nash just about the time when their first album was completed and has been with them ever since they started performing live. A brooding boy from the north country, Young has added a dark side to the group's sound, which partially accounts for the dramatic transition of their music from the first to the second album, *Déjà Vu*. Another factor in the shifting balance of the group is that most of its members have moved from Los Angeles to the San Francisco area. *Déjà Vu* varies a great deal in texture as compared with the first album, and there is an undercurrent of conflict which runs sporadically through the songs, breaking them apart, hurling them against one another, giving the album a sense of being jarred, startled, and, in parts, unsettled. It opens with another amazingly crafted Stephen Stills suite, "Carry On," with its shifting movements and fascinating instrumentation. My favorite, Graham Nash's "Teach Your Children," is a lovely melody enfolding a song for a child for all seasons. Jerry Garcia of the Grateful Dead plays a facile pedal steel accompaniment, making it one of the high points of the album. "Almost Cut My Hair" might not sound so blustery and cluttered had it not been placed directly after the fragile loveliness of "Teach Your Children." Neil Young's songs are alone and disturbing, fascinatingly introverted, and more imposing than the music

Crosby, Stills and Nash made without him. They are in the process of acquiring a heavier sound, and that transition accounts for some of the rough spots on the album. Live, they have worked out their individualities by doing the first half of the show acoustically, the second half electrically, with Dallas Taylor on drums and Greg Reeves on electric bass.

Déjà Vu includes Joni Mitchell's "Woodstock Song," the title song from the Warner Brothers movie of the legendary festival. Sung by Stephen Stills, it is more about the group than the festival. It was their second performance in public, and Stills had some graphic but unprintable remarks about their condition included in the film. Graham Nash's "Our House" is a timeless song of home and hearth, Stephen Stills solos on "4+20," a frighteningly quiet, tortured lament. "Country Girl" is a three-part medley through the life and times of Neil Young. The album closes with "Everybody, I Love You," a searing rock 'n' roll explosion, the harmonies gushing, the band working hard, the song swirling and crashing to an end in itself.

Buddy Holly, Mothers of Invention
Giant (Coral)
Cruising with Ruben & the Jets (Verve)
Saturday Review/March 29, 1969
"Nostalgia: Oldies but Goodies and a Last Ditch Attempt"

We are experiencing a rock 'n' roll revival, a pop boomlet of early rock styles and artists. Elvis Presley's recent TV special was received with enthusiastic acclaim by a national network audience, Jerry Lee Lewis's one-night stand at the Scene was a much-awaited event, and when the Everly Brothers played the Bitter End in Greenwich Village, even Bob Dylan came by to listen. Chuck Berry tore up New York's Fillmore East when he played there in February (as a last-minute replacement for Jeff Beck) and after three encores fans stood and wailed for more. The most emphasized aspect of the last Beatles album is the jivey tribute paid to their influencers, and Tiny Tim's latest single is a re-enactment of "Great Balls of Fire." Dale Hawkins's "Susie Q." was resurrected into a full-blown top-forty hit by Creedence Clearwater Revival, a San Francisco group; and Eddie Cochran's "Summertime Blues" is, at one time or another, a vital part of the repertoire of every rock band.

As the pop creative community becomes audacious enough to dig its own roots, it also elevates its own elder statesmen. The groundbreakers of pop—Elvis Presley, Buddy Knox, Jerry Lee Lewis, Chuck Berry, Little Richard—are experiencing the critical legitimacy of contemporary pop exponents, and with it new popularity.

An example of pop's inclination to erect its own monuments is the recent release of the remaining available tapes of the late Buddy Holly. *Giant* is a collection of material in the can, personal family tapes, and unfinished recording efforts by Buddy Holly. The production was carefully worked; strings and rhythm sections were pieced on. Holly's voice was dubbed in, and the entire intricate operation was performed like a heart transplant. As a result, there is a surprisingly contemporary balladlike interpretation of "Love Is Strange" and a full-blown rock 'n' roll "Good Rockin' Tonight," executed as if it were a complete, intact original. The latter and "Blue Monday" were built around homemade tapes. According to the liner notes, the original tapes had to be transferred to a multi-track recorder, and the additional accompaniment dubbed in by studio musicians.

It was no mean feat, and the results, while not perfection, are eminently passable and historically valuable. Despite technical shortcomings, *Giant* is a wonderful emergence.

Jerry Lee Lewis, the shrieking obscenity of the 1950s, is now a country artist. He's either outgrown rock or vice versa, for his new recording personality is as much a vital moving force as his original. Lewis characterized early rock 'n' roll and forecasted the sexual hysteria to follow with a shock of exploding hair, a double-fisted piano style, and a frantic finale during which he writhed on the floor, howling and clawing at his clothes. His two latest releases, "Another Place Another Time" and "She Still Comes Around," are sedate by comparison, but every bit as relevant.

Philips Records has announced the signing of Screaming Jay Hawkins, and Fats Domino is currently recording for Warner Brothers Reprise. The beat goes on.

The interest in early (post-Presley/pre-Beatles) rock is a peculiar sort of nostalgia. It is a significant backward glance into a culture a little over ten years old. The changes that have gone down in this last decade document the recognition of rock as a cultural entity and, by extension, the recognition of the young as a potent social force. The characteristic difference between a 1959 hit and a 1969 hit gives a vital insight into the sophistication of the children of rock 'n' roll. "Yakety Yak," a hit by the Coasters in the 1950s, is a disgruntled commentary on parental authority. The present-day pop protest expresses cool cynicism and flashing outrage against a more generalized and more formidable Establishment. The 1959 youngster had his curfew to cope with, today's draft-age youth argues for his own life, for humanity. Essentially, it is the same discontent, forced into sophistication by the weaponry that threatens it.

Rock has come of age in an era when norms are measured by extremes and the culture heroes are freaks. A nostalgic cycle in pop harking back to the hip swiveling, hot rod choking, lovelorn, sequined explosion of early pop is a yearning for innocence, as strange as that might seem. The realization that pop music has set the style for the most vital cultural element to affect the Western world since movies tantalized a Depression audience into material success orientation is nothing compared to hearing love songs to the accoutrements (blue suede shoes and tail-finned cars) of teentime in the 1950s. Remembering how young we once were is just as encouraging as reminding ourselves how far we've come, with a sense of humility and a sense of humor.

The oldies are their own satire; they document and caricature themselves and their descendants. Somewhere in the great absurd, Frank Zappa tuned in. *Cruising with Ruben & the Jets* (Verve), the latest release by the Mothers of Invention (graced with a high-school picture of Frank Zappa), is presented as "a last ditch attempt to get their cruddy music on the radio." It's an album of the Mothers as mad historians, caricaturing a caricature and making it work. They exult the sexual symbolism of early rock by calling the shots. "Cheap Thrills in the Back of My Car" wouldn't have gotten by the censors in the old days, but it sounds disconcertingly familiar now. The Mothers camp it up with reconstructed oldies spoofing the elusiveness and the immediacy that brought teeny-boppers out in droves to the Murray the K rock 'n' roll tours and the American Bandstand.

The Mothers of Invention reign as the prime purveyors of irreverent insight into American culture, and this time around, they are entrenching themselves. And as severe a reflection of the absurdity of itself as it is, *Ruben & the Jets* is a collection of good tunes. It has a beat and you can dance to it. It tells it like it always was, much to everyone's embarrassment, except theirs, and makes it fun to listen to at the same time. It's patently obscene without containing one dirty word. Now you've got to admit, that's class.

◆

Jefferson Airplane
Volunteers (RCA)
Saturday Review/January 31, 1970
"Where We've Been Today"

From the charged march that opens the album, the electric rallying cry of "We Can Be Together," it is clear that the latest Jefferson Airplane album, *Volunteers*, is something extraordinary. "We Can Be Together" is a chronicle of where we've been today by a group that's been all over this country and Europe, the group that wants to be the first rock band to tour the Soviet Union, a conglomerate of musical mischief-makers that has absorbed (even while they help create) the changes of turned-on youth and reflects them with such peculiar beauty that they've become an institution. In a uniquely personal way, they are one of the most beloved rock 'n' roll bands extant.

The Airplane has been around since 1965, an original San Francisco band that grew out of the community burgeoning during that time. They eventually eclipsed the scene that spawned them, got better, got worse, got growing, and got here—and only God knows how.

> *But we should be together*
> *Come on all you people standing around*
> *Our life's too fine to let it die*
> *And we can be together*

The Airplane and the people they gather around them are fun-lovers, slightly maniac, totally spontaneous, responsive, and totally human. The result is magnificent disorganization, sometimes awe-inspiring.

Nuttiness is a way of life for the Airplane crew. Their road manager, for instance, a veteran of the Merry Pranksters (the lovable "California crazies" about which Tom Wolfe's *Electric Kool-Aid Acid Test* was written), has been known to travel in an orange jumpsuit, alight from the plane, strap on a pair of roller skates, and proceed to zip on down to the baggage claim area.

The Jefferson Airplane takes off on nationwide performing tours and lets loose a musical theater that combines the magic and intensity of the times, the place, and the moment rising out of the social and political pressures that catalyze rock 'n' roll into the force it has become. The group has all the characteristics of its audience: wild abandon, vociferous desperation, messianic aspirations, and affluent brattishness.

Their music has taken many peculiar turns (as has their ethnobotanical environment), and not all of them have been successful. They started with a haywire, high-voltage, folky sound; got stranded in an abysmal sea of electronic disasters; barely rose above a drowning, bitterly nihilistic two-ton sound; and have now arrived at a point where all facets of the changes they've been through are organized, comfortable, open, rejuvenated, and exciting.

Volunteers is a beautifully paced album. Some of the songs ring with excitement; some lovely soothing tunes counterpoint the fray. Some are simple and perky and some are absurdly comical. It wouldn't be a Jefferson Airplane album if there weren't some sloppy moments, but the album as a whole is so sensitive and musical that it can dominate the moods of a moment in the nicest possible ways.

"Good Shepherd," an idyllic traditional ballad arranged and sung by lead guitarist Jorma Kaukonen, is melodic, blissfully lazy, and tender. "Hey, Fredrick" is a blistering, elliptical, sexual diatribe by Grace Slick.

Paul Kantner of the Airplane contributed to the creation of David Crosby's and Stephen Stills's "Wooden Ships," and the Airplane does an entirely different adaptation of the song, including a verse that Crosby, Stills and Nash don't sing, and an afterthought: "Go ride the music, c'mon and ride it, child." It is a simply breathtaking cut, full and flowing with both anxiety and rapture combined in an unforgettable manner.

Spencer Dryden, the Airplane's bucolic drummer, wrote no less than "A Song for All Seasons," a hilarious saga of the slings and arrows of fate that bemuse a rock 'n' roll band:

> *They say your drummer, he's crazy as a loon*
> *Last night they found him baying at the moon*
> *And as for your lead guitar*
> *He just cracked up his car*
> *But he should be out of traction very soon*

The group is comprised of outstanding musicians and vocalists who like to refer to themselves as "jazz weirdos." Often the group jams onstage, and various subsets of musicians perform separately when the group isn't touring. All this and Grace Slick, too.

Amazing Grace. She says she learned to sing from an electric guitar, and she wrote songs because songs were needed. Lesser musician-vocalists will work 'til they bleed and not touch the quality of songs and vocal transfigurations Grace Slick can produce offhand.

It is a strange time to be writing about the Jefferson Airplane. They have been around for the life span of approximately two and a half groups. They started as an instant local success, became the first rock band out of San Francisco to be hugely successful on a national level. Almost immediately they leveled out for a qualitative nosedive. They stayed together because there wasn't anything better to do, and very soon it became apparent that there never would be anything better to do than to keep Jefferson Airplane alive and kicking. They exhibited a kind of physical, mental, and musical stamina that is almost unheard of in the instant ready-mix atmosphere of the pop elite, and they have maintained the essence of what they started out to do, that is, merely turning on the world.

As it now stands, they do as many free concerts as their schedule will allow, literally spreading the wealth as far as it will go. With the Airplane, the community feeling didn't quit beyond the confines of Haight-Ashbury, and that community element in their music has endeared them to millions within their reach. With the best offers available to them, they still make a point of playing the American South because they feel they're needed there.

Above and beyond the musical experience, the group promotes a feeling of identity among the audience. They are the product of a lifestyle that they generously extend to any flexible head. In many ways, the byproduct of the group is as important as its music, and they've been able to sustain their appeal through many a rough time. Their recordings, more often than not, have not been able to communicate the group adequately, but with *Volunteers,* they have a representatively idiosyncratic classic. It is with no small measure of love, and just as much relief, that I recommend this album.

Certainly, there's something rattling around loose in the Jefferson Airplane. But at least it keeps good time.

Index